THE CANADIAN UFO REPORT

THE BEST CASES REVEALED

THE CANADIAN UFO REPORT

THE BEST CASES REVEALED

BY

CHRIS RUTKOWSKI
AND
GEOFF DITTMAN

A HOUNSLOW BOOK
A MEMBER OF THE DUNDURN GROUP

Copy-Editor: Jennifer Gallant
Design: Katherine Wilson
Printer: University of Toronto Press

Library and Archives Canada Cataloguing in Publication

Rutkowski, Chris

The Canadian UFO report : the best cases revealed / Chris Rutkowski and Geoff Dittman.

Includes bibliographical references.

ISBN-10: 1-55002-621-6
ISBN-13: 978-1-55002-621-4

1. Unidentified flying objects--Sightings and encounters--Canada.

I. Dittman, Geoff II. Title.

TL789.6.C3R87 2006 001.9420971 C2006-902688-2

1 2 3 4 5 10 09 08 07 06

Canada Council
for the Arts

We acknowledge the support of the Canada Council for the Arts and the Ontario Arts Council for our publishing program. We also acknowledge the financial support of the Government of Canada through the Book Publishing Industry Development Program and The Association for the Export of Canadian Books, and the Government of Ontario through the Ontario Book Publishers Tax Credit program, and the Ontario Media Development Corporation.

Printed and bound in Canada.
Printed on recycled paper.

www.dundurn.com

Dundurn Press
3 Church Street, Suite 500
Toronto, Ontario, Canada
M5E 1M2

Gazelle Book Services Limited
White Cross Mills
High Town, Lancaster, England
LA1 4XS

Dundurn Press
2250 Military Road
Tonawanda, NY
U.S.A. 14150

For

Chester Cuthbert, mentor of Chris Rutkowski,
and Gerry Archer, passionate writer.

TABLE OF CONTENTS

Transition Years

Towards the Millennium

... And Beyond

UFOs in Canadian Culture

PREFACE

Chris Rutkowski has been investigating UFO reports and researching the subject of UFOs since the mid-seventies. In the late eighties, he teamed up with Geoff Dittman to produce an annual study of Canadian UFO cases, called the Canadian UFO Survey. Since then, they have made their presence known in Canadian ufological circles through radio programs, TV shows, many posts to online UFO discussion groups, and travels across the country to lecture and conduct research and investigations.

Although they share a passion (or perhaps *obsession* would be a better word) for the subject, their views of and approach to ufology differ somewhat, so a collaborative venture such as this book will have its limitations. Although they together developed and discussed the contents of the entire book, they divided up the chapters according to their individual interests and, in some cases, the result of a game of rock, paper, scissors. The authorship of each chapter is explicitly indicated.

The result is a collection of essays that detail actual case investigations of UFOs in Canada. The stories will take you from sea to sea and from the Golden Triangle to the High Arctic.

ACKNOWLEDGEMENTS

From both of us:

Jan Aldrich, Errol Bruce-Knapp, Stanton Friedman, Don Ledger, Christian Page, and Brian Vike.

From Chris Rutkowski:

Vladimir Simosko, the Off the Wall Writers' Group, Luana at McNally Robinson Booksellers, Pat Goss, Geoff Currier, and Scott Young. Special thanks go out to my children, Vicki and Zach Rutkowski, for giving me inspiration and inducing perspiration.

And thank you, Donna.

From Geoff Dittman:

Joyce, Brian, Greg, Jody, and Cameron Dittman and David Williams.

INTRODUCTION

CHRIS RUTKOWSKI

Ten percent of all Canadians have seen UFOs. That is not a number frivolously picked out of thin air (pardon the pun) but a statistic based on polls and surveys of North Americans and specifically Canadians, done by various independent polling organizations and groups. When asked the question, "Have you ever seen a UFO?" one in every ten Canadians will say yes.

This is not an insignificant number of people. In 2003, according to Statistics Canada, there were 31.6 million people in Canada. Ten percent of the population is therefore 3.16 million people — definitely a lot of UFO witnesses. It's not that Canadians see more UFOs than people in other countries do; the percentage is the same in other developed countries such as the United States and Britain.

The significance of this data is that according to Statistics Canada, about the same number of Canadians has been diagnosed with high blood pressure: 3.25 million. By way of comparison, 2.1 million are afflicted with asthma, 1.3 million suffer from depression, and 1 million have arthritis. The difference is that great concern about the large number of people with high blood pressure, diabetes, arthritis, and depression has resulted in national programs to educate the public about the prevention and treatment of these conditions.

Yet, 3 million Canadians believe they have seen UFOs, and this does not seem to be of concern to educators, politicians, or the scientific community. If, as some suggest, people who see UFOs are imagining them or simply "seeing things," should it not be cause for some worry that one in ten people cannot trust their own eyes? Or if, as others believe, people are seeing spaceships from other planets, would an armada of 3 million vessels not cause some anxiety for military strategists?

Of course, the statistics need some expansion and interpretation. The term "UFO" is very ambiguous, being simply an acronym of the phrase "unidentified flying object." In popular culture, it has come to mean "alien spacecraft," but that is not necessarily what has been observed or reported.

Ufologists are people who investigate or research reports of UFO sightings. They do not study UFOs directly, because the reported objects are no longer around to be studied. Investigators use various techniques to try to explain or understand what the witness has seen based on his or her testimony. In this sense, ufologists are more like private investigators or members of an expert CSI: UFO team.

Through studies of case reports and investigations, ufologists have demonstrated that few UFO reports can be said to have no explanation. Many sightings of what witnesses believe to be unusual objects in the sky are found to have reasonable explanations such as military aircraft, advertising lights, brilliant meteors, scintillating stars, and fast-moving satellites. Only a small fraction of all UFO reports are sufficiently documented, well investigated, detailed by co-operative witnesses, and do not appear to have explanations after investigators have had time to analyze the data. Even then, this does not mean the UFOs in question were alien spacecraft — that would be an explanation, too! We can only state that there was no known explanation for what was seen and shrug our shoulders. This may not be satisfying or as sensational as tabloid TV would have us say, but it is the reality of ufology.

In Canada, there are a handful of dedicated UFO investigators scattered across the country, interviewing witnesses and collecting information about cases. Almost all co-operate in a national study called the Canadian UFO Survey, which compiles case data and publishes an annual analysis of UFO sightings reported officially in Canada. The 2005 Canadian UFO Survey was completed as this book was going into production. A chapter later in this book on the Canadian UFO Survey analyzes results from 1989 to 2004, during which period the number of UFO sightings reported in Canada increased dramatically. This was in direct contradiction to news reports that stated that the number of UFO reports is decreasing. The 2005 results do show a slight decrease in the number of reports from 2004, although the level is still the second highest on record. There were 882 cases received for study in 2004 and 763 in 2005, still more than two UFO sightings per day in Canada.

Remember, however, that this number represents raw UFO cases, and many turn out to be aircraft or satellites. Still, there are dozens of high-quality unknowns each year.

When someone asks, "Do UFOs really exist?" I respond with a decisive yes. If necessary, I explain that UFOs are merely objects in the sky that defy explanation by an observer. Obviously, such objects exist. Some stimulus is in the sky to cause an observation and thus a UFO sighting. The question that was probably intended is "Do flying saucers from other planets exist?" The answer to this question is one that has led many skeptics and believers to go at each other's throats in vicious arguments.

The phrase *flying saucer* is very liberally applied to UFOs by news media and most laypeople. The term was first coined in 1947, when pilot Kenneth Arnold claimed he had seen silver disclike objects flying near Mt. Rainier in Washington State. When asked by a reporter to describe what he had seen, Arnold replied that the objects moved as if they were plates or saucers skimming across water. From those words the reporter quickly formed the phrase *flying saucers*, and the name stuck in the public mind.

Arnold's objects were in a special category of what are called today *daylight discs*. These account for a minority of UFO reports; most UFO sightings are of objects known as *nocturnal lights*. Such objects are simply lights in the night sky that behave in ways that seem mysterious to their observers. Many of these turn out to be an aircraft, a satellite, a star, a planet, or a meteor.

What kind of people see UFOs? While some skeptics might answer that UFO witnesses are delusional, gullible, or uneducated, the reality is that the demographics of UFO witnesses cuts across all ages, socioeconomic status, educational background, occupations, and cultures, and furthermore, many witnesses are people with significant training in observation and judgement. Unfortunately, many UFO witnesses are reluctant to tell others of their sightings for fear of being ridiculed by skeptics. This attitude is changing, thankfully, and it appears that society as a whole is becoming more accepting of those who have had remarkable experiences.

What are UFOs, then? There are six basic categories of explanations for UFOs:

1. misinterpretations of conventional objects or common phenomena,
2. hoaxes,

3. unusual natural or poorly understood phenomena,
4. secret government or military projects,
5 hallucinations, or
6. something else.

Included in the last category is every speculative idea ever proposed concerning the extraterrestrial nature of UFOs and alien spacecraft. This quite naturally leaves the category wide open for anyone to propose his or her pet theory and innovation. These range from the relatively passive "man from Mars" to the extragalactic, and on through other dimensions and time travel. The motivations for "their" visits range from the benign — alien anthropologists watching our daily routines — to the sinister — preparation for oppression, colonization, or slavery.

It should also be noted that there is a great deal of modern scientific research and brilliant deductive studies in the emerging field of exobiology: life outside of the Earth. Hardly a month goes by without more analyses being completed on another sample of Martian soil or rock in a quest for evidence of extraterrestrial organisms. The duplication of amino acid formation in the early stages of Earth's history has convinced many scientists that life would likely arise on other planets and produce creatures somewhat similar to us.

We know with a high degree of certainty that other humanlike creatures do not exist elsewhere in the solar system. Speculation is rampant that primitive lichens and bacteria may exist on Mars, in Venus's atmosphere, or perhaps even on a large moon of Jupiter or Saturn. Regardless, our local star system has been more or less eliminated for extraterrestrial life, based on our knowledge of what conditions are necessary for life to be viable, such as heat, light, water, etc. Where else might it occur?

The next nearest star system to us is the Centauri triplet of stars right next door, only about 25 trillion miles away! (That's about 4.3 light years in astronomical terms; it takes light waves more than four years just to reach us from those stars, as the crow flies.) For various reasons, scientists have decided that the Centauri stars are unsuitable for life, so we must look elsewhere. Other nearby stars could be eliminated as well: Sirius is too hot, Ross 248 is too cool, and others bear only a passing resemblance to our own star, Sol, which is "just right" for life to evolve.

Some nearby stars, including Tau Ceti and Epsilon Eridani, were the targets of an attempt to establish radio contact with extraterrestrial beings in the sixties. Our messages apparently were not answered, so they didn't feel like answering, they weren't listening, or they're not there to begin with.

Let us suppose, though, that there are sentient beings somewhat like us (with whatever degree of sentience you would like to believe we have) on a planet circling a relatively nearby star, perhaps Tau Ceti. For some obscure reason, they decide to visit us and launch a rocket ship (or flying saucer) towards us with a select group of cosmonauts on board. If they travel with a top speed of the fastest space vehicle Earth engineers have themselves launched in various directions, the one-way trip to Earth from Tau Ceti would take approximately fifty thousand years. This is because although Tau Ceti is eleven light years away from us, light travels at 186,000 miles per second, a speed we can barely consider, let alone achieve.

It would be a long voyage, even if the Tau Cetians are placed in some sort of cryogenic suspension or stasis or if they are extremely long-lived. There is no guarantee that their equipment would continue to function properly over such a long period of time. Not only that, as they travel, their home planet and the Earth itself will age in normal time; drastic geological and biological changes will occur in the course of fifty thousand years. We (or their kin) may not be here. Our technology and society may have advanced to an unbelievable level, or perhaps not.

It is the technology that may be the important factor. A possible scenario would be the following:

1. IF their star began its planet-forming process before our own sun did, then they may very well be far in advance of us technologically; and
2. IF they are more advanced than we are, they may have been able to design spacecraft that can attain velocities far in excess of our own capabilities, perhaps even a significant fraction of the speed of light; and
3. IF they can obtain such velocities, then fifty thousand years could be condensed into a much shorter time span, perhaps only a few years or months; and
4. IF they decided that a trip was warranted, they might choose to visit Earth; then
5. their means of transportation here might be observed by us as UFOs.

Or not.

Canada has a rich history of folktales, legends, and myths embedded within its mosaic of many cultures. Stories of mysterious flying objects, "little men," and fantastic devices were part of ancient tradition as much they are retold in slightly different forms as UFO sightings and abduction stories today. Whether they have any basis in fact is not as important as the consideration that they are part our present-day culture and society. On TV, aliens have tried to sell us nasal decongestant and soda pop, while we were told in other ads that the new Volkswagen Beetle was "back-engineered" from a crashed flying saucer. Canada may indeed have been invaded by aliens, as judged by a sampling of our television programs, books, magazines, and other materials and activities to be found across the nation that have connections to UFOs.

UFOs have been sighted and reported by Canadians since they were first known as flying saucers, and before that when they were called ghost rockets, mystery aeroplanes, and balloons. Before that, they were simply unusual meteors, clouds, and odd lights in the sky. This book is a chronicle of the impact such observations have had on the lives of Canadians, whether they believe or disbelieve.

THE EARLY YEARS

CHAPTER ONE
THE HISTORICAL CONTEXT

CHRIS RUTKOWSKI

Ever since our ancestors first looked heavenward and wondered at the many points of light and larger orbs moving across the bowl of night, there have been UFOs. By definition, a UFO is simply an unidentified flying object — something in the air, in the sky, or moving through space that is not identifiable by its observer. Early hominids had no notion of stars and other astronomical bodies, so the lights in the sky were truly unidentified. Nevertheless, they formed many concepts about what they saw, calling them visitors, animals, gods, and spirits.

Once the Age of Reason was reached, scientific disciplines offered more down-to-earth explanations for the lights in the sky. We began to understand that the Earth was a rock in orbit around a fiery ball of gas and that there were many other such balls and rocks in the ocean of space. We identified comets, smaller planetoids, and meteors and began to classify what should and should not be in the sky.

Unfortunately, people still reported seeing things that did not easily fit the known scientific classification schemes. These puzzles were recorded by a host of historians, but because they were considered anomalous, they were often ignored or regarded as aberrations and of little interest since they failed to support the accepted view of the universe. After all, something that challenged the status quo could not be of much use.

In the beginning...

What may be the earliest recorded UFO sighting in Canada (or what would eventually be Canada) was described in a report by Jesuit missionaries living with the Algonquin people in New France in 1663:

> As early as last Autumn we saw fiery Serpents, intertwined in the form of the Caduceus, and flying through mid-air, borne on wings of flame. Over Quebec we beheld a great Ball of fire, which illumined the night almost with the splendor of day, had not our pleasure in beholding it been mingled with fear, caused by its emission of sparks in all directions. This same Meteor appeared over Montreal, but seemed to issue from the Moon's bosom, with a noise like that of Cannon or Thunder; and, after traveling three leagues in the air, it finally vanished behind the great mountain whose name that Island bears.[1]

They later also recorded some remarkable sun dogs on January 7, 1663, and again on January 14. Then, on September 1, 1663, there was a major solar eclipse that they recorded in some detail, too.

On February 5, 1663, a major earthquake shook the area, and the Jesuits described it in great detail, including its effects on people, animals, the physical geography, and the vegetation. Unusual lights were seen as well: "Beside the roaring which constantly preceded and accompanied the Earthquake, we saw specters and fiery phantoms bearing torches in their hands. Pikes and lances of fire were seen, waving in the air, and burning brands darting down on our houses ... without, however, doing further injury than to spread alarm wherever they were seen."[2]

Another early recorded UFO sighting in Canada took place in Manitoba long before it was a province. In the autumn of 1792, explorers David Thompson and Andrew Davy were camped on the shore of Landing Lake, near what is now Thicket Portage, and were startled to see a brilliant "meteor of globular form ... larger than the Moon." The object seemed to come directly towards them, lowering as it travelled, and "when within three hundred yards of us, it struck the River ice, with a sound like a mass of jelly, was dashed in innumerable luminous pieces and instantly expired."[3]

The next morning, when they went to see the hole it should have made in the ice, they were surprised to find no markings whatsoever. In some ways, the object sounds rather like a bolide — a brilliant meteor — which through a trick of the eye might appear to be nearby, although in reality it could have been many miles distant. However, it is interesting that the two heard a sound, something rare for meteors, and furthermore described the object as "globular" and that "it had no tail, and no luminous sparks came from it until it dashed to pieces." David Thompson goes on in his journal to describe a second such meteor, and this one again "passed close by me striking the trees with the sound of a mass of jelly." He thought its height was no more than eight feet above the ground, although dimensions can be quite deceiving at night, and this estimate could be incorrect. Nevertheless, we are left with an interesting historical account of a strange event in the northern woods.

Something was seen off the east coast of Canada, over the Minas Basin, Nova Scotia, at the head of the Bay of Fundy, in 1796. A Loyalist merchant and judge from Liverpool named Simeon Perkins (1735–1812) kept a diary of certain events. In an entry dated Wednesday, October 12, 1796, Perkins recorded (in Old English):

> A Strange Story is going that a fleet of ships have been Seen in the Air in Some part of the Bay of Fundy. Mr. Darrow is lately from there by Land. I enquired of him. He Say thet they were Said to be Seen at New Minas, at one Mr. Ratchford's, by a Girl about Sunrise, and that the girl being frightened Called out and two men that were in the House went out and Saw the Same Sight, being 15 Ships and a Man forward of them with his hand Streached out. The Ships made to the Eastward. They were So Near that the people Saw their Sides and ports. The Story did not obtain universal credit but Some people believed it. My Own Opinion is that it was only in Imagination, as the Cloud at Sunrise might Make Some Such appearence, which being Improved by Imagination might be all they Saw. Exceeding pleasent day and Evening.[4]

British explorer John Meares built the first ship launched from British Columbia and made many voyages across the Pacific Ocean. He established the settlement of Nootka Sound and was a keen observer of the local Aboriginal population. In his historical account, *Voyages Made in the Years 1788 and 1789, from China to the North West Coast of America*, he noted a legend told to him of an "extraordinary stranger from the sky."[5]

Meares asked the Native people how they discovered the use of copper and why they valued it so much. They replied that their ancestors had met a man from the sky who came to their land in a flying copper canoe. He told them he was from the sky, and he warned them that one day their nation would be destroyed and their people would die.

The visitor had many items made from metal, a substance foreign to them; they were amazed and believed it contained special powers. They killed the stranger out of fear and took his copper canoe and all the metal it contained.

CHAPTER TWO
AIRSHIPS OVER CANADA

CHRIS RUTKOWSKI

North America experienced what has come to be known as the Great Airship Wave between about 1896 and 1898. Many unusual aerial objects were reported floating or hovering in the skies, usually with accompanying descriptions of airships or gondolas suspended underneath large balloons. The reports were well documented, with many articles and some books devoted to the phenomenon. Accounts of observations of these objects appeared in hundreds of small-town newspapers across the continent. Some of the stories included personal narratives of meetings with the occupants or inventors of the vehicles. The strange craft often had bright lights or "headlights" that dazzled their observers, noiselessly sailing overhead and leaving as mysteriously as they came. Many of the stories were eventually determined to have been hoaxes written by newspaper editors in an attempt to boost circulation.

The first sightings considered part of the wave were reported in the fall of 1896. The *Sacramento Bee* carried a story on November 17, 1896, that a bright light was seen by hundreds of people.[1] The light was too distant for most observers to distinguish its shape, other than that it resembled a globe and travelled on an undulating course through the sky, against the prevailing wind, "like a ship through water." Other witnesses described an oblong or ovoid shape featuring propellers or a fan with a moveable light that swung back and forth, playing on the ground below. The witnesses were divided on whether the control or passenger cabin was on top of or beneath the craft. Whatever it was, the strange craft remained visible for nearly half an hour. Embellishments and speculation abounded, with some people claiming they heard voices coming from the craft, either laughing or giving orders to whoever was at the controls. The builder of the aerial vehicle was thought to be an inventor who lived in the Sacramento or San Francisco area and was highly secretive about his remarkable machine because his device had not yet been patented.

The *Decatur Daily Republican* of April 16, 1897, noted that on the previous night, an airship had landed near Springfield, Illinois. Farmhand John Halley and local vineyard owner Adolf Wenke said that it landed three miles west of the city and contained three people. A long-bearded man emerged and asked where he was. He said they usually rested during the daytime in remote areas in order to conceal the vessel's huge wings. When they asked the scientist his name, "he smiled and pointed to the letter M., which was painted on the side car." After bidding the farmers farewell, he pressed a button and the ship flew off.

The *Chicago Times-Herald* for Tuesday, March 30, 1897, described another sighting:

> The mysterious air ship was seen again last night by a number of Omaha people. It hovered in sight about the time church services were over and in half an hour had disappeared.
>
> This time the "air ship" came into view in the southeastern portion of the horizon. It was in the shape of a big bright light, too big for a balloon, and glowed steadily.
>
> It sailed over the city to the northwest and there disappeared behind the houses and bluffs. It moved very slowly and seemed to be quite near the earth. Nothing but the light was visible. A big crowd at Twenty-fourth and Lake Streets watched the trip of the visitor.

Canada experienced its share of such reports, as recorded in the newspapers of the day.

The first recorded airship sighting in Canada seems to have occurred before the airship frenzy hit California and the American Midwest. In Winnipeg on July 1, 1896, at about 6:00 p.m., many residents observed an odd "balloon" come from the west and make a "rapid journey some thousands of feet above the Earth." It was said to have been larger than a child's toy balloon but the same size as those used for "ascensions at River Park." Tethered balloon rides were a popular attraction and novelty in 1896.[2]

Manitoba was invaded by more American-style airships in 1897, when on April 14, a "specter" with attached lights "as large as the moon" flew from North Dakota towards Glenboro at an estimated speed of "365 miles per hour." Then on May 1, "the light of the strange vessel came into view about nine o'clock on the eastern horizon, near the St. Boniface Hospital." It moved over the city, then headed northwest, towards Stony Mountain. A witness reported that "only the bare outline of some dark object could be seen besides the strange, heavenly light, evidently from the 'masthead' of the aerial craft." This time, the strange vehicle was seen by "many reputable citizens," including the lieutenant-governor of the province, the Honorable James Colebrooke Patterson, who curiously enough had just completed a term as federal minister of militia and defence.[3]

Sightings were reported across the country. On August 14, 1897, the *Vancouver Daily World* prodded its readers:

> Have You Seen the Light in the Heavens? If Not You Are Not up to Date
>
> It has been hovering in the skies above Vancouver almost every night this week, and has been viewed by many. It was last seen on Friday evening and may be on view tonight, and again it may not. Last night the strange object in the skies was noticed to the north of the city across the city traveling in an easterly direction. The luminous ball of fire or airship as some call it was closely watched. It approached with great swiftness, paused in midair, then surrounded itself with flashes of color and moved towards the northeast.

It added:

> N. C. Schon of Burnaby saw the luminous body while on the steamer Rithet on Monday night. He states that it moved parallel to the sea far below the star line and looked like a bright red star surrounded by a luminous halo. It was cigar shaped and seemed to travel slowly and occasionally there seemed to drop a shower of sparks like the sputtering of an arc light.

The *Victoria Daily Colonist* of August 7, 1897, informed its readers:

> That strange aerial curiosity the fire balloon that has been completely mystifying people of the northwest during the past two or three months is evidently becoming bolder or more people are keeping late hours than formerly and in consequence have had the good fortune to catch a glimpse of it. What it is, or where it comes from or where it goes to, and who or what manner of men are responsible for its movements, remains just as much as a puzzle as when the bright light first made its appearance in the sky a few months ago.

The *Colonist* also noted that some firemen had watched the light for a considerable length of time:

> For upwards of two and a half hours Firemen North and Swain of the city brigade had opportunity to inspect the erratic visitor yesterday morning. However when it was finally lost to sight in the morning air they were completely mystified as to all its character as when they first sighted it.... It had no discernible form, balloon shape or otherwise, it was just a great light as large from the distance it was viewed as a drum from one of the hose reels, and brighter far, according to the two firemen than an electric light. ...
>
> Until four o'clock the brilliant body remained suspended in mid air passing slowly from east to west and back again three times and only disappearing with the coming of the day. At one time the firemen believed they saw a dark body outlined behind the circle of intense light but they could not identify it positively.

Its editors speculated:

> The favourite theory is that some local inventor is trying the product of his daring in the privacy of the night, preparatory to giving his secret to the world. It must be a fact that the inventor is the most successful keeper of a secret to appear on the scene for quite some

> time and yet this seems the most rational explanation put forward. Too many have seen the mid night visitor for people of common sense to doubt the presence of a mysterious something....

Sightings of odd aerial vehicles and lights continued through that summer. Many airship reports were fuelled by news stories of the announcement that a Swedish engineer, Salomon Andrée, would attempt a balloon flight over the North Pole from Scandinavia into Canada. In July 1897, Andrée's expedition left the island of North Spitzbergen in a large, well-equipped balloon. Some carrier pigeons were received from the explorers early into the voyage, and then nothing.

On August 9, the *Manitoba Free Press* carried a story that described lights in the sky over British Columbia and Manitoba and wondered if Andrée's airship could be off course and wandering throughout the north. It printed a letter from a reader:

> Douglas, Aug. 6, 1897. / To the Editor of the *Free Press.* Sir, — In case some of your numerous readers may have noticed something similar at some other point I would draw your attention to a peculiar matter noticed on the night of the 5th. About 11 p.m., just before retiring, a something that at first looked like a falling star appeared directly north of the residence of Mr. John Kyle, some four miles east of here. The person first to notice the strange object was led to call the attention of all in the house to the matter. For over half an hour we watched the strange visitor, as it seemed to rise and fall and sway from east to west, but gradually travelling further and further northward, until about 11:45, it disappeared from view. At times several of those watching the peculiar object, which all the while shone brightly, thought they could discern the shape of a massive balloon just above the bright light. It would be interesting to know if the circumstance was noticed by any others, and if so, what the impressions conveyed were. R.M. SCOTT

The editor added, "Any who have noticed similar objects are asked to inform the *Free Press*. If Andrée persists in floating about Manitoba barn yards let us find him."

Similarly, the *Manitoba Morning Free Press* for September 14, 1897, printed a letter from a correspondent in Scotland that explained that on August 5, 1897, a large light assumed to be a balloon passed over Prince Albert shortly after 6:00 p.m., heading west-northwest. To compound the mystery, the same paper on September 18 carried another account of a sighting:

> Was it Prof. Andrée?
>
> St. Petersburg, Sept. 17. — A telegraphic message was received here from Krasnoyarsk, in the interior of Siberia, which says on September 14, the inhabitants of the village of Antzifiroskoje, in the district of Veniselsk, Arctic Russia, saw a balloon, which is believed to be that of Prof. Andrée, the Swedish aeronaut, who left the island of Tromsoe shortly before 2:30 p.m., July 11, in an attempt to cross the Polar region. The balloon, it is added, was in sight for five minutes.

Over the next several months, people around the globe reported seeing Andrée's aerial expedition flying through the sky, but no actual trace of him or his companions was found. In 1939, the remains of the frozen bodies of the crew were discovered on a small island in the Arctic Ocean north of Spitzbergen. Investigators concluded that not long after they had launched, the balloon became covered in ice, and the crew was forced to make a crash landing on the rocky outcrop. Therefore, none of the sightings thought to be Andrée's balloon could have been that craft. The sightings could not have been fireballs or bolides because the durations were usually many minutes, too long for astronomical objects. On the other hand, the objects moved too swiftly to be misidentified stars or planets.

Comments made in the press in 1897 bear a strong resemblance to those made regarding modern-day UFO reports. Doubt was expressed over the veracity of the witnesses. Many people were unwilling to use their names in reports. Sky watchers speculated about craft built by secret organizations, and many people were outright skeptical and simply didn't believe that the objects could be anything but meteors. However, those who had witnessed an airship were adamant and insisted that they had definitely seen the thing, in the same way that UFO witnesses today insist that what they observed was really there.

Researchers have found that, although the idea of awkward and mechanical flying machines in the late 1800s is fanciful, the reality is that dozens of patents were issued to inventors of "aerial cars" and "flying gyrators" as far back as 1844, with a proliferation of them in the years following 1880. It is quite possible that some airship reports were indeed experimental vehicles, although there is no question that many simple observations of lights in the night sky were misidentifications of stars and planets, exactly as today.[4]

At the time airship stories were in circulation, the world was going through a rapid boom in economy, technological development, exploration, settlement, and communication. The atmosphere was rife for wild speculation about fanciful wonders in the skies. There was some skepticism, but there was also a wide range of speculation as to the airships' origin and mechanisms. The press noted that witnesses reacted with puzzlement and wonder to the strange sights in the heavens. A certain amount of ridicule was present, and there were satirical pokes at the witnesses by various institutions. The airships sold newspapers and products through their depiction in broadsheets and posters. Eventually, the sightings decreased in number (or, at least, the media lost interest), and reports slowly ceased being recorded.[5]

The airship wave of the closing years of the nineteenth century subsided, and the next era of strange sky wonders began.

CHAPTER THREE
THE GREAT METEOR PROCESSION OF 1913

CHRIS RUTKOWSKI

At 9:05 p.m. EST on the night of February 9, 1913, a strange phenomenon was seen in the skies over much of Canada and the United States. Beginning in Saskatchewan and heading to the east, a procession of brilliant lights made its way slowly and majestically overhead. Some witnesses described the sight as a red object with a long, fiery tail. Others saw two, three, or more sources of light travelling one behind the other, each with separate trails of sparks. As soon as these were out of sight, dozens of smaller lights in groups of twos, threes, and fours passed overhead on the same apparent path, from northwest to southeast, all with glowing tails. There were reports of the strange phenomenon as far east as Bermuda.[1]

Estimates of the total number of objects in the procession ranged as high as one thousand or more, although the best approximation was that ten or fifteen objects, each possibly composed of a number of smaller bodies, were seen over a twenty-five-hundred-mile path over the entire continent. The duration of the event was said to be as long as three and a half minutes.

Astronomer Dr. Clarence Chant presented a very detailed analysis of the meteor train, including many reports from eyewitnesses. He noted:

> The front portion of the body appears to have been somewhat brighter than the rest, but the general color was a fiery red or golden yellow. To some the tail

> seemed like the glare from the open door of a furnace in which is a fierce fire; to others, it was like the illumination from a "search light"; to others, like the stream of sparks blown away from a burning chimney by strong wind.
>
> Gradually the bodies became smaller, until the last ones were but red sparks, some of which were snuffed out before they reached their destination. Several report that near the middle of the great procession was a fine large star without a tail, and that a similar body brought up the rear.[2]

The spread of reports was very remarkable. Chant noted that the place farthest west from which a report had been received was Mortlach, about sixty-five miles west of Regina, Saskatchewan, where the lights were described as travelling from west to east. However, in Ontario, the meteors were described as travelling generally from northwest to southeast, and there were enough observations reported to allow triangulation and to calculate their true path.

From Campbellville, Ontario, the meteors passed directly overhead, travelling from northwest to southeast, and over Hespeler, they "seemed to go right over our heads." Sightings were also plotted for Elora, Guelph, Waterloo, Berlin, Georgetown, and Sheridan, where the meteors flew in a line about fifteen degrees to the west of the zenith.

Chant calculated that, based on the elevation angles and triangulation, the meteors were at a height of about twenty-five miles, just within the Earth's atmosphere, and travelling at a speed of somewhat less than ten miles per second. However, these values were debated among members of the astronomical community and a much higher altitude of about forty-five to fifty miles was later accepted.

The procession made its presence known through noise as well. Chant noted, "At Niagara-on-the-Lake the windows rattled, and at St. Davids, Rev. G. Mithro heard the sound and looked in vain up in the sky to see the cause of it."[3]

Similarly, near Sand Hill, Ontario, a witness reported, "Some had tails and some seemed to shoot a red vapor which threw a beautiful red glow. They came in bunches or groups. I counted ten in one group and I think there were 20 groups. As they disappeared in the east there was a loud report like rolling thunder, and then another sound like thunder, and a tremor of the earth."

And in Shelburne, Chant noted, "There must have been an earthquake the night before, that the vibration was quite perceptible, and the noise was like a series of blasts going off. In the *Shelburne Economist* it is stated that a man living 12 miles west of the town was awakened from sleep and thought that his horses were wrecking the stable. On investigating, however, he found the horses perfectly quiet."[4]

Other sample observations included:

> [Fort Frances, Ontario:] I saw them come slowly from the northwest; first, a string like candles, about forty of them; then, after 5 minutes, another string in the same line and about eight in number. They made the snow red quite a while after they had disappeared in the east. There was no sound, and they were lower than the stars. They went slow. A big one led the first string. I am sure you will hear something. It must be the end of the world. It was about 9 p.m. They did not pass overhead, but north of us.
>
> [Peterborough, Ontario:] The appearance was like that of an express train lighted up at night. The elevation was about 25°. Movement was slow and the duration about 3 minutes. In the first section there seemed to be from six to nine lights, with slightly spreading ends. Then, in succession, some three or four, not so brilliant sections passed. The most striking feature to me was the regular movement in an even plane. There appeared to be no curve whatever. No noise was heard. It was the grandest display I have ever seen.[5]

Beyond the objects seen that night, there were scores of other sightings recorded across North America on the days just before and after the procession, and in some cases minutes or hours before or after. Chant also noted a daylight sighting that may or may not have had something to do with the sightings of February 9:

> In conclusion I shall refer to a curious observation reported in *The Toronto Daily Star* for Monday, February 10. At about 2 p.m. on that date some of the occupants of a tall building near the lake front

> saw some strange objects moving out over the lake and passing to the east. They were not seen clearly enough to determine their nature, but they did not seem to be clouds, or birds, or smoke, and it was suggested at the time that, perhaps, they were airships cruising over the city. Afterwards it was surmised that they may have been of the nature of meteors moving in much the same path as these seen the night before.[6]

Many years later, the identity of the meteors in the procession was still being debated. In the journal *Popular Astronomy*, Vol. XLVII, No. 6, June–July 1939, astronomer C.C. Wylie argued that the procession was not a series of meteors in a long train. He stated, "The popular explanation of the phenomenon is that a cluster of fire balls traveled from Saskatchewan across North America, and over the Atlantic to the equator, a distance of some 5700 miles. Several considerations, of which we will mention four, make this explanation untenable."

He continued, "The meteoric display of February 9, 1913, was a shower of fireballs and shooting stars from a radiant in the north-northwest. It was not a procession of fireballs moving over an unusually long path. The most spectacular meteor of the display was a detonating meteor which fell in Ontario at 9:06 P.M., 75th meridian time."

Wylie's chronology of events is as follows:

1. A detonating meteor fell over Ontario on February 9 at 9:06 p.m. EST.
2. A shadow-casting meteor was observed from Ann Arbor, Michigan, at 10:15 p.m. CST (11:15 p.m. EST).
3. A spectacular fireball was observed from Bermuda at 10:00 p.m. AST (9:00 p.m. EST).
4. A shadow-casting meteor observed in Ontario on February 10 at 1:25 a.m. EST.

In addition to these spectacular meteors, several groups of shooting stars were observed, among them the ones over Fort Frances at 9:00 p.m. CST. A string of forty or so meteors, followed five minutes later by a string of eight, passed north overhead. Meteors were also observed over Pense and Mortlach, Saskatchewan ("Must have been hundreds"), and even as far afield as Watchung, New Jersey.

Charles Fort, the chronicler and collector of news reports of unusual phenomena for whom the field of Fortean research is named, also questioned the meteor train explanation. Indeed, if he had still been active when Wylie disputed Chant's conclusions, Fort certainly would have had some cynical comments to offer. In his book *New Lands*, Fort noted:

> It is questionable that the same spectacle was seen in Bermuda, this night. The supposed long flight from the Saskatchewan to Bermuda might indicate something of a meteoric nature, but the meteor-explanation must take into consideration that these objects were so close to this earth that sounds from them were heard, and that, without succumbing to gravitation, they followed the curvature of this earth at a relatively low velocity that can not compare with the velocity of ordinary meteors.[7]

CHAPTER FOUR
THE 1915 INVASION OF CANADA

CHRIS RUTKOWSKI

The headline of the *Toronto Globe* on February 15, 1915, read, "Ottawa in Darkness Awaits Aeroplane Raid." Call-outs in the body of the article warned, "Several Aeroplanes Make a Raid into the Dominion of Canada" and "Entire City of Ottawa in Darkness, Fearing Bomb Droppers."[1, 2]

One alarming series of headlines and secondary headlines told readers, "Machines Crossed St. Lawrence River, Passing Over Brockville — Two over Gananoque — Seen by Many Citizens, Heading for the Capital — One Was Equipped with Powerful Searchlights — Fire Balls Dropped." It appeared as though Canada was about to enter the war on its own homefront.

The excitement began on the night of February 14 at about 9:15 p.m., when many people in Brockville were startled to see the lights of unknown aircraft crossing over the St. Lawrence River and heading for Ottawa. The lights were seen even by the mayor and three city constables. The unidentified craft flying rapidly overhead was said to have made "unmistakable sounds of the whirring motor."

A second flying machine was heard as it crossed the St. Lawrence from the direction of Morristown, New York. As it passed overhead, three balls of fire were seen to drop into the St. Lawrence. Some observers thought these might have been bombs, while others worried they could have been flares used by enemy pilots to find their way across the border or over the ocean to the Canadian interior. Two more aerial invaders were reported to have passed over the east and west ends of Brockville, raising further fears.

The mayor said he also had seen a bright beam of light, like a searchlight, flash out from the aerial craft, lighting up an entire city block. The police chief, facing numerous inquiries from nervous citizens, called the mayor for instructions. He then relayed information to Ottawa's mayor and police chief, advising them of the approaching aircraft.

At approximately 9:30 p.m., the mayor of Gananoque contacted the Brockville police chief with the news that two invisible aircraft were heard quite distinctly passing overhead there. With so much activity over the seat of government, it was not long before advisors met with Prime Minister Robert Borden and evaluated intelligence information about the mysterious fliers. Borden and his caucus were concerned that the lights of Parliament Hill would make it an easy target for any invasion and ordered them to be turned off.

Under direct orders by the government, Parliament Hill went dark at about 11:15 p.m., and the entire city of Ottawa followed suit at approximately 11:20 p.m., including Rideau Hall and the Royal Mint. Shutters were secured and windows were darkened throughout the capital region. Military and police marksmen clambered to the roofs of government buildings in Ottawa and were given orders to shoot down any hostile aircraft. This was the first blackout and air raid in Canadian history, only one month after the first raid on Britain.

Ottawa was not the only target of an aerial invasion that night. Early in the morning of February 15, people living in a Toronto suburb notified police of a "strange aeroplane" hovering over their homes. Later, a man in Guelph saw "three moving lights passing over the agricultural college." He called out to other residents in his boarding house, who also watched the silent lights until dawn.

Meanwhile, far to the west, three people returning home from a late-night game of curling in Morden, Manitoba, heard a peculiar noise in the sky and looked up to see a bright light moving to the northwest. They, too, described it as an "aeroplane" travelling swiftly through the night sky.

It is important to note that there may have been an explanation for at least some of the objects seen in the skies over Ontario that night. It was reported that the hysteria in Ottawa was the result of a prank by a few jokers in Morristown. Supposedly, three balloons with fireworks attached were sent aloft in celebration of the hundredth anniversary of the end of the War of 1812. The fireworks created the impression of aircraft lights and engines, falling balls of fire, and the beam of light seen over Brockville.

At first, the government and its citizens refused to believe this. Even the profoundly skeptical Dominion Observatory rejected the explanation, noting that prevailing winds were from the east and would not have taken the balloons northeast towards Ottawa from Morristown. However, on February 15, a Brockville policeman found a paper balloon near Eastern Hospital, and a second paper balloon was later found along the river. This seemed to validate the explanation of fireworks, and afternoon media took advantage of the discoveries to poke fun at the morning dailies that had been so quick to fall victim to hysteria. Nevertheless, the next night, the lights of Ottawa were again turned out and guns were set up on rooftops.

Later research showed that at the time of these observations, only a handful of aircraft in the United States were actually capable of making the flight from the border to Ottawa, and none of these was capable of carrying searchlights.

CHAPTER FIVE
THE VILLAGE THAT DISAPPEARED?

CHRIS RUTKOWSKI

In books and articles about strange phenomena in Canada, the story of a village named Lake Anjikuni (or Angikuni) sometimes surfaces. Most versions of the story explain that in about 1930, more than twelve hundred people simply disappeared. Sometimes, the story includes details that investigators found pots still simmering on stoves and graves open and empty in the local cemetery.

The most widely accepted version of the story suggests that in the winter of 1930 a profoundly disturbing incident took place in Northern Canada. Trapper Arnauld Laurent and his son were tending their lines in a remote area when they observed a strange light (what we would now call a UFO) crossing the northern sky. It appeared to be headed in the direction of Lake Anjikuni in what is now Nunavut, west of Arviat and to the north of Manitoba. They described it to authorities as being cylindrical or bullet-shaped.

Meanwhile, at around the same time, another trapper, Joe Labelle, was also working his lines and had just reached the village of Lake Anjikuni. He was shocked to find that the community was completely silent, with no sign of any human activity. Even the sled dogs, which would normally have been excited to see strangers, were quiet and unresponsive. The huts were covered with snow and there were no fires lit, a very unusual situation for a winter night. All the villagers' kayaks were tied up on the shore of the lake.

Inside the homes, Labelle found meals left hanging in pots over long-dead fires, all grown old and moldy. They looked abandoned in the midst of cooking. Most shockingly, the men's rifles were still standing by the doors. This was particularly disturbing because such weapons were very precious to those living off the land and would not be left behind by any reasonable person.

When Labelle made it back to civilization, he reported his discovery to the Royal Canadian Mounted Police, who investigated the villagers' disappearance. By the time they arrived, the dogs had died of hunger. They had all been chained to a tree, and their bodies were now covered by a snowdrift.

The most terrible discovery was that the town's graveyard had been emptied. The bodies had all been exhumed and there was no sign of the former occupants.

As the story goes, even to this day the RCMP continues to consider the case open and unsolved, despite extensive air and ground searches. No trace of the twelve hundred missing men, women, and children was ever found.

One of the most recent tellings of this tale was in the science-fiction novel *Majestic* by Whitley Strieber (1989). The story is contained in a fictional "National Board of Estimate" document by an "Office of Research and Analysis," titled "Intelligence Estimate On Flying Disk Motives" and dated July 8, 1947. The names of the trappers are given, as well as the details of the discovery of the abandoned village. The document's fictional author asks, "Were the hardy Eskimos moved to some other world, to plant the human seed among the stars?"[1]

A more embellished version of the story can be found in *The World's Greatest UFO Mysteries* by Nigel Blundell and Roger Boar. These authors include details of conversations between Laurent and the RCMP and note him as having not one but two sons. Then, the authors claim, when Joe Labelle finds the abandoned village and sends a telegraph to the RCMP regarding his discovery, "every available officer was despatched to the Anjikuni area."[2]

A web page on Jeff Rense's extensive "Sightings" site describes the incident as "The Village That Disappeared." In his version, the discovery was made in November 1930, and Anjikuni is called a "thriving fishing community of about 2,000 residents," significantly more than in other versions.[3]

In 1994, the story was discussed in detail within the Internet newsgroup alt.paranet.ufo among UFO buffs fascinated with Strieber's mention of the incident. Ufologists James Easton, Chris Rutkowski, and others participated in the review of case details. One of the newsgroup's contributors, Patricia Welsh, pointed out that an elaborate version of the story was in a book by Frank Edwards, a popular author of flying saucer books. This early version contains much speculative material such as Labelle's personal thoughts and feelings as he explores the abandoned village of Anjikuni.[4]

However, the origin of the story appears to be an article by "Special Correspondent" Emmett E. Kelleher in the November 29, 1930, edition of the *Halifax Herald*. The story was picked up by newspapers across North America and overseas. In this, the original story, a small community of twenty-five people living on the shore of Lake Anjikuni vanished under mysterious circumstances. Labelle found two starving dogs and the bodies of several others near the tents. Inside, he found parkas, deer bones, boots, pots and pans, and a rusty rifle. He figured that it had been a year since anyone had been in the camp.

The newspaperman wrote that Labelle began panicking because he recalled the Eskimos' fear of an evil spirit named Tornrark, who was often cited as a tormentor. His anxiety increased when he stumbled upon an Eskimo grave near the campsite, correctly described as a pile of stones, not as a six-foot-deep hole as in modern Western tradition. The stones had been scattered and the body was indeed missing. The story was accompanied by a photograph that depicted several teepees and the faces of some Inuit.[5]

John Robert Colombo, a Canadian editor and writer extraordinaire, noted this origin of the story in his book *Mysterious Canada*. He concluded, "The truth, which is much more interesting than Joe Labelle's tall tale and Kelleher's journalistic hoax, is that within two months of its publication the RCMP had debunked the tale."[6]

After the story was published in newspapers, the RCMP understandably received many letters from people wanting to know more about the case. On January 17, 1931, not even two months after the story broke (showing the true efficiency of the RCMP), Commissioner Cortland Starnes released a report by Sergeant J. Nelson of the RCMP detachment in The Pas, Manitoba. Nelson spoke with the owner of a trading post at Windy Lake in the Northwest Territories, who said there were no other trappers or Inuit who could confirm the story. An investigation of Joe Labelle found that he was new to the North and was known only to have been running traplines in north-central Manitoba, far from Anjikuni.

As for Kelleher, he was apparently known for writing "colourful stories of the North" and embellishing details. Nelson noted, "I consider the whole story fiction." Even the photograph was found to be misleading; it was taken in Churchill in 1909 by an RCMP officer who said Kelleher borrowed it when he was visiting him one day, as proven through comparison with the original negative.

Fortean writer Dwight Whalen did some additional investigation for an article on the case published in November 1976 in *Fate Magazine*. He found that the story was that of "an inexperienced trapper told to an imaginative and not too conscientious newsman."[7]

Although the story still finds its way into books and articles today as an unsolved mystery, there are many clues that it is a hoax. As one contributor to the UFO newsgroup on the Internet noted, "A mass abduction of 1,200 humans was difficult enough to accept, but robbing the local graves as well was just a little too extraordinary to be credible." James Easton asked, "Did the story of 1,200 people disappearing have its roots in a true story of 30 people disappearing, or are both fireside tales?"

Even today, the relatively large Northern town of Baker Lake, near Anjikuni, contains only about fifteen hundred people, so the story of twelve hundred or two thousand people in a remote settlement is rather unlikely. The apparent exhumation after interment is also a tip that the story has some fictional elements. The addition of Arnauld Laurent's sighting of a mysterious object over the exact spot where the villagers vanished suggests that it was included for the sole purpose of attracting UFO buffs to the story.

Unfortunately, with the passage of time comes the loss of history. In the eighties, UFO buff Gary Overman pursued the story independently and asked the RCMP for information. He was told by an RCMP historian that the story was not true but that it began with the publication of Edwards's version in the fifties. This "history" is provided by the RCMP even today, despite the fact that they themselves debunked the story more than twenty years before Edwards put pen to paper. An official RCMP website explains:

> The story about the disappearance in the 1930's of an Inuit village near Lake Anjikuni is not true. An American author by the name of Frank Edwards is purported to have started this story in his book *Stranger than Science*. It has become a popular piece of journalism, repeatedly published and referred to in books and

> magazines. There is no evidence however to support such a story. A village with such a large population would not have existed in such a remote area of the Northwest Territories (62 degrees north and 100 degrees west, about 100 km west of Eskimo Point). Furthermore, the Mounted Police who patrolled the area recorded no untoward events of any kind and neither did local trappers or missionaries.[8]

In summary, we can be safely assured that the story of the vanishing village of Lake Anjikuni was not based on a real event. However, confusion by writers over the years and by an apparent lack of memory on the part of the RCMP has served only to promote the story as truth.

EXCITING DECADES

CHAPTER SIX
SAUCER-SPOTTING PARTIES

CHRIS RUTKOWSKI

In his books and articles on evidence concerning crashes of flying saucers and their subsequent cover-up by American military officials and government, ufologist Stanton Friedman notes that newspaper coverage of a particular incident on July 7, 1947, differs between western and eastern parts of the continent. His observation is that only evening newspapers in the western United States carried details of a press release sent at noon in New Mexico, which advised editors that debris from a flying saucer had been recovered by the military. A few hours later, according to Friedman, the air force hastily called a news conference to cover up the event and inform reporters the saucer was nothing more than pieces of a balloon. This was too late for the evening papers on the west coast, and only editors of morning newspapers on the east coast had time to prepare stories based on the later information. Californians, therefore, read that evening about a recovered flying saucer, while New Yorkers read the next morning about a balloon.

Friedman suggested that other UFO researchers examine microfilms of North American newspapers to see the difference for themselves. When papers from Canadian cities are examined, a few turn up some surprising articles and coverage of flying saucer stories.

The night the Roswell saucer story emerged, Canadians were themselves witnessing an aerial display. Under the headline "Mystery of the Flying Discs Deepens," the *Winnipeg Free Press* reported on Monday, July 7, 1947, "What appeared to be six of the 'flying saucers' were seen flying north over Mount Royal, P. Q., Saturday by J. Duffield of Montrose N.J., visiting Montreal. 'They were quite visible and the sun glinted off their shiny surfaces,' Mr. Duffield said. 'They were going northwards and were flying in formation, like ducks.'"[1]

In Winnipeg, "one local citizen, who refused to give his name, insists he saw the flying saucers whirling overhead while he was sitting in the legislative building grounds with a lady companion Saturday night. They kept passing from east to west, he said, and all disappeared behind the Golden Boy." The paper further noted:

> In one of the earliest reports, about a month ago a trapper at Bruno, Sask., reported seeing a mysterious object which he was convinced was a meteor. He said it crashed.... A flying saucer was reported at Port Hope, Ont., Sunday night by a railway employee. He said it had a slight reddish tinge but was not a shooting star. He said it sailed high over Port Hope at three o'clock in the morning, "against a clear sky."

There were other sightings noted, including one from Village Green, Prince Edward Island. Experts were quick to offer their opinions, which varied greatly: "In Syracuse, N.Y., Dr. Harry A Steckel, psychiatric consultant, discounted the element of mass hallucination in connection with the reports. 'They have been seen by too many people in too many different places to be dismissed so lightly,' he said in a radio broadcast."

Local experts included D.R.P. Coates, president of the Royal Astronomical Society of Canada, Winnipeg Centre, who said, "Some kind of flying device, still on the secret list, is definitely being tested somewhere on the continent. Earlier reports would be more authentic than recent ones. There are persons who would now call any flying object a 'disc.' One or two reports suggest meteors, but that is not the answer. Experimentation, that's it."

Winnipeg's mayor, Garnet Coulter, suggested, "I think it's a Martian contractor at work. These flying saucers are probably a new type of construction material he wants us to use when we build the new city hall."

His employee, assistant city clerk G.I. Gardner, disagreed. He was quoted as saying, "Flying saucers ... phooey! Too much indulgence in wild moose-milk!"

Meanwhile, the *Winnipeg Free Press*'s competition, the *Winnipeg Tribune*, was at work with a different approach. Its reporter Victor

Murray enlisted the services of a "Prof. Roberts" in setting up a "flying saucer observation station" on the roof of the *Tribune* building. Equipped with binoculars and a canteen of "barley water," the unabashed reporter and his assistant kept watch in the sky, in between several catnaps. Their headline on July 8 read, "Dr. Murray Scientific Expedition Probes 'Flying Saucers.'"[2]

Obviously, there was some difference in editorial opinion and approach to the subject of flying saucers.

CHAPTER SEVEN

SKY CLEAVAGE: THE FIRST CANADIAN UFO PHOTOGRAPH

CHRIS RUTKOWSKI

On July 10, 1947, at about 5:30 p.m., two Pan American Airways mechanics and a third witness were driving up a mountain road six miles south of Harmon Field, a U.S. Air Force base near Stephenville, Newfoundland. Messrs. J.E. Woodruff, J.N. Mehrman, and A.R. Leidy reported seeing a silver disc-shaped object flying high overhead at an estimated altitude of about ten thousand feet. The object was flying in a horizontal arc over the base and towards the north-northeast. Its size was comparable to a C-54 transport aircraft. As it flew past, it left behind a bluish-black trail about fifteen miles long. One of the witnesses (not specified in the report but thought to be Woodruff) had a camera with him and managed to take two Kodachrome pictures of the trail.[1]

Copies of these photos are part of the official Project Blue Book files. Although very poor reproductions, they nevertheless show the odd smoke trail in the sky. Weather records confirmed scattered clouds between eight thousand and ten thousand feet, which supports the original altitude estimate.

This case was investigated by Army Air Force Intelligence and was of particular concern to military officials because of a perceived threat that the Soviets may have been behind the appearances of flying saucers. If this was the case, then it was obvious that in order to spy on the U.S.A., flights from the U.S.S.R. would have to pass over Canada. The initial report was filed by Harmon base intelligence officers on July 16, with a more detailed report received at the Pentagon on July 21.[2]

Air Force Brigadier General George F. Schulgen, then Chief, Air Intelligence Requirements Division, Office of the Assistant Chief of Staff, A-2 (Intelligence), ordered intelligence officers at Wright Field in Dayton to go to Harmon Field to assess the situation and report directly to the Pentagon. The Wright T-2 chief, Colonel Howard M. McCoy, dispatched a team by July 30.

The T-2 investigation report on the Harmon Field case noted, "The bluish-black trail seems to indicate ordinary combustion from a turbojet engine, athodyd motor, or some combination of these types of power plants. The absence of noise and apparent dissolving of the clouds to form a clear path indicates a relatively large mass flow of a rectangular cross-section containing a considerable amount of heat."[3]

The report did not consider that a meteor or fireball had made the trail, even though this explanation was the official conclusion on the case file. However, Blue Book documents showed that the Pentagon was still focused on a Soviet connection. As noted in a report on the case, "Wright Field investigators spoke with the commander of Harmon Field and others to make sure that no British or Canadian aircraft had been in the area at the time. And since they knew no American aircraft were to blame, they privately concluded something of 'foreign origin' made that curious split in the clouds over Newfoundland."[4]

What we are left with is a well-witnessed and intensely investigated UFO case, reported long before the term "UFO" was coined by the American military. In the early years of the Cold War, the Soviets were suspected, since the object seen was not "friendly." The photographs show a very strange rocket-like exhaust trail or contrail, proving that something definitely was seen by a number of qualified observers that day. It was the first photograph of an unidentified flying object reported over Canadian soil.

CHAPTER EIGHT

DUCK, DUCK...

CHRIS RUTKOWSKI

In the heart of Labrador is a rugged area known as Happy Valley, at the western end of the Hamilton River and Lake system. In 1941, the United States built an air force base there at Goose Bay, a strategic location leading to the ocean. It facilitated anti-submarine exercises and the staging of aircraft on overseas flights. A set of Distant Early Warning (DEW) Line sites was constructed in Labrador during the Cold War and monitored at a NORAD site at Goose Bay beginning in 1953. The 641 Aircraft Warning and Control Squadron was based there and began flying missions for "surveillance, identification and interceptor control." Given this mandate, when the flying saucer phenomenon began flourishing in the forties and unidentified aircraft were being reported over the Rock, Goose Bay seemed to be a major hot spot. It was not surprising that an American air base on Canadian soil might be the site of many saucer sightings, just like so many other bases worldwide.

What is perhaps a bit surprising, though, is that there were so *many* saucer sightings at Goose Bay. In the forties and fifties, there were twenty known reports, a considerable number for such a remote base. Most civilians were unaware of what was being seen and reported by pilots and other military personnel, although rumours of events persisted over the years.

The first known sighting near Goose Bay took place in the summer of 1948 and was described by a military witness who came forward much after the fact and related his story to UFO investigators. He provided few details but painted a picture that can be easily visualized, showing the reaction of the intelligence community and the command chain.

Major Edwin A. Jerome, USAF (Ret.), stated that in the summer of 1948, a high-ranking inspection team was visiting the base's radar facilities as part of a tour looking at refuelling and servicing capabilities for all military and civilian aircraft on North Atlantic air routes. During the generals' inspection of the USAF radar shack, the operator painted a high-speed target on his scope going from northeast to southwest, with a computed speed of about nine thousand miles per hour. This caused considerable concern, since the base personnel wanted to look good in front of the inspection team and such a calculation must have been an error.

Jerome noted, "The poor airman technician was brought to task for his apparent miscalculation." However, when the target appeared a second time, the brass saw the target on the screen themselves. They dismissed the reading as being due to poorly calibrated American equipment. They then went to the Canadian side of the base to inspect the RCAF facility and learned that the equipment there had also just tracked the same or a similar object. The inspecting officers branded the incident a coincidence. The anomalous target on both scopes had been moving at speeds faster than anything known to be possible.

Jerome was an intelligence officer at the base and was ordered to make a report on the incident. It had been suggested that the object was a meteor, but when he interviewed the radar operators on both sides of the base, he found the object was tracked as it maintained an altitude of sixty thousand feet throughout its flight, and he believed this ruled out a meteor as a possibility. While conducting his investigation, he was shocked to learn that the very next day, both radars again reported an anomalous object, this time moving slowly over the base at about ten miles per hour at forty-five thousand feet. This time, the anomaly was explained as "high-flying seagulls."

One can only reflect on the fact that this case occurred long before rockets and jet aircraft were capable of such speeds and high-altitude helicopters were possible. The consternation of the inspectors and the embarrassment of the radar technicians must have been considerable and would have been talked about in the mess hall for many weeks.[1]

If a radar case is explained as being due to faulty equipment, technicians point out that the same equipment is used to track known military operations without malfunctions. You can't have it both ways; either the equipment was working — or it wasn't.

Through the rest of the decade, there were four more known sightings at Goose Bay. Three of these were October 27 and 31 and November 1, 1948, with little information available on the first two other than that they were noted in Project Blue Book.[2]

Donald Keyhoe, a noted journalist and author of several UFO books, described the cases, citing the third case as well:

> Following this, I asked the Air Force for typical reports and conclusions, from 1948 up to date. One of the first cases, involving three separate incidents, took place in Labrador, at Goose Bay Air Force Base. About 3 a.m. on October 29, 1948. An unidentified object in slow level flight was tracked by tower radar men. Two days later, the same thing happened again. But the following night, on November 1, radar men got a jolt. Some strange object making 600 m.p.h. was tracked for four minutes before it raced off on a southwest course. At the time, weather conditions were considered as a possible answer. But in the light of the new temperature inversion revelations, this obviously must be ruled out.[3]

The fourth sighting took place on September 9, 1949, at 9:56 p.m. AST. It was noted by Project 1947 (a private UFO research project) that a military aircraft pilot saw an egg-shaped object disappear into a cloud at high speed.[4]

Then, on September 14, 1951, at 9:30 p.m., another Blue Book case occurred, listed as No. 969 in its files. Technical Sergeant W.B. Maupin and Corporal J.W. Green were witnesses when two objects were tracked on radar on a collision course. One of the radar operators attempted to warn the objects of the imminent collision and was surprised to watch one avoid danger by moving to the right upon the request. No aircraft were known to be in the area. A third unidentified track then joined the first two. The entire incident lasted more than fifteen minutes.[5]

It's difficult to say what might have transpired in the radar booth that night. It's likely that someone there remembered the unfortunate incident with the visiting dignitaries just three years earlier and wanted to avoid another reprimand. So, he logically deduced that the unknown objects were aircraft and handled them as unidentified traffic, vectoring them to safety. It appears rather unlikely that two spacecraft from another planet would need flight directions from a terrestrial radar operator.

The next year, another weird "something" was reported over Goose Bay. Edward Ruppelt, former head of Project Blue Book, said that one night early in 1952, the pilot of an air force C-54 about two hundred miles southwest of Goose Bay contacted the tower to report that a large "fireball" had buzzed his airplane. It had come from behind and the pilot had not seen it until it was "just off the left wing," an estimated one hundred or two hundred feet away. The base officer of the day, also a pilot, was in the flight operations office and overheard the report. He went outside and saw a light coming from the southwest. In the blink of an eye, it flew over the airfield, increasing to the size of a "golf ball at arm's length." The object seemed so low and close that the officer and the driver of his command car dropped to the ground and hid under the car because they were sure it was going to hit the ground nearby. But as they watched, the "fireball" made a ninety-degree turn over the airfield and flew off to the northwest. In the control tower, the technicians saw the object make its right-angle turn and were certain it was not a meteor.[6]

This incident was discussed during a briefing Ruppelt had some time later in the Pentagon with General Samford, the director of intelligence, some members of his staff, two navy captains from the Office of Naval Intelligence, and other officials. He was recounting some outstanding "unknown" UFO reports he had investigated and noted that they were increasing in number. Even though the reports were detailed and contained a great deal of good data, he said they still had no proof that UFOs were real. An officer used the Goose Bay sighting as an example of an unexplained case and noted that it, too, could not be accepted as proof of alien spacecraft. Ruppelt noted, "I said that our philosophy was that the fireball could have been two meteors: one that buzzed the C-54 and another that streaked across the airfield at Goose AFB. Granted a meteor doesn't come within feet of an airplane or make a 90 degree turn, but these could have been optical illusions of some kind."

The colonel asked, "What are the chances of having two extremely spectacular meteors in the same area, traveling the same direction, only five minutes apart?" Ruppelt's response was that he "didn't know the exact mathematical probability, but it was rather small..."

The colonel went on:

> "Why not assume a point that is more easily proved?"

> he asked. "Why not assume that the C-54 crew, the OD, his driver, and the tower operators did know what they were talking about? Maybe they had seen spectacular meteors during the hundreds of hours that they had flown at night and the many nights that they had been on duty in the tower. Maybe the ball of fire had made a 90 degree turn. Maybe it was some kind of an intelligently controlled craft that had streaked northeast across the Gulf of St. Lawrence and Quebec Province at 2, 400 miles an hour.
>
> "Why not just simply believe that most people know what they saw?" the colonel said with no small amount of sarcasm in his voice.[7]

On June 19, 1952, another radar/visual saucer sighting occurred at Goose Bay AFB. It was described in a number of sources with slightly differing details, but the substance of the case is interesting. At 2:37 that morning, "2nd Lt. A'Gostino and unidentified radar operator saw a red light turn white while wobbling. Radar tracked a stationary target that suddenly enlarged then returned to previous size, possibly a disc rotating to present wider reflective surface."[8]

Another version notes:

> On June 19 radar at Goose AFB [sic] in Newfoundland picked up some odd targets. The targets came across the scope, suddenly enlarged, and then became smaller again. One unofficial comment was that the object was flat or disk shaped, and that the radar target had gotten bigger because the disk had banked in flight to present a greater reflecting surface. ATIC's official comment was weather.[9]

Not to be left out, journalist Donald Keyhoe had his own version of the story:

> On the night of June 19, 1952, Goose Bay Air Force Base, in Labrador, came in for a brief observation. Just as radar men picked up a UFO track, ground men outside saw a strange, red-lighted object come in over the field. The radar blip suddenly enlarged, as if the device

> had banked, exposing a larger surface to the radar beam. At the same moment the watching airmen saw the red light wobble or flutter. After a moment the light turned white and quickly disappeared. Apparently the unknown craft had gone into a steep climb...[10]

Keyhoe notes his source was a USAF intelligence report, although which one it was is unclear. He commented on this case again in his *True Magazine* article:

> On June 19, 1952, a new incident occurred at Goose Bay Air Force Base — the fourth to date. Just after midnight, a weird red light appeared, holding a southwest course. At the same time, tower radar men caught it on their scope. After hovering briefly at 4,000 feet, the light suddenly turned white. At about this instant, the blip on the scope "brightened." This effect, familiar to operators, is seen when a plane banks, the larger surface exposed to the radar beam causing a sharper return.[11]

There are some obvious inconsistencies in the stories, however. Was the radar blip stationary or moving? If it was stationary, it could not have been the red object that "came in" over the airfield.

Two brief notes in UFO researcher Brad Sparks's list of Blue Book cases allude to additional sightings at Goose Bay in September and November 1952. He lists Case No. 622 on September 28, 1952, mentioning only that physicist James McDonald noted it in his list of important UFO sightings. Then Sparks noted Case No. 656 on November 26, 1952, in which at 2:30 a.m. an F-94 chased a manoeuvrable disc that changed colour from white to red as it climbed and turned. Canadian UFO writer Gregory Kanon, in an article about Maritime UFOs, noted that the object on November 26 easily eluded jet interceptors.[12]

This meagre information perhaps does not do justice to what actually happened. A former radar operator told the story in a fascinating account published on the Internet. Although his memory is vague about the date, he certainly seems to know more about the incident. He posted the information on a website devoted to military reminiscences, hoping to find answers to some of his questions from half a century ago.

Bob Jones was stationed at Goose Bay AFB during 1952–53 and was the radar maintenance technician on duty at the American radar site when the encounter occurred. He wrote that in late December 1952 or early January 1953, a severe winter storm was raging and winds were gusting up to seventy miles per hour. The storm was so intense that all of the F-94 jet interceptors were tied down to prevent them from being damaged by the high winds. No air traffic had been detected by the radar through the storm, with heavy snow and visibility of less than twenty-five yards. Jones noted the radar at Goose Bay was of Second World War vintage and could not cancel out ground clutter, which prevented tracking objects accurately within about twenty to forty miles of the antenna.

Around 11:00 p.m. a target appeared on the radar screen, about ninety miles to the north and approaching the base at about ninety miles per hour; the radar could not determine its altitude. Jones noted:

> The fact that the target was approaching from due north (0 degrees on the radar screen) was very unusual since no military or civilian airfields were located in that direction. Its slow speed of travel was equally strange. Most aircraft that approached Goose Bay from a northerly direction were flights coming in from Thule, Greenland, where the United States was building an air base and radar site.[13]

The object proceeded south at a constant speed and heading and was classified as "Unknown." Because of this, despite the weather, the F-94 interceptors were ordered to scramble. Because they were all tied down, it took forty-five minutes to get them airborne, and by that time the object had entered the ground clutter and tracking was lost.

Only a few minutes later, two more objects appeared on the radar screen, at the same range but this time on a bearing of forty-five degrees. The radar operators directed the F-94s to intercept them. But although the aircraft had nose-mounted radar and could usually locate targets with that, none of the jets was able to detect a target, although the ground radar controller was able to track all six targets on his screen. At one point, the ground controller guided one pilot toward a target so that the jet and the target merged on the screen, yet the pilot could not see it either visually or on radar. The interception exercise seemed fruitless.

About an hour later, the three unknown targets reappeared on the ground radar screens. They were in formation and heading southeast towards Newfoundland. Jones figured that Goose Bay "had been used as a rendezvous and the first target had waited overhead for forty-five minutes until the second and third targets joined it, at which time the three of them established a new southeasterly course."

Another attempt was made to intercept the unknown objects. This time, six F-94s were scrambled and flew throughout the area looking for any aircraft, without success. The targets continued on, oblivious to the frenzied search underway, and eventually disappeared one hundred miles southeast of Goose Bay. The jets were recalled to the base. The pilots' frustration was evident from radio chatter in which they complained that the ground radar operators needed to clean their radar screens. This was not unexpected, as they had been scrambled to fly in dangerous weather conditions and had even been directed to fly into locations where other aircraft might have been flying.

Jones noted, "There was definitely something in the sky that night that was under intelligent control. The three craft used Goose Bay as a rendezvous point and as a reference point for establishing their new course to the southeast. Their slow speed and how they navigated in such terrible weather remains a mystery."[14]

A number of other cases occurred over Goose Bay over the next few years. On April 6, 1953, at 7:00 p.m. AST, between Goose Bay and Sondestrom AFB in Greenland, a USAF transport pilot and his co-pilot saw a white light at fifteen thousand feet on a steady course descending in a shallow turn.[15] Then, on May 1, 1953, at 11:35 p.m., the annotation for Blue Book Case No. 2555 is that a pilot and a radar operator of a USAF F-94 jet interceptor, as well as a control tower operator, all saw a white light, which evaded interception by F-94s scrambled to intercept. The sighting apparently lasted for thirty minutes, during which time some kind of triangulation wasattempted on the object.[16]

Sparks notes four more cases at Goose Bay in 1953. Three of these were grouped together in a listing for his case No. 734, occurring on May 2, May 12, and June 11.[17] Another Blue Book entry on June 22 involved a jet interceptor. At 2:10 a.m., for five minutes, the pilot and radar operator of yet another USAF F-94 jet interceptor saw a red light flying at 1,000 knots 1,100 miles per hour), eluding pursuit.[18]

Perhaps the most cited UFO incident over Labrador, however, occurred more than a year later, on June 30, 1954. This involved not just a military aircraft but also a commercial airliner with many passengers who witnessed the object as well. Eleven crew members and the pilot of a BOAC Stratocruiser all shared the experience, and the pilot was driven to write about it at length in his routine flight report.

Captain James Howard was flying the airliner, approaching Goose Bay just after sunset at around 9:00 local time, on an otherwise uneventful New York to London flight. Suddenly, he saw a large black object "like an inverted pear suspended in the sky." There were six additional objects in formation ahead and behind the main UFO, all "keeping station not less than five miles away." Querying the Goose Bay tower, he was told that there were no other aircraft in the area. As he watched with his co-pilot, the primary object changed its shape into a "flying arrow — an enormous delta-winged plane turning in to close with us." It paced the airliner for more than fifteen minutes and about eighty miles of flight, during which time other crew members and passengers also observed the strange phenomenon.[19]

Goose Bay, as in the other cases, again scrambled a jet fighter to intercept the odd formation, but as the fighter approached, the satellite objects "appeared to return to their base ship." Shortly thereafter, the cluster of objects simply "faded away." The objects had no vapour trails and did not have any lights on them. At no time did any of them appear on radar.[20]

James McDonald, a physicist who studied UFO cases in depth, believed the BOAC case to be one of the strongest on record, with no satisfying explanation. In his analysis he noted:

> No meteorological optical phenomenon could reasonably account for the reported phenomena.... To suggest that a natural plasmoid [ball lightning] could keep pace with an aircraft at that speed and distance seems entirely unreasonable. The speed and motions rule out meteors. The peculiar maneuvering of the smaller objects and the curious shape changes of the larger object suggest no conventional explanation.[21]

Interestingly, Blue Book does not have an entry for this case, even though it was reported that a Goose Bay aircraft was vectored to give chase. It is not clear how this could be possible, given the rather thorough listing of Blue Book cases that is now available.

Finally, two other sightings are recorded for Goose Bay during the rest of the fifties. On February 12, 1956, at 11:25 p.m., for one minute, an F-89 pilot and a radar operator both saw a green and red object rapidly circling the jet, which was tracked on radar. No further details are available.[22]

Three years later, on August 10, 1959, on the Goose Bay AFB at 1:28 a.m., RCAF pilot Flight Lieutenant M.S. Mowat watched a large starlike light crossing fifty-three degrees of sky in twenty-five minutes.[23]

CHAPTER NINE
THE STEEP ROCK LAKE WATER BANDITS

CHRIS RUTKOWSKI

One of the most persistent Canadian stories about little men and flying saucers is an incident that is said to have occurred on July 2, 1950, in Sawmill Bay on Steep Rock Lake in Northwestern Ontario. The story originally appeared in the September/October 1950 issue of the *Steep Rock Echo*, the in-house publication of Steep Rock Iron Mines, Ltd. In a letter to the editor, an anonymous writer claimed that he and his wife had a very unusual experience while fishing in the bay.[1]

Early that evening, they had grounded their boat and were having a snack when "the air seemed to vibrate as if from shock waves." They climbed on some rocks to get a better view of the lake and saw "a large shining object resting on the water" about a quarter of a mile away.

The object looked like "two saucers, one upside down on top of the other." Along the rims were black portholes spaced about four feet apart. The upper surface had what appeared to be open hatch covers, and moving around on the hull were ten queer little figures. They were each about three and a half to four feet tall, and "moved like automata, rather than living beings," in that when they turned, they seemed to just change the direction of their feet. They were each wearing a metallic vest of some kind, and their legs and arms were covered with a dark material. Their faces were never seen clearly.

The couple watched the creatures and the object through a cleft in some rocks. They could see a hoop-shaped object, like a directional rangefinder or antenna, rotating slowly above the craft. When it rotated to face their hiding spot, it stopped and the creatures froze in their activities. When a deer emerged from a point near them by the water, it appeared as though the creatures had detected the deer and understood it was not a threat, so they resumed their business. The couple breathed a sigh of relief.

As they continued to watch, one of the "midgets" picked up a bright green hose that led down into the lake. Suddenly, there was a loud humming noise that seemed to be caused by the hose siphoning up water. This continued for some time, and the couple eventually withdrew to talk about what they were experiencing. When they returned to their lookout spot, they found that the craft was no longer on the water but several feet in the air and there were no creatures to be seen. There was a rush of wind, and the saucer was gone.[2]

Some Canadian newspapers reprinted the story and authors of UFO books were quick to add it to their collection of classic UFO cases to prove that aliens are visiting Earth.[3] Apparently, no one made any attempt to investigate the story, even after some writers pointed out that the Steep Rock case bore a remarkable resemblance to an earlier case that was described in a letter to a UFO researcher in 1966. In the letter, William Kiehl claimed that in 1914 he was with several others "on the banks of Lake Ontario at Georgian Bay," when he saw a metallic, disc-shaped craft resting on the water. It, too, was manned by small figures that were using a hose to siphon water from the lake.[4, 5] (It should be pointed out that Lake Ontario and Georgian Bay are not directly connected.)

In the mid-seventies, Robert Badgley, a Scarborough, Ontario, member of the Tucson-based Aerial Phenomena Research Organization (APRO), found that Steep Rock employee Gordon Edwards had made up the entire story.[6, 7]

Explained away or not, according to one contactee organization that believes UFO sightings are proof of alien visitation, the Steep Rock case is consistent with what they believe is true about alien technology:

> This Awareness indicates that this appears to be valid. This Awareness indicates that it appears the ship was transferring fluid from within the ship, giving out what might be referred to as a kind of sewage, on the one hand, and taking in a certain amount of water on the other hand. It appears that this was circulating or replacing water of one type that had been overused

and taking in fresh sea water. It does not see anything other than this as a purpose for this action. There are certain chemicals that are taken from the sea water and used in the ship for various reasons and purposes as well as the use of the water after the chemicals have been extracted.[8]

CHAPTER TEN
CANADIAN SAUCERS IN THE FIFTIES

CHRIS RUTKOWSKI

On October 21, 1950, the *Toronto Telegram* carried a letter from a reader in Moose Factory at the mouth of James Bay. The author, Don Delaplante, claimed that several unusual incidents had occurred in that region over several months. These included the sighting of a mysterious red light that remained stationary in the sky above Nemiscau, a trading post on the Quebec side of the bay. It had been observed by the local factor and his assistant. They described it as resembling a traffic stoplight and insisted it was not a star. Just west of Nemiscau, some First Nations people saw two objects with bright lights like airplanes, although also stationary in the sky. The most peculiar claim was that "strange white men" were seen by First Nations people farther north near Fort George. These "men" would run away and hide when discovered by local residents.

According to Delaplante, RCMP officers investigated these stories and interviewed the witnesses. "But nervousness prevails here," he noted in his letter, "for the vast unpatrolled coastline of James Bay and Hudson Bay makes a landing by any hostile invader an easy one."[1]

On June 1, 1951, at about 7:00 p.m., two young boys about five years old were playing ball in front of Fleming Elementary School in Brandon, Manitoba. One of the boys was distracted by something he saw in the sky and pointed it out to his companion. They both watched as an unusual aircraft descended slowly from the clouds, approaching them silently. The object was saucer-shaped, about six feet in diameter and three feet in height. Its bottom half was black and its top half was a clear glasslike canopy with a square black box inside of it. There were no markings on the object, and there was no visible means of propulsion.

The object continued to descend until it was only about thirty feet away from the frightened boys. It remained motionless for a few minutes and then moved slowly over them and took up a position above some power lines, wobbling slightly as it hovered. While the object was motionless, one of the boys became brave enough to throw a rock at the saucer, but it was too high. After about fifteen minutes the craft started to move slowly away and ascended into the clouds.

The next morning, just before sunrise, one of the boys was awakened by a sound "like many bees buzzing." He was shocked to see small dustlike particles swarming at the foot of his bed. The particles converged into the form of a ghostlike man wearing a black suit, with white hair in a pompadour. He didn't speak but moved his right arm slowly upward as if to say hello. The boy was so scared that he retreated under the covers of his bed in terror. He apparently fell back asleep, and when he woke up again the entity was gone.[2]

On October 23, 1952, about thirty-four miles southeast of Seal Island off Nova Scotia in the Atlantic, the crew of an American fishing boat came upon a mysterious fiery object bobbing on the water. Thinking a ship was in distress, the captain altered course and prepared for a rescue operation. However, when he reached the object, he and his crew were confounded to see only a bright light. The ocean waves repeatedly washed over the object, which gave off a loud crackling noise and seemed to skip about the surface of the water. Even the ship's searchlight didn't give them a good view of the strange flotsam. They watched it for about thirty minutes, then turned back to their course.[3]

Across the United States, 1957 was a banner year for flying saucers. The number of sightings reported was identified as a major wave that swept the country. A study of press coverage of UFOs noted more than 1,000 UFO reports had been received by the U.S. Air Force in 1957, compared to 670 in 1956 and 545 in 1955. After the peak in 1957, reports dropped to 627 in 1958, and only 390 in 1959.[4] Canada also experienced an increase in cases, suggesting it was a continental effect and not confined to one country.

On January 8, 1957, at approximately 5:20 p.m., a yellow light was seen north of Prince George, B.C., by some residents. Another bright light, this one orange in colour, was seen in the east and low on the horizon. The lights seemed to radiate from their tops and bottoms, but not from their sides. A total of eight witnesses, some with binoculars and members of a local flying saucer club, watched the lights for ten minutes before they moved into the distance and out of sight. From then on, sightings of flying saucers really seemed to take off and were common for the rest of the year.

The peak month for sightings, however, was November, when 349 reports were filed with the USAF. The month started slowly, with a few cases trickling into public attention. Around 7:00 p.m. on November 3, for example, a driver and two companions were travelling to Calgary and had just reached the small town of Sibbald when they saw a light "like the blinking beacon at the airport" appear suddenly over the car. This object was moving "very fast in a curve that carried it toward the northwest horizon." The driver was startled to find that as the object passed over her car, its motor coughed and the headlights flickered. "At the time, we chalked it up to loose wiring," she noted.

On November 5, at 6:45 p.m., a civilian meteorologist at Gimli RCAF Station watched a small object the size of a pencil point that was stationary in the sky. Initially white in colour, it began to move from the south to the north and changed colour to a reddish orange as it finally disappeared over the horizon five minutes later. During the observation, personnel at Gimli contacted the 916th radar base at Beausejour, where observers confirmed the sighting and watched it on a southwest to northeast track between the two bases. To observers at Beausejour, it was a pinhead flying slowly through the sky and was in sight for five minutes. According to Project Blue Book files, "It is very possible a balloon was launched from any one of the numerous airfields located in the area of [the] sighting. They are usually launched just prior to the time of [the] sighting."[5] One could ask, however, why a meteorologist and military personnel would report such a benign object as a UFO.

The peak of the 1957 wave in North America occurred on November 6, when sixty-one reports were received. Canada's main contribution was a most remarkable UFO encounter at Lake Baskatong in Quebec, about one hundred miles north of Ottawa.

At about 9:00 p.m., Jacques Jacobsen and three friends were discussing their hunting exploits of the day in their lodge near the lake. They were listening to a battery-powered radio, as there was no electricity to the area. One of the men was just returning from the outhouse when he pointed out a strange light in the sky. In the southeast, a brilliant yellow sphere seemed to hang over the top of a hill a few miles away. Since the sky was completely overcast, the object must have been relatively low in altitude.

From the top and bottom of the sphere, two beams of light shot out, shining down on the trees below and the underside of the clouds above. It was motionless and made no noise; binoculars could not resolve the object further.

They noticed that their AM radio was now filled with static, despite the clear reception it had received just a moment or two before. They then tried a shortwave radio they had for emergencies, and it, too, was filled with static — except for one signal: a single modulated, pulsed tone like Morse code that seemed to be jamming all other radio signals in the area.

After fifteen minutes, the UFO slowly ascended into clouds towards the south. Once it was out of sight, the radios were found to be working perfectly.

At about 8:00 p.m. that same night, six people in downtown Toronto watched a yellow light in the eastern sky over Lake Ontario. It moved slowly from south to north, and people reported interference on their television sets while it was in the sky.[6]

CHAPTER ELEVEN

THE FORT MACLEOD INCIDENT

CHRIS RUTKOWSKI

Shortly before sunset at about 7:20 p.m. MDT on August 27, 1956, RCAF Squadron Leader Robert J. Childerhose and Flight Lieutenant Ralph Innes were attempting to set a cross-Canada speed record in their F-86 Sabre jet. They had taken off from an air base at Gimli, Manitoba, and were heading for Vancouver. They were flying west over the Canadian Rockies near Fort Macleod, Alberta, at an altitude of thirty-six thousand feet on the far left side of a formation of four F-86 Sabre jet aircraft. While approaching a large thunderhead at a ground speed of about 400 knots (460 miles per hour), Childerhose observed, at a much lower altitude than his aircraft, a "bright light which was sharply defined and disc-shaped" or "like a shiny silver dollar sitting horizontally."[1]

As the squadron continued flying west, the object was left behind them and was visible at an "eight o'clock low" position before it was lost to sight. This was significant because it meant the object was stationary in the sky and not a reflection. Its altitude was judged to be below the upper layer of clouds at thirteen thousand feet but above the lower layer of clouds at ten thousand feet, according to verified weather conditions at the time. The object was observed against the dark clouds and appeared to be "considerably brighter than the sunlight."

As Childerhose and his companions flew past the object, he decided to take a photograph to record the unusual phenomenon. To do so, he had to quarter-roll the aircraft in the direction of the object.

The duration of the sighting was estimated to be between forty-five seconds and three minutes. After pointing the object out to the flight leader, Childerhose took a 35-mm colour slide (Kodachrome) of the object. The sun was off the left edge of the film, which was about thirty degrees to the left of the object, based on calculations of shadows on clouds made by other clouds in the photograph. He took a second photograph that did not contain the object to illustrate the position of the other aircraft.

A number of explanations were proposed for the case. One suggestion that it was merely a brightly illuminated small cloud was ruled out because the object in the photograph is equally as bright on its right side as it is on its left, and clouds in the same photograph are darker on their right sides because the sunlight is coming from the left. Also, the object is brighter than the brightest clouds. Others simply considered the object to be a ball of plasma or ball lightning. A number of researchers expended considerable effort to calculate the luminosity and radiance of a ball of plasma that could create such an object. Most discounted that explanation based on the size of the object. However, one researcher noted that ball lightning tends to be roughly spherical, with a diameter of about four inches, although a few witnesses have reported sizes up to five feet or more. If the Childerhose object was well over one hundred yards, as calculated, and was ball lightning, it was a unique case. And, since physicists do not have a completely satisfying theory of how ball lightning is created and sustained, explaining a UFO as ball lighting is not much of an explanation at all.[2]

Optical experts ruled out the possibility that the UFO was a sun dog because of the large angle between the direction to the object and the direction to the sun, and also because the object appeared below the aircraft and at one point was hidden from the sun behind a cloud. The object seemed to be a definite light source and was not a reflection in a lake.[3]

Childerhose wrote about his experience in an article published in a popular magazine based on entries in his logbook. He noted, "On landing at Vancouver a short while later, the members of the section discussed the light briefly. Everyone agreed that it was an unusual sight. Nobody had even encountered a similar orb of light; nobody had any reasonable explanation to offer; nobody suggested that it might have been a 'Flying Saucer.'"[4]

Later in his career, Childerhose became an avid UFO investigator and contributed numerous articles on the subject to magazines and other publications.

THE SIXTIES

CHAPTER TWELVE
THE FALCON LAKE INCIDENT

CHRIS RUTKOWSKI

Note: This chapter was originally written and produced as a privately circulated essay in 1980. The information is based on extensive interviews with Stefan Michalak and his family, military personnel, and other investigators, as well as scores of official notes and documents on record with the National Archives, National Research Council, and Ufology Research of Manitoba (UFOROM) files. It is reproduced in its entirety here, edited slightly.

The Whiteshell Encounter

On May 20, 1967, Stefan Michalak left the Falcon Lake Motel very early in the morning and headed north into the bush, intending to indulge in his hobby of amateur prospecting. Around 9:00 a.m., he found a quartz vein near a marshy area, close to a small stream, and began inspecting the rock formation. At 12:15 p.m., Michalak was startled by the sounds of some geese nearby, agitated by something. He looked up and saw two cigar-shaped objects with bumps on their upper surfaces. They were about forty-five degrees in elevation, glowing bright red, and descending in his direction. As they approached, these strange objects seemed to become more oval and then disc-shaped.

The farthest one of the pair stopped its advance and hovered in mid-air, while the other drew nearer, dropped down, and appeared to land on a large flat rock about 150 feet away. The one in the air stayed for a short while, then departed, changing colour from red to orange to grey as it flew into the west, where it disappeared behind the clouds.

The craft on the ground started changing colour, too, from red to grey, until finally it was the colour of "hot stainless steel" and surrounded by a golden glow. As he watched the craft with fascination, Michalak knelt behind a rock cropping, trying to remain hidden from sight. For the next half-hour, he stayed there, making a sketch of the object and noting things like waves of warm air radiating from the craft, the smell of sulphur, the whirring of a fast electric motor, and a hissing, as if air were being expelled or taken in by the craft. Because he had been chipping away at the rock before the arrival of the craft, he was still wearing his welding goggles to protect his eyes from rock chips. This was fortunate, because brilliant purple light flooded out of slits in the upper part of the craft, and he would have been blinded otherwise.

Suddenly, a door opened in the side of the craft and he could see smaller lights shining out of the opening. Michalak warily approached to within sixty feet of the craft and was able to hear two human-like voices, one with a higher pitch than the other. Convinced the craft was an American secret test vehicle, he brazenly walked up to it and called out, "Okay, Yankee boys, having trouble? Come on out and we'll see what we can do about it." The voices stopped abruptly and, feeling brave enough now, Michalak walked closer to the craft, ending up directly in front of the open doorway. Poking his head through the opening, he saw a maze of lights on some sort of panel and a group of lights flashing in a random sequence.

He stepped back from the craft and noted that the wall was about eighteen inches thick. Abruptly, three panels slid over the opening in front of him, sealing it completely. He took this opportunity to examine the outside of the craft and reached to touch it with his gloved hand. There were no signs of welding or joints; the surface was highly polished and looked like coloured glass. It was also apparently quite hot, because his rubberized glove began to melt.

Without warning, the craft rotated and Michalak was now facing the grid of an exhaust vent of some kind. Then, a blast of hot air hit him in the chest, setting his shirt and undershirt on fire. In a lot of pain, he tore them off and threw them to the ground. He looked up to see the craft rise up and fly off, feeling a whoosh of air as it ascended.

Michalak noticed that some moss and leaves had been set on fire by the blast of hot gas, and so he stamped out the smouldering debris.

When he went over to where the object had been, he immediately felt nauseous and his forehead throbbed from a headache. Piled up in a circle fifteen feet in diameter was a collection of pine needles, dirt, and leaves. As he looked around his headache became worse, and he decided to head back to the motel. He managed to stagger out of the woods. He came upon an RCMP officer. The officer, however, felt Stefan Michalak was drunk, and Stefan was left to fend for himself. At 4:00 p.m., he entered the motel coffee shop to inquire whether or not a doctor was available, as he was now in considerable pain. He decided to return to Winnipeg and took the next bus home. His son met him at the terminal and took him to the Misericordia Hospital.

When word of his experience got out, he was interviewed by TV, radio, and newspaper reporters and eventually UFO investigators. He was tested for radiation contamination, since some radiation was found at the site where Michalak said he had his experience. He did exhibit some very unusual ailments, including reported weight loss, peculiar burn marks on his chest and stomach, charred hair, an odd rash, and recurrent dizziness. He was interviewed by the RCAF and RCMP. He led officials to the site, where the Department of Health and Welfare found such high levels of radiation that they considered cordoning off the area for a short while.

Michalak spent a great deal of his own money travelling to the Mayo Clinic, as it was not covered by medicare. The results of the tests were negative; the physicians could find no explanation for his symptoms, and psychiatrists concluded he was not the type of person who would make up such a bizarre tale. If it was a hoax, it is the most contrived on record, involving radiation, contaminated soil, medical examinations, and a flurry of interrogation by government officials at many levels.

In the report of the United States government-sponsored UFO project, the Condon Committee, Michalak's experience was labelled "unknown," meaning there was no explanation for his experience. The concluding remarks were impressive: "If [the case] were physically real, it would show the existence of alien flying vehicles in our environment."

The Site

Investigators from the USAF and the University of Colorado Condon Committee found cause for concern with Michalak's inability to find the site while in the presence of officials. Michalak visited the area twice after recovering from his encounter before finding the site with Mr. G.A.

Hart, a personal acquaintance. Some writers point to this fact as a prime reason for labelling the case a hoax. However, Michalak has stated that locating the site presented several difficulties. First, when the incident occurred, the trees and bushes were devoid of leaves. When brought back to the area, Michalak said he was disoriented because the foliage was lush and full. This is a common complaint of individuals who hike in wooded areas and can be regarded as a logical reason for experiencing difficulty in finding the site. In addition, Michalak said that for the first expedition, he was transported to the area by helicopter and was told to find the site from the location where they landed. The second expedition began from a point suggested to be Michalak's exit from the bush following his encounter. It too was unsuccessful because of the increased vegetation and Michalak's unsettled state of mind and body. These explanations can be accepted as reasonable and are sufficiently sensible so as to eliminate a negative judgement on the case based solely on the inability to locate the site with official investigators. Disorientation in the wilderness can definitely be a problem in locating specific sites.

There is no question, however, that the site can be easily located with proper trailblazing. The usual method of finding the site is to head north from the Falcon Lake townsite and follow a creek around large rock outcroppings until the bare rock face is seen. The numerous beaver dams and claims markers in the area can be used as reference points. Also interesting is that the actual site was within direct view of a forest ranger tower. However, the forest ranger on duty at the time of the incident did not observe either the landing and flight of the UFO or the smoke that resulted from the ignition of grass by the landed UFO. While this would seem to be a serious flaw in Michalak's story, one must remember that the individual in the tower would not be looking in the direction of the site constantly. Yet, if the object was landed for at least forty-five minutes, and if it gleamed in the sun or emitted an "intense purple light" (as it was said to have done), it is puzzling that the individual in the tower did not notice it.

Another problem the Condon Report found was the reported direction in which the object departed. This direction was 255 degrees, which would have had the object fly away from most corroborating observers, but within a mile of the local golf course. No golfers reported seeing the UFO.

Barrie Thompson, an APRO investigator, was one of the first to accompany Michalak to the site. He reported that finding the site was not that difficult and that the early expeditions to the site were led astray by basic errors. Thompson also noted a large amount of destroyed vegetation around the site, including circular lesions on many leaves in the area.

Radiation

Much was made of the finding of radioactive debris at the site. This suggested to some people that Michalak was possibly suffering from radiation poisoning.

The radiation was detected in soil samples brought back to Winnipeg by Michalak and an associate after they had finally located the site. They had placed Michalak's torn shirt and tape measure in plastic bags and put these together with the soil samples in the same knapsack. When the items were given to officials for examination, the shirt and tape measure were naturally found to be radioactive as well.

Michalak claimed that Stewart Hunt of the Department of Health and Welfare informed him that the soil analysis showed radiation. Hunt's own report noted, "One small area ... contaminated ... across the crown at the rock. There was a smear of contamination about 0.5 x 8.0 inches on one side of the crack. There was also some lichen and ground vegetation contaminated just beyond the smear. The whole contaminated area was no larger than 100 square inches."

The origin of this radiation is in some doubt. Whatever its cause, it was of sufficient quantity for the federal Radiation Protection Division to consider restricting entry to the area. Beyond the areas located by Hunt, there was no radiation above the normal background. A more detailed soil analysis showed a significant level of radium 226, for which there was no explanation. It was suggested that the radium could have come from a luminous watch dial scraped onto the site. However, no evidence could be found to support this contention.

Analyses performed by the federal government's Whiteshell Nuclear Research Establishment (WNRE) showed that the radioactivity in the samples was that of "natural uranium ore." This included counts of both alpha and gamma particles. One 190 KeV photopeak was originally thought to be due to enrichment of uranium 235. While this would seem to indicate something other than natural uranium, the isotopes were later found to be present within the normal ratios.

To check further on the soil radiation, in June 1979 a reanalysis was carried out by physicists at a Canadian university. A lithium-drifted germanium detector showed that all the energies detected could be adequately explained by the decay of natural uranium. It is speculated that confusion may have resulted from overlooking the fact that U-238 decays eventually into radon, a gas. Radon decays further into other elements, but the observed energies indicated a lower abundance than what would be expected. The reason for this, though simple, may not have been immediately obvious: radon is a gas and will dissipate. Therefore, abundances of elements later in the decay chain will be much less than if the previous elements were solids.

Why this would not be immediately obvious to experts at a nuclear laboratory is not clear. Identification of the 190 KeV peak as "abnormally high" may have been an oversight. The theory of radium 226 was related to this peak. Assigning elements to each of the peaks is a trying job, and often two elements give nearly the same peak, often at the same intensity. This process is much like solving a jigsaw puzzle and somewhat open to luck and interpretation, as it depends on variables such as the resolution, efficiency, and capability of the analyzer used. The observed radioactivity could be considered to be due to natural uranium decay.

This, of course, raises the question of why the Department of Health and Welfare would consider closing off the area from such radioactivity. The early tests in 1967 have not been located. These would be helpful, since it is possible that at that time, there may have been different peaks detected from elements with short half-lives. It will be noted, though, that the Whiteshell results, done in 1968, showed nothing other than the 1979 run, so this may suggest that the early analysis yielded the same results.

There exists some disagreement, however. A Canadian Aerial Phenomena Research Organization investigator claimed that Hunt's check of the site showed a much higher level of radiation than was reported. It was suggested that the bulk of the radioactive material was in a rock fissure across the site, which was either missed or ignored by official investigators. This is most relevant to a review of the metal analysis.

The Metal

The metal samples recovered from the site are quite curious. A year after his encounter, Michalak returned to the landing site with an associate. With a Geiger counter, they found two W-shaped silver bars, four and a half inches in length, and several other smaller chunks of the same material. All this was found two inches below some lichen in a crack in the rock over which Michalak said the UFO hovered. Analysis showed that the silver was of high purity and contained low amounts of copper and cadmium. The University of Colorado noted that the composition was "similar to that found in commercially available sterling silver or sheet silver." UFO investigators directly contradicted this, saying the silver concentration was "much higher than would normally be found in native silver or commercially produced silver such as sterling or coinage." The reported percentage of copper, however, at 1 or 2 percent, is similar to that of commercial silver.

The metal showed signs of heating and bending, and it was speculated that it had been molded into its present shape. Support for the heating theory also comes from the fine quartz crystals that were imbedded in the outer layer of the silver. The sand was similar to typical foundry sand, covering all of one bar and half of the other. But the very odd thing about the silver bars was their radioactivity. The bars were covered with small crystals of a uranium silicate mineral and pitchblende, as well as feldspar and hematite. These particles were held to the silver by a sticky substance but could be removed by washing with ethanol and brushing with a soft camel hair brush. The problem is that Department of Health and Welfare officials went to the site on more than one occasion and checked it thoroughly. Why was the silver not discovered by them?

Physiological Effects

The most noted elements of the incident are the many severe physiological effects Michalak experienced during his encounter. When the object took off, Michalak was burned by a blast of heated gas that came from a grill-like opening in front of him. His shirt and undershirt caught fire, burning his upper chest. He tore off these items and stamped them out, not wanting to cause a forest fire. Walking back to where the object had been, he felt nauseated and had a strong headache. He broke out in a cold sweat and began vomiting. Red marks began to appear on his chest and abdomen, burning and irritating. He set out for Falcon Lake in search of medical aid, bare-chested.

He eventually made it back to Winnipeg, where he was examined at the Misericordia Hospital on May 20. He told the examining physician that he had been burned by "exhaust coming out of an aeroplane." On May 22, Michalak's family physician examined him and decided the first-degree burns on his abdomen were not very serious. He prescribed 292s for the pain and seasickness tablets for the nausea. On May 23 Michalak went to a radiologist, who found no evidence of radiation trauma. A whole-body count taken a week later at the Whiteshell Nuclear Research Establishment also showed no radiation above normal background. The burns on Michalak's abdomen were diagnosed as thermal in nature. Later, the curious geometric pattern of the burns led one skeptic to speculate that Michalak had fallen onto a "hot barbeque grill."

Over the next few days, Michalak reported that he lost 22 pounds from his normal weight of 180. Judging from the fact that Michalak reported an inability to hold food down, in one week his weight loss could have been considerable. However, his physician could not verify the weight loss, since he had not seen him for over a year. Also reported was a drop in his blood lymphocyte count from 25 to 16 percent, which returned to normal after a period of four weeks. These two counts were six days apart but were associated with normal platelet counts on both occasions. This speaks against the theory of radiation exposure. A UFO investigator claimed that the actual drop was from 25 to 6 percent, although this is not supported by medical documentation.

There is some evidence to indicate that the red welts or burns went through periods of fading and recurrence, a most unusual medical situation. Because of the suggestion of radiation at the site, it was quickly suggested that the welts were radiation burns. This was not supported by the evidence, either.

Radiation was also blamed for an "awful stench" that seemed to come from within Michalak's body. It was suggested that a quick dose of gamma rays may have deteriorated the food he had just eaten for lunch, giving him a vile odour and causing him to vomit "green bile." Individuals consulted on this, however, say that such a strong burst of gammas would have deteriorated *Michalak*, not just his digested food.

Another physiological effect was the rash that appeared on Michalak's upper body. The University of Colorado reported that the rash was "the result of insect bites and was not connected with the alleged UFO experience." An RCAF investigator reported that he had been bitten by black flies when he was with Michalak searching for the site. Medical reports show that Michalak had "skin infections" with "hivelike areas with impetiginous centers." Later he had "generalized urticaria" (common hives) and felt weak, dizzy, and nauseated on several occasions. Several times in intervening years he went to a doctor for numbness and swelling of the joints.

A hematologist's report showed that Michalak's blood had "no abnormal physical findings," although there were "some atypical lymphoid cells in the marrow plus a moderate increase in the number of plasma cells." This is in some contradiction to several published accounts that claimed that there were "impurities" in Michalak's blood. It is obvious that the reported irregularities in his blood would not in themselves be the cause for his condition.

The swelling of his body, however, strongly suggests an allergic reaction of some sort. After an apparent recurrence of his swelling while at work on September 21, 1967, Michalak reported that doctors diagnosed his affliction as "the result of some allergy." The symptoms leading up to this diagnosis were burning sensations around his neck and chest. Then, there was a burning in his throat, his body "turned violet," his hands swelled "like a balloon," his vision failed, and he lapsed into unconsciousness.

Later, he described how sometimes his wrists swelled so much that they filled his shirt cuffs. Exactly what sort of allergy could Michalak have had?

The Mayo Clinic

In August 1968, Michalak went to the famed Mayo Clinic in Rochester, Minnesota. The purpose of his visit was to undergo tests to determine exactly what was ailing him, as the doctors in Winnipeg appeared to be unhelpful. It is worthy of note that Michalak paid for the Mayo tests entirely on his own, as Canadian medicare would not cover such a trip. He went and stayed at a hotel near the hospital, walking across the street each day and attending as an outpatient. He reported that he was given a thorough physical and psychological examination by various doctors and then sent home.

Michalak showed investigators bills from the Clinic made out to "Mr. S. Michalak" and his registration card. He waited for several weeks but received no word on his results. UFO investigators were anxious to learn the results as well and sought the aid of medical consultants to accelerate the process. They then received a letter from the Clinic that bluntly said that Michalak had never been registered there and that they didn't know anything about him. This immediately spurred shouts of "cover-up!" from UFO buffs, as it appeared to be a deliberate attempt to mislead the investigation.

Was this a cover-up or just a matter of incompetence? It perhaps was neither.

Medical ethics is a very serious concern, and few realize that the so-called red tape has been set up for the protection of both doctor and patient. There is a very great danger in releasing confidential files to unauthorized personnel and this certainly applies to other fields as well as ufology. Another letter was sent to the Mayo Clinic, this time accompanied by a release form signed by Michalak, and the report came immediately.

Michalak had been found by them to be in good health but with neurodematitis and simple syncope (fainting spells caused by sudden cerebral blood pressure losses). The report suggested that the syncope had to do with hyperventilation or impaired cardiac output. This is interesting, as Michalak did indeed have heart problems later in his life.

The psychiatric section of the report showed that despite the usual generalizations normally assigned to individuals giving a detailed UFO encounter story, there was no other evidence of delusions, hallucinations, or other emotional disorders. It seems that there was nothing wrong with Michalak. He had no ailment directly related to an encounter with a UFO.

Investigations

Michalak called the *Winnipeg Tribune* late Saturday afternoon on the holiday long weekend, after returning home from the hospital. The next evening, May 21, reporter Heather Chisvin was the first one to talk to him about the experience, and her story must be considered the first account uninfluenced by later documentation.

The first investigator on the scene, however, was Barrie Thompson, who had read the account in the newspaper and immediately contacted Michalak. Thompson's investigation, on behalf of APRO, began the series of civilian UFO investigations. Michalak noted, "After hearing my story, [Thompson] stated his belief that the craft was not an earthly creation." Michalak praised Thompson on several occasions because "he was the first person who took my story seriously."

Soon, however, the Michalak household was in turmoil. Calls (crank and otherwise) came in at all hours of the day and night, people dropped in at any time, and letters poured in by the bagful.

UFO investigators took Michalak to get a body radiation count at the WNRE and encouraged him to take other tests. One misleading bit of information said that Michalak had been to a clinical hypnotist and that he had been hypnotically regressed. In fact, the clinical hypnotist had only interviewed Michalak and not put him under. A tape of a hypnosis session with Michalak is in existence, but the session was conducted, apparently, by an amateur who was a reporter for the *Winnipeg Free Press* at the time. (This issue is not fully resolved, as others insist that a clinical hypnotist was involved. Until the original hypnosis tape and/or transcript is published or given voluntarily to present-day researchers, the case still has gaps that need filling.)

The RCAF investigations were under the direction of Squadron Leader P. Bissky, who was of the opinion that the case was a hoax. However, many relevant documents are contained in Department of National Defence (DND) files on the case and have been obtained by several ufologists. A rather carefully worded statement is in the National Research Council's Non-Meteoric Sightings File, DND 222, noting, "Neither the DND, nor the RCMP investigation teams were able to provide evidence which could dispute Mr. Michalak's story." Further, RCMP analysis by its forensic lab was "unable to reach any conclusion as to what may have caused the burn damage" to Michalak's clothing.

Cover-up?

The Mayo Clinic "cover-up" aside, the Canadian government seemed to refuse access to information on the case. On June 29, 1967, it was reported that MP Edward Schreyer asked about UFO investigations during a question period in the House of Commons. The Speaker of the House "cut off the subject without government reply." Then, in response to requests by several cabinet members to obtain information on the incident, on November 6, 1967, Defence Minister Leo Cadieux stated, "It is not the intention of the Department of National Defence to make public the report of the alleged sighting." On November 11, 1967, Schreyer formally placed a written question on the Commons order paper seeking information on UFOs.

This closed-mouth attitude of the government prompted several comments by the press. About the case, one editor noted, "The attempt to keep it concealed can have only one effect — it will give the UFO legend another boost." Of course, he was precisely correct.

On October 14, 1968, House Leader Donald MacDonald again refused an MP, this time Barry Mather, access to reports on the Michalak case. However, on February 6, 1969, Mather was given permission by a member of the Privy Council to examine their file on UFOs, "from which a few pages have simply been removed." It was reported that outright release of the file "would not be in the public interest" and might "create a dangerous precedent that would not contribute to the good administration of the country's business."

Psychological Effects

The psychological aspects of an encounter with a UFO, if true, would be substantial. Michalak's reaction and thoughts about his experience are quite interesting.

By the time Michalak made it back to his motel, he said, he was exhausted:

> I did not go inside the motel for fear of contaminating people around me … I felt detached from the rest of the world … The pain was unbearable … the odour seemed to come from within me, and I could not escape it … I was afraid that I had ruined my health and visualized the resulting hell should I have become disabled … my mind centered on the possible consequences … there had to be some way of getting medical attention … I thought of the press. Things that happened to me were definitely news, if nothing else … I did not want to alarm my wife, or cause a panic in the family. I phoned her as a last resort, telling her that I had been in an accident…

Michalak felt that it was his duty to report the incident and was initially unafraid of ridicule. Later, he and his family became somewhat defensive about the incident and were irritated to read skeptical accounts.

It is this writer's personal impression that Michalak was a very sincere individual. Also, it should be emphasized that psychiatrists could not find any evidence of emotional or mental illness in the man. He was not considered someone who would make up stories for notoriety or personal gain.

Hoax?

Would Michalak have gone to so much trouble to perpetrate a hoax? There is no question that he became seriously ill and experienced lasting effects. If we can assume that Michalak burned himself while concocting his hoax, would he have then repeatedly pursued medical assistance and gone to the Mayo Clinic in a belaboured effort to make it look good?

One physics professor at a major Canadian post-secondary institution believed that Michalak was experimenting with toy rockets that exploded because of mishandling. He also suggested that he was amateurishly trying to hit two chunks of uranium together to make a homemade bomb, the gridlike pattern of burns on his body caused by the grill he used as a support. This totally unfounded theory ignored most of the known facts of the case, yet was seriously proposed.

An RCAF spokesman was convinced that Michalak was drunk and had fallen on a hot barbeque grill. One immediate objection to this is that contact burns would give exactly the *reverse* impression of those found on Michalak's body. Others suggested the case was a hoax because Michalak could not find the site when with the Condon investigators.

Roy Craig, the Condon Committee's investigator, concluded, "If [Michalak's] reported experience were physically real, it would show the existence of alien flying vehicles in our environment." However, he noted "inconsistencies and incongruities" and said that even with some of the other evidence associated with the case, he would have to stick to his initial conclusion, namely that "this case does not offer probative information regarding inconventional [sic] craft." Despite this the index of the Condon Report lists the case as an "unexplained" sighting.

Craig also found reason to question that the metal samples found by Michalak would have been missed by early investigators at the site. Stewart Hunt of the Department of Health and Welfare described his examination of the area as "a thorough survey," using three different radiation counters. It is definitely odd that the metal chunks were not found until Michalak's visit to the site a year later. Thompson remarked that the samples were deeply buried inside the crack in the rock and that some effort was expended in getting them out. He also remarked that most of the radiation detected was inside the fissure. A close examination of soil samples showed that small silver particles were present in the mixture, suggesting that someone did not simply plant the silver bars. However, this is not conclusive, as native silver particles occur naturally in the area in small amounts, and their presence in the soil samples does not eliminate the possibility of planting.

There is no doubt that the metal samples are very suspicious. They even had an obvious seam that suggested fabrication, as if someone molded the silver in a definite shape. Did Michalak produce these himself? Or did someone *else* produce them and plant them at the site to make it look more convincing? Even without the metal samples, the case was a significant one, needing no support. In fact, the samples tend only to confuse the case. An amateur UFO buff probably would have thought that the samples would enhance the case. Since the case attracted many such individuals, it would be difficult to determine who this might have been. One cover-up theory has the government fabricating the samples themselves. However, evidence for this idea would be difficult to obtain and essentially impossible to prove. If true, it would raise the question of why the government would deliberately enhance the case and then create an aura of secrecy, lending itself to suspicion. Other hoax theories can be postulated, but all need the necessary proof, including a motive for their devices.

Conclusions

Something very unusual occurred on May 20, 1967, north of Falcon Lake. Stefan Michalak came back from his prospecting trip badly burned and seriously ill, claiming that he had encountered a strange craft. But is the account true? Can this case be proved beyond a shadow of a doubt? The evidence includes the following:

- An eyewitness account of a vehicle behaving in ways not attributable to conventional craft.
- Physiological damage to the witness, the mechanism of which is not immediately obvious.
- A visible landing site consisting of a ring of loose soil on a bare patch of rock, plus some unusual radioactive materials including relatively pure metal bars.

Does this prove that an alien craft landed near Falcon Lake? No. If we assume that Michalak's story was truthful (and we have no immediately obvious reason to suppose otherwise), then we have a solid report of a landed UFO, complete with physical and physiological effects. What could it have been?

A host of explanations have been offered by writers on the subject. Journalist Yurko Bondarchuk suggested that Michalak was burned by "an intelligently guided craft of unconventional structure and of unknown origin." He also found evidence of government intervention in the case and noted that the publication of Michalak's book, which to some suggests a hoaxer's methods, was financially not a successful venture, and the experience proved to be more costly to Michalak than a boon.[1,2]

Author Palmiro Campagna, on the other hand, is of the opinion that Michalak was burned by a secret American test vehicle, essentially a version of the AVRO "flying saucer" that had been in development and reportedly cancelled in the early sixties.[3]

This writer is hesitant to give a final evaluation to the case. Personal interviews with the Michalaks showed them to be sincere people not prone to irrational acts. They were intelligent, level-headed individuals and were well read on many subjects. Their annoyance at their notoriety was apparent, and their defensiveness at further prodding showed they had been subjected to severe ridicule and criticism since the incident first hit the media in 1967.

Debates over the merit of the case are continuing. If officials were convinced Michalak was a hoaxer, why was he not prosecuted for public mischief? Was there no definite evidence towards this end? It certainly would have been an interesting court case, arguing about the existence of UFOs in Canadian airspace.

It is possible Michalak would have won.

A&E & Me: Reflections on the Falcon Lake Incident, Thirty Years Later

In 1996, producers from the Arts & Entertainment Television Network (A&E) contacted me to arrange a preliminary interview and work out details on their coverage of the Falcon Lake case for a series titled *Unexplained*. Only one show in the series was slated to be about UFOs, and there would be only five cases included. These represented, in their opinion, the cases with the best evidence and most accessible investigative background materials in the history of ufology.

These few best cases were to be about the Belgian triangles, the Rendlesham encounter, the Michigan radar case, and the Falcon Lake incident. The fifth segment would be on the Roswell affair, condensed for brevity. All this in an hour, including commercials!

Originally, A&E said they were going to fly me down to their studios in June, but that plan fell through because of scheduling problems and because they had a change in producers. The end result was that the new A&E producer, Bill Neal, would fly into Winnipeg in mid-August to do some interviews and arrange some location shoots.

On Thursday afternoon, August 15, I met Bill at the home of Stan Michalak, the son of Stefan Michalak. Bill had been picked up by Steve Hladkyj, a friend of mine who was possibly the best videographer in the business. (Hladkyj produced a TV special on the Manipogo monster that July, for which I was narrator and host.) Bill wanted to interview Stan Michalak because the elder Michalak was ill and not up to on-screen appearances.

Stan recounted how his family was affected by his dad's experience. Although he had been only ten at the time, he remembered that the way TV and radio reporters were often coming around was tempered by their constant presence, interfering with his life. He testified how sick his father had become and recalled seeing the burns. He remembered especially "the smell like rotting eggs and burned electrical circuits which seemed to come out" of his father, "through his very pores."

Stan argued that there was no way his father could have made up the story and concocted such an elaborate hoax. "He was simply not that kind of guy," he said.

It's not generally known that Stan and I went to school together. I remember playing with him as a child and have a vague recollection that his dad had been sick at one point, but when you're prepubescent, that kind of detail is not that important. We kept in touch through the years, occasionally crossing paths when he was an on-air TV personality and also in radio. He's also a fine artist; his paintings of real-life scenes are reminiscent of Hopper and are clearly a result of his father's talented genes. (Stefan Michalak's excellent landscape paintings are known to only a few.)

Steve Hladkyj set up the camera on Stan's patio with his friend Greg as the soundman. Bill interviewed Stan for about an hour, carefully getting him to cover several important points. I hung around as the gofer.

I had urged the original A&E producer to interview Peter Warren, an investigative journalist with an abrasive on-air radio personality but a warm, witty persona underneath. Peter had been the news editor at the *Winnipeg Tribune* when Steve Michalak showed up to relate his story, and I thought he would be an excellent character witness since he had always supported Michalak whenever he was mentioned over the years.

However, somewhere in the planning process, Peter was dropped from the list. I told Bill that Peter would still be a good person to get on-camera, and he asked me to see if Peter was available. As it happened, Peter had been out the entire day investigating a story about pasteurized milk and didn't return until suppertime. But since the interview with Stan took longer than expected and Steve also had to shoot some still photos and maps, by the time we were done Peter was available.

We zipped out to Peter's house: a beautiful, well-appointed home with a large front yard and a backyard that dropped steeply down to the river. Inside, a baby grand piano sat in an atrium next to the patio and deck, adjacent to the bright, well-stocked kitchen. While we waited for Steve and Bill to arrive, Peter offered me a glass of his homemade wine and we chatted in his living room.

When the others arrived (Steve had lost me in traffic), we went out onto the deck overlooking the river. Steve quickly set up and then Bill asked Peter what he remembered about the case. Bill said Peter was "fantastic." His glowing comments about Michalak's character were almost too flattering. At one point, Bill asked him if he thought Michalak might have been lying about his experience, and Peter pointed his finger at Bill. "You'd be more likely to be scamming me than Steve Michalak!" he retorted.

Bill was very impressed with the Michalak case. He could not understand why it had not received more attention from researchers and did not consider that Michalak had hoaxed the incident. However, he did say that he expected skeptic Roy Craig to "come up with something" when he spoke with him during the coming weeks.

The next morning, they picked me up at my home just outside of Winnipeg. From there, it was an easy hop onto the freeway straight out to Falcon Lake. Steve drove the van, with his brother-in-law Terry beside him. (Terry was hired to play the role of Steve Michalak in the recreation of the event.) Greg and Bill were in the row behind them and I was assigned the back of the bus.

During the one-and-a-half-hour trip into the Canadian Shield, we talked about where we would go and how we would approach the shoot. Bill wanted to find a nice open area in which to film the recreation of Michalak getting burned. The plan was to actually set a shirt and dummy on fire and make up Terry to look as if he had been injured. I didn't think that setting a fire inside a park was a good idea, especially during a forest fire season. We thought about doing it at a campground, but it would be best to do it on private property where government and park regulations would not apply.

We arrived at Falcon Lake right at noon and proceeded directly to the parking lot of the Falcon Creek hiking trail. My plan was to park there and hike into the area near the main creek, less than a mile up the trail. Since the A&E expedition was not designed to reach the exact site but only to find a suitable area for filming a recreation, the actual site was not necessary.

We travelled up the trail about a quarter of a mile, over a bridge, across rocks, past a boulder the size of a mobile home, through dense underbrush, and finally out onto immense, flat shale lit by the bright sun. Bill decreed that one flat area was perfect for the shoot and that the natural lighting was optimal, so we stopped and set out the gear.

The first step was to recreate Michalak examining some rocks for signs of silver or other ores. There was a natural cleft in a rock at the side of one flat spot, so that's where Steve set up the camera. Terry donned a cotton undershirt and plaid shirt that matched Michalak's old clothing, then added the old-style cap, goggles, and rubberized gloves. A little talcum powder added to his hair by Steve and me, and Terry looked somewhat like a fifty-year-old Michalak.

The shooting went very well, although scenes were done over and over again, and from several angles, with close attention paid to continuity. The one scene where Michalak first sees the UFO must have taken two hours by itself. Then, the fun stuff: Michalak touches the side of the craft and is burned by exhaust as it lifts skyward.

We weren't going to do the pyrotechnics there, but Terry re-enacted getting knocked down by the exhaust and getting set on fire. For the close-ups of his body, I skilfully used oil pastels to create singes, charring, and burns on Terry's chest and stomach to match those that had appeared on Michalak's body.

Terry faked being blasted with hot gas and rolled, staggered to his feet, and acted disoriented while Steve did hand-held close-ups and point-of-view shots, following him around the site. Greg ran along beside them with the boom mike, capturing every one of Terry's moans and gasps.

After what seemed an eternity, it was finally time for my part. Bill had wanted to interview me out at Falcon Lake for an air of credibility. We found a relatively flat rock and Greg miked me up. Bill sat on a rock across from me and when Steve had the camera in place began asking me about my involvement with the case and my view on what had really happened.

The major sticking points for the few outspoken skeptics of the case are the inability for Michalak to find the site in the company of *Life* magazine journalists and the Condon investigators, the few discrepancies in the story, and the view that Michalak's physiological effects were nothing more serious than insect bites.

The third objection is the easiest to deal with; Michalak's injuries were obviously much more serious than insect bites, and the rashes that later appeared could not conclusively be explained as allergic reactions. The second isn't that much of a problem; Michalak's own basic story hadn't changed significantly over the past thirty years, and the only real incongruities are those that arose during the various civilian, military, and other official investigations.

There remains the one issue of finding the site, however. Stan Michalak explained that the site is not all that easy to locate, even with good orienteering skills. The trees all look the same, there were no trails in or out at that time, the rock faces appear similar, and the terrain is fairly rugged. Furthermore, Michalak was still very ill when he was asked to lead the official expedition. It can be argued that these and other factors could have made finding the site more of an effort than had been thought.

But to the contrary, the main expedition included members of the RCMP as well as RCAF, and one would think that they would be pretty good at wilderness orienteering. Finding a thirty-foot circular patch of radioactive vegetation should have been a piece of cake. Of course, according to the map in RCMP files, the team had to search an area of twenty square miles.

Curious, also, is Craig's claim that Michalak suggested the search be called off only an hour or so after they started, shortly after noon. Given that they still had another four or five hours of daylight at that time of year, that is a bit odd. But it could be explained by the fact that Michalak was ill and tired easily. As I noted earlier, Michalak must have been very disoriented after his encounter to wander so far west of the site before reaching the highway.

The fact that the site was found by Michalak and a family friend a few weeks later can indeed suggest to skeptics that the site only existed after he had created it himself as part of a hoax. But would the RCMP and RCAF not have checked Michalak's movements previous to his finding the site and tried to pin a public mischief charge on him if they were convinced he was having them on? The numerous searches must have cost a great deal of money at the time.

Furthermore, what could a hoaxer have been doing in the wilderness that could have resulted in a peculiar pattern of chemical and heat burns? Why go to the media with a story that couldn't be supported? Why not just shut up about the whole thing?

So many aspects of the hoax theory don't add up. It raises more questions than it answers. In some ways, it's easier to believe that Michalak was burned by a flying saucer.

Anyway, I answered Bill's questions as best I could, saying that I did not think the case has been satisfactorily explained. Maybe a clever editor could get me to say that it was a prelude to *Independence Day*, but there's always a danger of that.

After my interview, we packed up and headed out of the woods. Bill had an idea that the riding stable's owner might allow us to film on his property. He went into the office while I went over to the stable, where a teenage girl was getting some horses ready for riding. She asked me what we were doing and I told her we were doing a piece about the guy who was burned by a UFO.

"Oh, you mean the place on the ridge," she said. "I've been there lots of times."

Apparently, the place is a mecca. Everyone in the area knows about it. In fact, a UFO buff once organized a public trip out to the site that attracted nearly 150 hikers. According to some people at the riding stable, "the crowd really made a mess of the site."

Bill returned with the owner, who agreed to let us film somewhere on the property. The first order of business was to shoot a close-up of gas jetting out of the UFO's exhaust grid. Bill and Steve had cleverly manufactured this with a cookie sheet and a fire extinguisher. Steve had found a rusted cookie sheet, polished it clean, and drilled an array of holes in its surface. It was mounted on some tripods, and Bill held a carbon dioxide fire extinguisher behind it. That took several tries. The best effect was when Terry held a cardboard box between the nozzle and the sheet to disperse the flow slightly. He got a little cold, admittedly, but that's showbiz. (Remember, this was done in the parking lot of a riding stable.)

Then it was time for the action shots of Terry as Michalak getting blasted, with real smouldering shirts and vegetation. I now fully understood the reason for bringing along the fire extinguisher.

Bill spotted a rock face and scrambled up a cliff to the top of a ridge about thirty feet up, just beside some log cabin–style cottages. He declared it a good spot and we went and got the gear. Terry and I had stuffed another shirt with yellow insulation. The idea was to use a blowtorch to start it on fire then put it out with gloved hands and leave it smouldering. We did this all on the ridge, with amused cottagers looking down on us. (Literally and figuratively.)

The first series of shots, though, had Terry on the ground and getting blasted with the fire extinguisher "smoke." I have to admit, it looked pretty good for Roger Corman. (Aside: the A&E producer's son worked for Corman.) Again, Steve used hand-held shots to make the effect more dramatic.

Then Steve and I set up the stuffed shirt and Terry lit the torch. The shirt burned easily — too easily, which was when we found out that Bill shouldn't have done so many takes of the exhaust grid shot. All we got from the fire extinguisher was a gasp of air. We ended up stomping on the shirt and some moss that had also ignited.

On the tape, though, this all looked rather impressive. With proper editing, Bill thought the entire recreation would look great.

Finally, the shoot was over for the day. It was nearly 7:00 p.m. and we had missed both lunch and dinner. Steve had to return the camera equipment by about 8:30, so we packed up and headed back to Winnipeg.

On the way back, we discussed the case, and Bill agreed that the site would not have been that easy to find. If Michalak was a hoaxer, other hoaxers should tip their hats to his groundbreaking efforts. If he had a real experience, the case was very puzzling. Perhaps the initial sighting was bona fide but a UFO buff fabricated evidence in order to make it seem more robust. If one was into conspiracies, one might even believe that the military had created the site and muddied the effects to cover up a real landing of something. (After all, their investigation was hardly thorough or objective.)

Being directly involved with an outside view of the Falcon Lake case gave me a new perspective on the incident. Although I had already done a lot of research on the case, I appreciate now how much more can be done and also what is missing from the original investigation reports. For example, where exactly did Michalak emerge from the bush? Where in the RCMP report are the comments from the officer whom Michalak met on the highway immediately after his experience? What path did Michalak take out of the woods? Steve Hladkyj noted that a real police investigation would have tried to track Michalak's movements between the time of his encounter and the time he found the site in order to rule out tampering.

As skeptical as I am of most UFO cases, the Falcon Lake case is intriguing. All things considered, it's a strange case. If it is a hoax, it's got enough complications to make it one of the best on record. As a scientist, I can only judge a case on the available evidence. There is, of course, no proof that the object Michalak encountered was a flying saucer. It could have been a military test craft of some sort, I suppose, and that might explain the official interest in the case and why their investigation seems incomplete.

All we have is a record of actual injuries to a man who claimed he was burned in a close encounter with a strange craft in a sparsely populated part of the Canadian Shield. It's a single-witness case, yet it does come with some physical evidence. It may be inconclusive evidence, but it's there nevertheless.

Michalak's family supported him completely. Wouldn't they have grown tired of the whole charade after all these years and called him on it? They gained nothing and suffered greatly. With all the attention and the number of people involved in the case over the years, wouldn't an accomplice have finked on them at one point?

CHAPTER THIRTEEN
NOVA SCOTIA'S UFO CRASH

GEOFF DITTMAN

By now most people are familiar with the story of Roswell, New Mexico's alleged UFO crash. It has been endlessly debated both within the UFO community[1] and outside. Hollywood has even produced several movies featuring the crash.[2] In 1997, for the fiftieth anniversary, people from around the world flocked to the small town to pay homage and party, much like how fans of Elvis pilgrimage to Graceland. What most people don't know, however, is that Canada has its own Roswell in the form of Shag Harbour, Nova Scotia. The story was generally ignored until two ufologists named Chris Styles and Don Ledger began chasing it in the nineties. In 2001, Ledger and Styles published their findings in the definitive study of Shag Harbour, *Dark Object.* Shag Harbour is now considered one of the more important of the alleged UFO crashes.

Something fell from the sky late one night in 1967, and this fall was documented not only by the Royal Canadian Mounted Police but also by the military. It began in the early evening of October 4, 1967. People all around Quebec and the Maritimes began to see something strange in the sky over Canada. First, over the southeastern part of Quebec, pilots of an Air Canada DC-8 saw a large, brightly lit rectangular object, estimated to be flying at around twelve thousand feet, followed by a trail of smaller lights flying in a parallel flight path. At around 7:19 p.m. ADT, and then again about two minutes later, an explosion seemed to occur around the UFO. The smaller trailing lights began to move erratically. The Air Canada crew watched the display for a few minutes longer until it drifted out of sight.[3]

About half an hour later, people in the Maritimes began observing strange sights in the sky. Two brothers near Shearwater, Nova Scotia, saw a bunch of lights moving from the northeast to the southwest.[4] Then around 9:00 p.m. ADT, the captain and crew of a fishing vessel near Sambro, Nova Scotia, saw several red lights over the water. Not only did they see the lights visually, but they also picked them up on radar. The RCMP, communicating with the captain via the Canadian Cost Guard, were curious enough about the event to request the captain file a report when he returned to port.[5]

Witnesses on mainland Nova Scotia began to report sightings around 10:00 p.m. ADT. Chris Styles saw a disc-shaped object glowing orange and drifting up the Halifax Harbour. After running closer to the object, Styles could see that it was an orange ball, roughly fifty feet in diameter, moving slowly over the water. No sound could be heard.[6]

Styles wasn't the only witness in the area at that time. Others also reported seeing the orange ball drifting in a southeasterly direction. Sometime after 10:30 p.m., Will Eisnor saw something strange over Lunenburg Village, also in Nova Scotia.[7] He observed three lights in the sky in a triangular formation. A professional photographer, Eisnor managed to take photos of the lights. While interesting, the lights cannot be definitively identified from looking at the photo.

Observations continued around the province. At about 11:00 p.m., just southwest of Waymouth, Nova Scotia, a police officer and two game wardens observed a fireball just above the trees.[8] Approximately twenty-five minutes later, the strange sights finally found their way to Shag Harbour. Five youths observed an object descending at a moderate pace.[9] With a swishing sound, the object fell out of the witnesses' sight, seemingly crashing into the harbour. Moving to the harbour to see what happened, the youths could see the object floating in the water, about two hundred yards or more from the shore.

At this point, the machinery of government began to move. Thinking the object might be a crashed plane, the youths called the RCMP. The local RCMP dispatched a car to the scene. The local police also contacted the Halifax station, the headquarters for the surrounding area. In turn, Halifax contacted the national headquarters in Ottawa. Ottawa then filed a UFO report with the air force.

The air force, suspecting a downed plane, completed the circle by contacting the Rescue Coordination Centre back in Halifax.[10]

Meanwhile in Shag Harbour, the local RCMP began to think of ways to reach the object, whatever it was.[11] Three RCMP officers were at the scene (one of whom saw the lights in the sky earlier). For several minutes the officers were able to see a strange yellow light off the shore. With the help of binoculars, the officers were also able to see what appeared to be yellow foam around the light.[12] Local fishermen were awakened, and the Mounties were able to secure at least two boats. Unfortunately, by this time the object had sunk beneath the surface.

The boats travelled out to where the object was last seen. While the would-be rescuers didn't find the object or any occupants, they did find something else. Thick yellow foam was floating on the surface in the vicinity of the crash site. The foam was estimated to be about three inches thick and covered an area about eighty feet wide and a half-mile in length. Bubbles could be seen coming to the surface, and the smell of sulfur was in the air. Travelling through the foam naturally made the boats' occupants nervous, not knowing its composition or density.[13]

Other fishing boats joined the first two in the search, and by 12:30 a.m. the Canadian Coast Guard had arrived on the scene. The search continued, but by 4:00 a.m. many of the searchers, including the coast guard, had temporarily thrown in the towel.[14]

The search began again the next morning, this time with the help of a navy dive team. Four scuba divers, later to be joined by three others, searched the depths of the harbour in hope of finding the object that fell from the sky.[15]

The military was puzzled as to what could have crashed into the water. In an air force memorandum dated October 6, 1967, it was indicated that "the Rescue Coordination Centre conducted preliminary investigation and discounted the possibilities that the sighting was produced by an aircraft, flares, floats, or any other known objects."[16]

The search continued through to Monday, when it was finally called off. Officially, nothing was found. Unofficially, however, rumors circulated that something, or at least pieces of something, were recovered and sent to a naval base in Dartmouth. One witness believed he saw divers pulling material with the appearance of aluminum out of the water.[17]

And here the story sat for some time, with an object apparently crashing into Shag Harbour, only to disappear. But then UFO researchers Chris Styles and Don Ledger began to hear of an apparent second crash, this one around Shelbourne Harbour. Naval vessels searched the area with the help of scuba divers and remained in the area for a good week.[18]

Ledger and Styles managed to link the two incidents at Shag and Shelbourne harbours. Seemingly, the two crashes were one and the same. According to a confidential informant, NORAD tracked the object from where it first entered Earth's atmosphere over Siberia to where it crashed into Shag Harbour. It floated in the water for a while, only to submerge and then apparently move under its own power northwest, where it eventually came to rest in Shelbourne Harbour.[19] The navy moved in and the search began. Styles suggests that a barge was moved into the area to remove anything that was recovered.[20]

Explanations?

Officially, nothing was recovered from the waters off the coast of Nova Scotia in the search for what crashed back in October 1967. The Condon Committee examined the case (Case #34 in its report). After a brief review of events, the report concluded the case: "No further investigation by the project was considered justifiable, particularly in view of the immediate and thorough search that had been carried out by the RCMP and the Maritime Command."[21] No explanation for the sightings was even attempted by the committee.

Thirty-five years after the events is it possible to come up with an explanation? One suggestion put forward was that the object was either a downed satellite or meteorite. This explanation brings to mind another alleged UFO crash incident that has been explained by some to be the recovery of Soviet space debris. This incident, in Kecksburg, Pennsylvania, in 1965, like Shag Harbour in 1967, involved a large number of witnesses and documented evidence of the presence of the military. Such factors tend to differentiate Shag Harbour and Kecksburg from most other alleged UFO crashes, which tend to have very few first-hand witnesses and no documented interest from the military. But is a downed satellite or space debris an acceptable explanation for what happened at Shag Harbour? An immediate problem for such an explanation is the eyewitness testimony. Eyewitnesses reported behaviour (such as floating on the water) that is inconsistent with space debris. While eyewitness testimony is frequently wrong, one must nonetheless question the strength of the space debris hypothesis based on the testimony.

Another explanation offered for Shag Harbour is that it was simply a hoax. For example, after Discovery Canada aired a segment about Shag Harbour on a special UFO show, they received an email from an angry viewer who offered them a slightly different version of the story. The email reads as follows:

> Subject: Shag Harbour UFO sighting in 1967
> On Oct 4 and again on Oct 11, 1967 three men doing nightwatch at the rock-weed processing plant just north of Shag Harbour in Woods Harbour, set off signal flares, which arched southward out over the water west of Shag Harbour. These were observed and interpreted as UFO's. When the controversy arose, the men were afraid to confess for fear of losing their jobs. (There may have been liquor involved as well.)
>
> One of the men confessed this information to my father-in-law when they were both in hospital some time ago. My father-in-law is in his 80s. Two of the participants have since died and the remaining one is not in good health.
>
> I believe that the one remaining could be convinced to confess for the record, if he were assured that he would not suffer ill consequences. I would be willing to make introductions in the event that someone were interested in conducting a legitimate investigation without excessive publicity.
>
> [Name withheld] was the fisherman who took the RCMP out to investigate the night of the sighting. I remember him commenting on the unusual greenish foam streak on the water in the vicinity of the sighting that night. Unfortunately, no one thought to take a water/foam sample at that time.

Much like the astronomical explanation, flares leave much to be desired. Multiple witnesses would have to be grossly mistaken as to what they saw. And it seems unlikely the military would have spent as much time as they did on the search looking for something that was only flares.

As it stands right now, there is no adequate explanation for the Shag Harbour case. After more than thirty-five years, it seems unlikely that we will ever have a suitable explanation.

CHAPTER FOURTEEN
UFOS AND BLACKOUTS

GEOFF DITTMAN

Back in the sixties and seventies many UFO researchers came to believe that UFOs were interested in certain kinds of human infrastructure. Some argued this was because the aliens were determining our military strengths and probing for our weaknesses. This seemed somewhat plausible, as it sounded like something we humans would do, and the places of interest that were put forward were frequently of vital strategic importance. For example, nuclear weapon storage facilities were described as being regularly visited by flying saucers. Other apparent areas of interest included power plants. Accounts from all over the world popped up of UFOs hovering over or around various energy-generating facilities. Then some researchers began linking power failures to UFO sightings, which was not such a great leap given that by this time there had been many documented cases of UFOs seemingly being involved in small, isolated electromagnetic disturbances, like causing individual cars or homes to temporarily lose power. But could UFOs cause large-scale power failures, and is there any evidence that they have done such a thing?

With the incredible amount of electricity used every day in North America, the Canadian and American governments have had to develop a fairly complex system to ensure power is continuously available. The answer to their power problems was the creation of a distribution grid. This grid is essentially a network of power stations over a large geographical area. The various stations are connected with high-voltage transmission lines, allowing the stations to share power and therefore share the demand for electricity. Together the stations are able to more efficiently and effectively handle peaks and troughs in the demand for electricity across the network.[1]

Unfortunately, the network is susceptible to certain kinds of failure. If the conditions are right, these failures can lead to the widespread collapse of the entire network. The last major collapse occurred in 2003; the first was in 1965. It is this first blackout from 1965 that is of interest to us because it allegedly involved UFOs.

The beginning of the blackout was traced to 5:16 p.m. on November 9, 1965. In Ontario, near Niagara Falls, power lines were running north from the massive Sir Adam Beck Generating Station. A massive, unexpected power surge caused a relay in the Beck station to trip in response (somewhat like a circuit breaker in your home). This shut down the line. The power was then sent to the remaining four lines. These each in turn became overloaded and within three seconds all had to shut down.[2] The power had to go somewhere, and according to the Federal Power Commission, the electricity that had been heading north to service the Toronto area "reversed and was superimposed on the lines south and east of Niagara. It was this tremendous thrust upon the transmission system in western New York … which exceeded its capability and caused it to break up."[3] A cascade effect occurred throughout the northeastern power grid, as generating stations were forced to shut down to protect their turbines. Between areas shut down because of excess supply and lines shut down due to an inability to handle an increased demand, much of the Canada–United States Eastern Grid shut down and some 30 million people, spread out over eighty thousand square miles, lost power.

People today know what to expect from a large-scale blackout. Back then, however, it was something new. Traffic was snarled because of non-functioning traffic lights. People were stuck in high-rise elevators. Subway trains were paralyzed between stops, trapping people in the tunnels. Some airports didn't even have runway lights. Gradually power was restored, with much of Ontario being back to normal within three hours. New York City, however, was without power into the night.[4]

But what caused the initial surge in power? No one knows. Some people's attention has been focused on the many UFO sightings that were made that night. Could UFOs in some way have caused the blackout?

The first UFO report occurred at about 4:30 p.m. local time over Tidioute, Pennsylvania. Pilot Jerry Whitaker and his passenger George

Croninger observed two jets seemingly chasing two shiny, unknown objects. Before the jets could get too close, the UFOs sped off at a high rate of speed.[5]

Less than an hour later, at 5:22 p.m., six people were driving from the Syracuse airport on their way to Rochester when they observed some strange lights in the sky. They watched for several minutes before the lights disappeared behind some hills.[6]

Over Syracuse at this time was private pilot Robert C. Walsh, who happened to be the deputy city aviation commissioner. After the power went out, he was able to safely land his plane (as the airport had emergency power). Upon landing, he began to discuss the blackout with some friends who had gathered along the runway. Suddenly, they saw a fireball approximately fifty feet in diameter seemingly rise up from the ground off in the distance. It rose quickly and then just vanished.[7]

At the same time in New York City, the blackout had begun, and so had the UFO sightings. Witnesses in the Time and Life Building could see a round object over the city giving off a strange glow. Several pictures were taken, one of which was printed in *Time* magazine.[8]

The most interesting sighting of the night occurred back in Syracuse. Shortly after Walsh saw the first fireball, a flight instructor named Weldon Ross and student James Brookings were approaching Hancock airport after finishing a training flight. They observed what they first took to be a building on fire but quickly realized was a flying fireball, approximately one hundred feet in diameter. What is really interesting is that the witnesses believe they saw it over the Clay power substation.[9] This substation moves electric power from Niagara Falls to New York. Before laying blame on the Beck substation in Ontario, authorities first said the source of the blackout was Clay.

Shortly after the blackout, some in the media began to point fingers at UFOs as a possible source of the blackout. The *Indianapolis Star* urged the government to consider the UFO angle.[10] The *Syracuse Herald-Journal* reported the Ross/Brookings sighting, likely to the dismay of the government, which by that time was focusing on Clay. On November 15, even the Associated Press picked up the story. But then the government announced they had solved the mystery of the blackout. Author Donald Keyhoe explained: "Suddenly, the UFO discussion ended — eclipsed by a news flash from Washington. The great blackout, stated the FPC [Federal Power Commission], was now explained. The mystery which had baffled all the top experts had a simple explanation: a broken relay, a circuit breaker, in a Canadian power plant."[11]

After almost a week of focusing on the area around Clay, and just after the UFO sightings there began to receive national attention, the authorities said the Beck power station, not Clay, was the source of the blackout.

Was this a sleight of hand meant to divert attention away from Clay and the UFO sightings? It probably wasn't anything that devious. But it should be noted that the explanation of a broken relay was also wrong. It came out some time later that the relay was not broken but tripped by an unknown surge in electricity.[12]

As for the source of the surge, no one knows. Several prominent UFO investigators of the day followed up on the UFO reports. One such investigator was atmospheric physicist Dr. James McDonald. He went to the FPC offices in Washington, D.C., to see if he could get more information. He was told only that it was a "random fluctuation." They could not tell him the size or strength of the fluctuation or provide him with technical details. Interestingly, the FPC did indicate that it had received many UFO reports from around New York City.[13]

Not impressed by what he was told by the FPC, McDonald still considered UFOs a possible source for the power surge and blackout, though he was far from convinced. In testimony before the House Committee on Science and Astronautics on July 29, 1968, McDonald had this to say: "I am saying there is a puzzling and slightly disturbing coincidence here. I'm not going on record as saying, yes, these are clear-cut cause and effect relations."[14] Basically, McDonald felt that while perhaps the evidence linking UFOs to power failures was weak, it nonetheless deserved some looking into. The FPC, on the other hand, seemed to prefer to completely ignore the potential problem.

So did UFOs cause the great northeastern blackout? The principle of Occam's razor comes to mind: The simplest explanation is likely to be the right one.[15] In other words, don't push a complicated hypothesis when a more simple argument will suffice. The Canada–United States Eastern Grid is an incredibly large and complicated network, encompassing eighty thousand square miles and tens of millions of people, which means we don't have to resort to blaming aliens from space to account for unusual power surges. Nonetheless, the possibility can't be discounted out of hand. Especially since, as will be discussed later in the book, there have been numerous incidences of more localized power failures that have seemingly been traced directly to UFOs.

CHAPTER FIFTEEN
THE LANDING ON ALLUMETTE ISLAND

CHRIS RUTKOWSKI

On May 11, 1969, near the village of Chapeau on Allumette Island in the Ottawa River west of Ottawa, farmer Leo Paul Chaput was awakened by the barking of his dog at about 2:00 a.m. He looked out the window and saw a brilliant light that appeared to be close to the ground, bathing the field in white light. The source of the light seemed to be a domed craft with a flat bottom, only about five hundred feet away. He later described the object as resembling a military helmet worn by French soldiers during the First World War. Chaput looked away briefly, and when he turned his gaze back, the object had vanished completely. However, he could hear what sounded like a motor whirring coming from the direction of where he had seen the craft, getting fainter as if it were slowly moving away.

Chaput had a restless sleep after that and was anxious to look for evidence of the object's passing in the morning. When he went to explore the area, he found a large circular indentation in the ground, six hundred feet from his home. The impression was thirty-two feet in diameter, and Chaput insisted it had not been there the previous day. The marking of scorched grass was a ring two and a half feet wide. Inside, the vegetation had not been damaged but there were three impressions that Chaput noted formed a perfect equilateral triangle, fifteen feet on a side. These were each about eight inches in diameter and three inches deep, suggesting that something very heavy had created them. The suggestion was that these impressions were caused by a "landing tripod" of some kind.

A short distance to the southwest, Chaput discovered a second circle, this one only 27 feet 6 inches in diameter but with the same ring of scorched grass. It, too, had a triangle of three indentations in its centre, but this triangle's sides were not equal. Two were 13 feet 9 inches in length, and the third was 14 feet 6 inches in length.

Chaput then found a third ground marking, this one only a semicircle, near the second. Within the semicircle was a pile of rocks that had been gathered from the field. The semicircle itself was scorched like the others. An explanation offered for the markings was that they were fairy rings, concentric rings of darker grass caused by fungi. However, such rings take years to achieve any significant size.[1]

THE SEVENTIES

CHAPTER SIXTEEN
THE 1973 INVASION OF QUEBEC

CHRIS RUTKOWSKI

Around midnight on October 5, 1973, a couple living near St-Mathias-de-Chambly were walking along a road and saw a bright light like a searchlight playing about in an adjacent field north of their farm. Because there had been some cattle rustling in the area, they assumed the light was from police keeping watch in the field. They continued home to their farmhouse without giving the light much thought.[1]

The next morning, the woman was hanging clothes out to dry and saw a thick column of smoke rising from the field towards the north part of their property, where they had seen the light the night before. She watched the smoke for a while with two workmen who had arrived at the house to do some repairs.

At 11:35 a.m., their attention was drawn to an object shaped like an upside-down bowl resting on the ground about half a mile into the field. It was yellow in colour and an estimated twenty yards in diameter. They assumed the object was a tent of some kind and were surprised to see a smaller object of the same colour seemingly split from the larger and travel about sixty yards away to the known location of a small spring. They believed this second object was a bulldozer moving topsoil over the fallow field.

Then, one of the witnesses noticed something much more unusual. Between the two objects, moving about the field, were five "little people" performing various actions. Now believing the main object was in fact a tent, the witnesses assumed the small figures were boy scouts.

These "scouts" were thought to be four feet in height, although they were mostly obscured by the tall grass, which was about two feet high in that area of the field. They moved back and forth between the two objects, apparently diligently at work on some important task, bending down, waving their arms, turning, and walking to and fro. Upon closer scrutiny, the figures appeared to be wearing some kind of helmets, and their clothes or suits were the same yellowish colour as the "tent."

Because they figured the tent and scouts were not all that mysterious, the witnesses became casual observers, concentrating on their own work and only glancing now and then towards the field. After about twenty minutes, they saw that the objects and figures had disappeared. It was only then that the witnesses became perplexed, because the only road to the field ran by the house and no vehicle had come by during that time.

About a half-hour later, the daughter of the woman arrived at the house, and after hearing her parents' story, decided to enter the field and find out who had been out there. She found a large circular patch of recently burned and crushed grass, about fifteen yards in diameter. Two tracklike marks, each about six inches wide, ran from this burned patch to a smaller one about four feet in diameter near the spring. By the time the daughter returned to the house to report what she had discovered, she had started to feel ill, with a bad headache and nausea.

A month later, UFO investigators were able to visit the area and examined the burned patches as well as the track between the two sites. They also found three unusual depressions in a triangular pattern about ten yards apart within the larger of the two circles. Because of the proximity of the second site to the spring, it was believed by the investigators that aliens had landed to "refuel" and obtain hydrogen for their propulsion system.

Another case involving an apparent entity associated with a UFO sighting occurred on November 18, 1973, near the town of Tracy, not far to the north of the location of the October incident. After dinner that night, four women began a drive south of Tracy toward the village of Contrecoeur. They were surprised to see a "watermelon-sized" ball of yellowish light suddenly appear over a pylon about a quarter of a mile ahead of them. As they passed the light, it started moving westward over the St. Lawrence River on their right. They were able to get a good view of the object, which seemed to change shape as it flew, becoming alternately larger and smaller, dimming and growing in intensity. They soon realized that the light was actually following them as they wove in and out through wooded areas, moving away as they drove through a town then approaching again as they came into the open. Its altitude also seemed to vary from the height of the telephone poles to as high as the cloud ceiling. Eventually, the object was lost to sight as the women drove into Montreal.[2]

The most curious facet of the case, however, concerned events that occurred during the observation of the UFO, while the women were driving just past Contrecoeur. At this point in their journey, they encountered a high volume of traffic, almost bumper to bumper, caused by a pink cloud about twenty yards in diameter lying across the highway. Each car in turn slowed as it passed into and out of the cloud, but there did not seem to be any effect on the cars or on the occupants.

However, immediately upon exiting the cloud, the women saw a small human figure standing directly in the middle of the highway on the white dividing line. The driver had to swerve to avoid the man, who made no attempt to get out of the way and took no notice of the cars passing dangerously close to him. This odd person seemed to be sweeping the highway, slightly bent over and facing away from the women's view, and holding a stick with a wide end piece like a vacuum cleaner and intently pushing it back and forth on the asphalt. He was about five feet tall and wearing a dark green uniform with a peaked cap hiding his face. Once the women had passed the figure and pink cloud, they drove through to Montreal without any further incidents.

More than thirty unusual UFO sightings and encounters were reported in southern Quebec that month. Many were more significant than simply observations of lights in the sky. A third example to highlight this flap occurred on November 21, just outside the town of Joliette.

At about 2:00 a.m., a woman having a bout of insomnia decided to go into her kitchen to have a cigarette. She didn't turn on the light because a streetlight was shining into the room from outside and she could navigate well enough without any additional illumination. However, as she sat there, she was startled by a bright white light flooding into the room from her yard. She went to the window and encountered a glowing figure, not much more than three feet tall, staring at her with two round eyes. It had a round head with a halo of some sort, and what appeared to be whitish flames emanating from its body. No mouth, nose, or ears were visible. It had no shoulders, but its body fell away from the head at a forty-five-degree angle, and there were laces tied around its neck.

The woman admitted she was not scared at all and in fact was somehow attracted by the creature at her window, transfixed by its appearance. After what she judged was fifteen seconds, the figure moved away suddenly and the spell was broken. She ran into the bedroom to wake her husband, and he quickly dressed and ran outside but there was no sign of any intruder or trespasser.

That same night, local police and a Catholic priest all were witnesses to UFOs in and around a local quarry. Once word spread, hundreds of people parked their cars at the quarry during the next several evenings, hoping to catch a glimpse of the alien invaders, but nothing was seen again. Skeptics dismissed the sightings as being related to army helicopters on manoeuvres, but townspeople and witnesses of the lights and craft strongly disagreed with the explanation.

As quickly as the flap began, the number of UFO sightings in the area dropped off, and the Quebec townships became peaceful once again.

CHAPTER SEVENTEEN
DID FLYING SAUCERS CREATE CROP CIRCLES?

GEOFF DITTMAN

"You gotta be nuts! That's impossible!"[1] That's the response Edwin Fuhr got when he told his family his story. His encounter with crop-circle-making UFOs was just too much for the farm family.

These days crop circles are well known and tend to be associated with Mel Gibson movies, British pranksters, and assorted New Agers. Back in the mid-seventies, however, farmers never expected to find geometric patterns in their crops. They certainly never expected to find their farm being invaded by something that was seemingly from out of this world!

It was a cool rainy morning around Langenburg, Saskatchewan, back on September 1, 1974. Edwin Fuhr, a thirty-six-year-old farmer with property just northeast of town, was out harvesting his crop of rapeseed. Knowing that he was coming up to a rough spot in the ground, he looked up from his machine. He was startled to find a large object ahead of him. Initially thinking it was only a goose blind left there as some sort of joke by his neighbour, Edwin jumped down from his swather to investigate. Upon closer inspection, however, he realized it was no goose blind! The object was hovering just off the ground and revolving in a clockwise direction. The texture seemed to be rough, the colour of brushed steel.

Stunned, Fuhr slowly backed away, never turning his eyes from the strange sight. Back on the swather, he noticed the object wasn't alone. Four other objects were nearby, all revolving and hovering.[2]

Fuhr just sat there, taking in the strange spectacle in front of him. He could see that something, possibly a probe, was coming out of one of the objects and was being stuck repeatedly into the ground. He could hear no sound emanating from the craft, but with the swather still running, it could merely have been drowned out.

Fuhr had been watching the objects for fifteen minutes, when suddenly they rose up into the sky, still revolving in a clockwise direction. He could see exhaust fumes coming from underneath the craft. With a sudden blast of air, the objects disappeared into the clouds.[3]

While the craft may have departed, they left something behind: five circles of flattened vegetation. The grass was not burned or otherwise dead but merely flattened in a clockwise direction.[4] Two of the rings seemed to have marks inside them, apparently the result of the probe.

Still in a state of shock, and unsure of what to do next, Edwin Fuhr continued to swathe, not returning home for a good hour. After some prodding from his family, who could clearly see something was bothering Edwin, the witness told his story.

Skeptical, Edwin's father had to go see for himself the evidence of the encounter. The skepticism turned to bewilderment, however, upon sight of the mysterious circles. The old man began crawling around on his hands and knees, examining the strange pattern in front of him.[5]

Later that evening, Edwin's brother-in-law heard of the occurrence. While he too was skeptical, the brother-in-law felt obligated to inform the authorities. First thing the following morning, Constable Morier of the RCMP visited the Fuhr farm. It was obvious to the constable that Fuhr was still shaken up by the event, and he didn't know what to make of the ground markings.[6] He placed a call to his commanding officer to inform him of his observations and took several photos of the scene. As far as he could tell, it was not an obvious hoax on the part of Fuhr. In his report, Morier wrote, "The witness Fuhr has been known by a member of this detachment for a period of four years.... He is a responsible person and his information is considered reliable."[7]

Morier's commanding officer suggested to Fuhr that it would be best if he kept the event "under his hat."[8] But as can be expected in a small town, word quickly got out about the strange happenings on the farm. Soon hundreds, if not thousands, of people had trampled all over the poor farmer's property. The *Regina Leader-Post* was the first paper to break the story, publishing an article on September 10. News of the story eventually found its way to an American UFO research group, the

Centre for UFO Studies (CUFOS), headquartered in Chicago, Illinois. Ted Phillips, a well-known and respected researcher, visited the scene about three weeks after the event. Phillips interviewed the witnesses and several family members in an attempt to find an explanation for the event.

A Solution?

Nothing has come to light that would suggest Fuhr was responsible for a hoax. His character as described by those who knew him did not indicate that he would make up such a tall tale. As noted by Phillips, the alleged event occurred at harvest time, exactly when a farmer wouldn't want hundreds of people trampling on his crops.[9] Furthermore, it wasn't the witness who first contacted the media. So it isn't likely that Fuhr was hungry enough for his fifteen minutes of fame to concoct such a wild story.

If Fuhr didn't stage the event as a hoax, is it possible that other earthly pranksters could have been behind it? The complexity of the sighting, most notably the observation of five fairly large objects, would have to be explained. It seems unlikely that anyone would have the desire or the ability to put together such a complex scheme for no apparent reason.

Ignoring the sighting and the objects, could there be a natural explanation for the strange rings found on the ground? The federal government thought so. The National Research Council of Canada (NRC), which at the time was the semi-official clearing house for UFO reports, indicated that the markings were no more than fairy rings, that is, the result of fungi.[10] It should be noted however that the NRC didn't do any sort of investigation. Research was limited to reading the RCMP file on the case. And an analysis of the soil found no evidence of anything unusual. Furthermore, fairy rings usually take some time to develop. And of course the NRC explanation ignores the observation of the objects.

Other Sightings

Other unusual occurrences happened in the same area around the same time. While Fuhr was witnessing the strange craft, cattle in a nearby field became agitated and broke through a fence.[11]

The night before, the Fuhrs' neighbours' babysitter was unnerved by normally quiet dogs barking and growling outside.[12] The dogs acted up again on September 2. The following morning, a sixth circle was found alongside the first group of five. And on September 15 one more circle was added to the group. [13] Over the next few weeks, more circles were found around Langenburg, as well as in the towns of Young, Peebles, Lake Lenore, and Dinsmore.[14]

Sightings continued over time, though their frequency significantly declined. Another flap, however, did occur in 1989. On the evening of October 11, six youths across the street from the RCMP detachment station observed a classic flying saucer that at its closest was estimated to be hovering only about two hundred feet in the air and about four hundred feet away from the witnesses. Two days later a woman on a farm outside Langenburg described seeing a similar UFO, approximately thirty feet in diameter, slowly and silently moving around her property. An interesting aspect of this case is that cattle and a dog were near the object but appeared to not notice, or at least not to be bothered by, the UFO.[15]

Postscript

During the nineties, Fuhr agreed to several interviews, bringing to light new allegations. Fuhr stated that the government examined the site in the eighties and found an abnormally high amount of radiation. People would come on to the property, take soil samples, and perform various tests and measurements. He also said he believed that during the encounter back in 1974, he experienced a period of missing time, perhaps the result of an abduction.[16]

This sighting has become one of the better-known cases in the history of Canadian ufology. Like most things Canadian, UFO cases here tend to be ignored by our American neighbours. But the Langenburg case caught the attention of a large American group. As such, it has received quite a lot of publicity, which has continued even decades after the event. There can be little doubt that Fuhr's memory of the incident has become clouded over the years or perhaps even influenced by the attention he has received. This likely explains the discovery of missing time years later. But the basic story remains the same after all this time. The Langenburg close encounter case can be considered one of the more interesting cases of the seventies.

CHAPTER EIGHTEEN
THE FALCONBRIDGE RADAR/VISUAL UFO CASE

CHRIS RUTKOWSKI

On November 13, 1975, NORAD issued a press release concerning an incident near Sudbury, Ontario:

> At 4:05 pm, Nov. 11, the Canadian Forces radar site at Falconbridge, Ontario, reported a radar track of an unidentified flying object about 25-30 nautical miles south of the site, ranging in altitude from 25,000 to 72,000 feet. Persons at the site also saw the object and said it appeared as a bright star but much closer. Two F-106 aircraft of the US Air Force Air National Guard's 171st Fighter Interceptor Squadron at Selfridge ANGB, Michigan, were scrambled, but the pilots reported no contact with the object.[1]

By itself, the story was quite amazing, apparently involving a UFO tracked on radar, observed from the ground and causing enough concern that NORAD recommended interception by American jet fighters. In fact, one writer described the Falconbridge incident as "probably one of the most significant modern examples of suspicious unknown air activity possibly affecting national security."[2]

Interpretations of the incident varied, as might be expected. It is interesting to sort through the information known about the case in order to try to understand, in retrospect, what really occurred that night.

UFO document retrieval researchers Lawrence Fawcett and Barry J. Greenwood, in their book *Clear Intent*, discussed government cover-up of UFO sightings and published documents about the Falconbridge case retrieved through Freedom of Information Act requests. A recovered entry in the NORAD regional senior director's log read, "1205Z 11 November 1975 Received unusual sighting report from Falconbridge AFS, Ontario, Canada. Info passed to NORAD Command Director, Intelligence and Weather."[3]

The first curious thing to note is that the time of the report differs from that given in the press release. 1205Z is Greenwich Mean Time, which is five hours ahead of EST, Sudbury time. That would make the time of the report 7:05 a.m., not 4:05 a.m. The next entry read:

> 1840Z 11 November 1975 Actions pertaining to scramble of JL08 and 09 due to unusual object sighting. With Director of Operations approval. Scrambled JL08/09 at 1745Z, airborne at 1750Z. NORAD Combat Operations Center notified of Falconbridge AFS incident. Aircraft over Falconbridge flying over incident, point no sighting. 1831 aircraft still in area, no radar aircraft or visual contact. Falconbridge AFS still reporting object at 26,000 feet.[4]

According to these entries, it took more than five hours for the air force to scramble jets in response to the report. Furthermore, the pilots were sent up after lunch, when the sun would have overwhelmed the light coming from any aerial source. It is no wonder that they were unable to see anything, even if the ground radar was still painting an object.

It is important to understand that the Falconbridge incident took place in the context of a major North American wave of UFO reports. Arch-skeptic Phil Klass also pointed out that on October 20, 1975, NBC had aired *The UFO Incident*, a recreation of the Betty and Barney Hill UFO abduction story, which he believed contributed to the public's heightened interest in UFOs. This had been followed by three weeks of "an abnormal number of reports of sightings of unidentified objects in the sky." Furthermore, according to Klass, it was because the Falconbridge AFS had received phone calls from several people regarding UFOs they had seen in the early morning of November 11 that they turned on their height-finder radar and looked specifically towards the south, where the witnesses said they had seen the objects. Klass said, "In doing so they observed a target at a distance of about twenty-five miles south-southwest (in the direction of Sudbury), at an altitude of about 36,000 feet, moving slowly from west to east."[5]

Klass then noted that Jupiter was an evening star that month and also that Venus was very bright, rising about 2:30 a.m. local time. He concluded that most of the sightings of UFOs were probably one or the other of these astronomical objects.

Fawcett and Greenwood provided additional documents to support their contention that the objects seen that night were truly anomalous. The commander-in-charge of NORAD sent a message to all NORAD units in North America that night:

> This morning, 11 Nov 1975, CFS Falconbridge reported search and height finder radar paints on an object up to 30 nautical miles south of the site ranging in altitude from 26,000 ft. to 72,000 ft. The site commander and other personnel say the object appeared as a bright star but much closer. With binoculars the object appeared as a 100 ft. diameter sphere and appeared to have craters around the outside.[6]

The rather large difference in altitude is curious, as is the estimate of size if the object was really as far away as thought. One could hardly judge the diameter of a light source that was thirty miles away and between five and fifteen miles in altitude!

These estimates of the distance to the object are worth examining in detail. Another source with information about the observations comes from an ATC Log Book, classified as "SECRET" and released through the National Archives of Canada.[7] The relevant entry on November 11, 1975, reads:

> 1118 CFB Falconbridge [illegible] called re: UFO over the base and also rep of UFO over OPP bldg downtown Sudbury. Brilliant color — like looking at a large gem with colored lights all around it.
>
> 1123 North — Cape activity. Intel 0 ([??] little). Stand-by DO (Col. OECHSLG) Advised.

1147 Maj. Oliver fm. Falconbridge called re: UFOs. Report is as follows:

> Time 1115Z-1129Z — sighted 2 UFO brilliant lights - one at 200E fm. CFB Falconbridge, the other at 180E but much further aways. Maj Oliver took 3 snapshots with Brownie camera (no results) as of this time. Other observers were Capt. Calson and Cpl. Lawelenceson of CFB Falconbridge — They observed the closest object through binoculars and object was rising vertically at tremendous speed — they had it on ht. finder at two cuts of 44,000′ and again at 72,000′ — object circular — well lighted and what appeared as two black spots in the centre.

1231 Warnship: DTG 11/1023 TrackII One faded position 67.30N,005.00E″11/1152 notified Col. Oechsley & Maj. Little

1303 Startover Cont. To insert to octals

1310 Warnship: DTG 11/1023 Track II one reappeared 64.00N,001.00W, one UK F-8 scrambled 1235

Apart from the fact that trying to take a photograph of a distant light with a Brownie is quite ridiculous, it seems as though there were many witnesses of the UFO, including OPP officers and some base personnel. In this document, however, the time of the report is given as 1118Z, or 0618 local, again differing from other records. Not only that, but the UFO was painted on radar at between 44,000 and 72,000 feet, whereas other altitudes are given as 26,000 and 36,000 feet. It is no wonder that airborne jets couldn't find anything when the object's location couldn't even be reckoned with any consistency or accuracy.

A report of the sighting appeared in the *Winnipeg Tribune* on November 13, 1975:

> Ontario police sight 4 UFOs
>
> Sudbury, Ont. (CP) — Police reports say unidentified

> flying objects were sighted over Sudbury and Halleybury, about 90 miles northeast of here.
>
> Reports on the sightings were compiled by regional police, provincial police and staff at Canadian Forces Base Falconbridge.
>
> Regional police constables Bob Whiteside and Alex Keable said they saw three objects in the sky Tuesday, and later spotted a fourth.
>
> Regional constable John Marsh said he saw lights in the sky to the southwest while on patrol on Highway 17 near Coniston, (a few) miles east of here.
>
> He said the object moved in a jerking manner, had pulsating lights and "was different from what you would normally call a star."
>
> Four persons at the Canadian Forces Base Falconbridge said they had sighted objects in the sky and on radar.[8]

UFO investigator Michel Deschamps located information on a host of other witnesses to objects certainly related to the Falconbridge event. Six members of the nursing staff at Pioneer Manor in Sudbury reported an object that seemed to hover over Sudbury Stadium. One object was very bright and very low at first and suddenly shot into the sky. It had been observed for nearly two hours and was still visible when Sudbury Regional Police arrived at 0955Z. An object seen for this long is almost certainly astronomical in nature, and this would bear out Klass's suggestion that the Falconbridge UFOs were likely Venus and/or Jupiter. The observation time would have been between 2:55 and 4:55 local time, and if the police arrived at about 5:00 a.m., it would make sense that they would watch it for a while and then report their sighting to CFS Falconbridge. This would make the time of the police report between 5:00 and 6:00 a.m., and Falconbridge personnel would then have begun observing the object at about 6:00 a.m., in agreement with the ATC Log Book record of the UFO being observed at 1115Z, or 6:15 a.m. local time. As for the impression that the object "suddenly shot into the sky," there are several possible explanations, one of which is that the witnesses had lost track of the initial object and mistook it for a higher object in the sky.

In total, seven members of the Sudbury OPP observed UFOs that night. Constables Chrapchynski and Deighton reported:

> 4 objects were observed clearly in the sky. The brightest in the east remained in a stationary position. One on the southwest moved at times in a jerky motion. One in the northwest remained stationary. The one in the northeast was the dimmest, also stationary. They were still plainly visible after day break when all regular bright objects in the sky had disappeared. Seen intermittently for 1 hour.

Given that the stationary objects were probably stars, the only one in some doubt was the object in the southwest, which could very well have been Jupiter, observed with some illusory autostasis effects. Note also that they only observed "intermittently" (probably because they were also attending to more important police duties), so it would have been easy to get confused over the objects' movements or lack thereof.

Constables Keable and Whiteside reported only one object, observed with binoculars: "At times it appeared to be cylindrical with shafts of light bright enough to light up clouds in immediate area it appeared at times to travel in circles. At one point, it came quite close. It was still visible to the naked eye after the sun came up." If this was Venus or Jupiter, it was certainly bright that night. But why did these two witnesses not see the other objects?

Constable Marsh reported:

> ... one very bright star-like object moving in a jerky circular manner. When covered with clouds, it was still bright enough to shine through as well as light up an area around it. While observing this object he saw two other similar objects, one in the south and one southwest of Coniston. All seemed to be moving in a jerky circular manner. They seemed to emit a pulsating type of light varying in colours. Easily distinguishable from the stars.

This last sentence is almost certainly incorrect. The other point to note is that there were scattered clouds that night, which would have interrupted continuous observation, made the lights wink on and off, and also become greatly scintillating, leading to the impression that they were moving in a jerky manner.

Constables Ryan and Lederoute noted only that they saw a single bright object that "appeared to be over the north end of the city of

Sudbury, moving in a north westerly direction at a high rate of speed." They watched it for about one minute before it was obscured by a large cloud.

Meanwhile, at Falconbridge, Captain Carson Master Corporal Kreutz and Corporal Lawrenson reported "a circular object, brilliantly lighted with tow black spots in the centre, moving upwards at high speed from 42,000 to 72,000 ft. with no horizontal movement. This object was sighted visually and by radar bearing 210 magnetic at 30 nautical miles from CFS Falconbridge. A similar object was sighted by the same observers bearing 270 magnetic but at too great a distance to provide details."

A further note said that Major Oliver (who had been the one to take the photographs), Captain Carson, and Corporal Lauritsen saw an object that was "spherical shaped and appeared to be rotating." The object "appeared to have surface area similar to the moon and was ascending and descending." They watched it for two hours, although their view of it was intermittent because of the cloud cover. Its position was reported as "210 degrees 30 miles alt. 42,000 ft. at 1115Z, and 200 degrees 30 miles alt. 50,000 ft. at 1120Z, then 190 degrees 25 miles alt. 72,000 ft. at 1129Z."

This last batch of data on the object's rise over time suggested to UFO researcher Brad Sparks that "this translates to a climb rate of 1, 600 ft/min the first 5 minutes then about 2, 400 ft/min the next 9 minutes, and an almost due eastward course at about 70 mph then northeast at about 60 mph." He thinks the evidence points to "a balloon that has been caught in the east-flowing jet stream, having been launched at about 6 a.m. apparently somewhere in the general Sudbury region."

Like Klass, Sparks also believes the OPP observations were likely stars and planets:

> Sunrise was at about 7:20 a.m. Venus would have been very bright in the SE sky before sunrise and for some time after, rising above the horizon almost due east at about 3:08 a.m. The first sightings with times reported were "very low" over Sudbury Stadium from about 3:00 to 4:55 a.m., then apparently continued for some indefinite time afterward. Jupiter was very bright in the western sky and set beneath the horizon at about 4:30 a.m. Mars and Saturn were very high up in the SW and SE skies. The brightest star Sirius was high in the southern sky.[9]

What about the radar targets, if the visual sightings were only stars and planets? When the pilots were eventually dispatched six hours later to the area where the UFOs had been seen, Venus was long gone, as was any balloon that would have travelled at least four hundred miles east and much higher than the planes were flying by that time. Klass reports that the pilots could find only "high-altitude clouds laden with ice crystals that reflected sunlight.... Such clouds would return radar energy and produce blips on the Falconbridge height-finder radar." This contradicts the balloon hypothesis but does give us a second possible explanation for the radar observations.

Finally, if the visual observations were really of stars and planets, how do we explain the descriptions of the objects as having craters like the moon and "two black dots"? When binoculars are improperly focused, starlike objects will appear to be mottled spheres because of effects of the optics and the internal aqueous humor of the eye. And if binoculars are focused on Saturn, it can appear as an extended object with the gap between the rings and planet visible as black areas, which can be interpreted in many ways if the observer does not know he is looking at a ringed planet.

In summary, the so-called classic Falconbridge radar/visual UFO case is much less mysterious than has been claimed. While there is no way to determine if all the objects seen that night were stars or planets, it seems as though many might have been misidentified. Why experienced radar operators would not be able to distinguish between clouds and truly anomalous tracks is somewhat odd, as is sending USAF fighters up to investigate potentially unknown targets after more than five or six hours had passed.

CHAPTER NINETEEN
CHARLIE REDSTAR AND FRIENDS

CHRIS RUTKOWSKI

The number of UFO sightings in Canada increased rapidly as the seventies progressed. Although the first few years of the decade had respectable numbers of UFO reports, they still didn't match the dozens recorded for the 1967 to 1969 flap. But then a handful of sightings in Manitoba in early 1975 became precursors for a major UFO "invasion."[1]

In February 1975, a farmer was walking to his barn north of Lundar when a basketball-sized light swooped down over his head. While gazing up with astonishment at the object, he felt a sensation as if hot plastic had been poured on his face. He said he felt suffocated and that he couldn't think straight while it was over him. This may have been the first sighting of what came to be known as "Charlie Redstar," the strange red light that was frequently seen bobbing over the hillsides near Carman, Manitoba, about forty-five miles southwest of Winnipeg.

Although the majority of sightings in the Carman wave were observations of distant lights in the night sky, many involved more significant objects, including classic flying saucers. People reported seeing disc-shaped objects at close range, near enough to see what looked like portholes on the sides or underside of the strange craft. There were reports of "ferris wheels" in the sky, with many coloured lights moving in slow, ponderous action, very like the vehicles depicted in the movie *Close Encounters of the Third Kind*. However, the sightings at Carman predated that movie's special effects.

When considering UFOs, some sightings obviously carry more weight than others. If more than one person sees a UFO, this is perhaps more reliable than a single-witness incident. Also, if a photograph is taken, this sometimes is considered to support the observation of the witnesses. And if there are physical traces left in the area, the case is similarly regarded in higher profile.

All of these characteristics were true of the Carman wave of UFO cases. Dozens of people were witnesses to the same objects in several instances. Many photographs were taken of unusual objects in the sky and film crews were able to document the movement of lights overhead. "Landing rings" were found in a number of farmers' fields, leading to speculation that aliens were visiting the normally quiet rural area.

The sighting that seems to have started the Carman wave of "Charlie" reports occurred on March 27, 1975, near Graysville, Manitoba, southwest of Winnipeg. A young girl woke to the sound of a "shrill, pulsating siren" at about 2:00 a.m., accompanied by a trembling "like an earthquake." She looked out her bedroom window and saw a red ball of light zip by her window. She thought it had set her house on fire because there was so much light flooding in the window and it looked "like the sun was coming up." The light flew over the house from the north heading south.

A few weeks later, just east of Graysville near Carman, on April 10, 1975, Bob and Elaine Diemert were walking from their farmhouse to Friendship Field, their private airfield. They saw what was apparently the same object that had been seen earlier, a large red light moving slowly along the treeline. They noted, "It was close enough already that you could see the dome on the top." The disc-shaped object flew towards them from the west, then turned north and disappeared out of sight after about five minutes.

The Diemerts had several more UFO sightings that month, but things really got going the next month, beginning on May 7, when they started seeing unusual objects in the night sky literally every night for several months. That summer, once word got around, people would gather nightly at the tiny airstrip, watching and waiting for the appearance of Charlie Redstar as he scooted along over trees on the horizon. The light sometimes would baffle onlookers by deviating unexpectedly from its course, zooming over their heads and then disappearing as quickly as it came.

Throughout the summer of 1975, spectacular sightings were the rule rather than the exception. For example, on May 9, Constable Ian Nicholson of the Carman detachment of the RCMP was called out to the Diemert's farm at the request of concerned citizens. He, too, saw "an object in the west, three or four miles away, and at about 1000 feet [altitude]." Nicholson was the most unbiased and objective observer to that point, and his vivid yet matter-of-fact report was very useful in understanding what was occurring in the Carman area. He said that as he arrived in the general area, he thought he would drive away from the crowd in order to get a less cluttered view of the phenomenon. He noted in his report:

> I drove a mile north … then another mile west, where I stopped the car. Off to the northwest there was an oval-shaped red light … [with] an x-shaped white halo around it.… The light was somewhat the colour of … a stoplight.… I sat there for two or three minutes just looking at the object, which appeared stationary at the time. Then I decided to get a closer look at it. I drove west … and I can say I was moving pretty fast. As I was going west, the object seemed to be flying in a northeasterly direction.… I continued for approximately 12 miles, keeping the object in sight, trying to get somewhat abreast of it so that if the opportunity presented itself, I could have driven north toward it.… About 16 miles west of Carman, I stopped the car. I'd seen there was no way I was going to catch up to it. So I just stopped the car and watched the object go out of sight over the tree line on the horizon.

It should be noted that the object was ostensibly behaving like an aircraft on a descent into Winnipeg, following a flight path commonly used by planes en route to the city towards the northeast. The object's apparent stationary position could have been an illusion caused by his moving parallel to its movement without accurate reference points, especially as it may have been turning from the north to the northeast during its descent. However, one would expect that a police officer upon whose excellent observing capabilities we rely every day would be able to discern the difference between a UFO and an incoming aircraft.

The best case during the Carman wave, however, involved multiple witnesses, simultaneous observations from differing directions, television news footage, and physical traces in the form of radioactive soil. There were many people involved, and the events took place over a wide area over more than two hours. It has been difficult to collaborate all the observations and interpretations of what was seen during the event, complicated by conflicting witnesses' accounts and statements. Regardless, there is no doubt that something unusual was witnessed and recorded on the night of May 13–14, 1975, a few miles northwest of Carman.

A few days earlier, Bob Diemert contacted CKY-TV in Winnipeg in the hope that filming the UFO would definitively prove what was being reported. He told the news team that if they sent a camera crew to Carman, they would definitely be able to film Charlie and get some exciting footage. Station employees Bill Kendricks, John Berry, and two others went to Carman on May 11, 1975, but to the chagrin of the Carman UFO enthusiasts they saw absolutely nothing of interest. Their curiosity aroused by the locals' determination, they went out again on May 12 and saw what was defined by the UFO buffs as a "Light At The End of the Road" (LATER), a "boring" kind of UFO that sat stationary directly ahead of observers on country byways, rapidly zipping backward when anyone tried to approach it. Wanting to see the effect for himself, Berry got in his car and tried to approach the light, but as predicted, it moved away and disappeared ("blinked out") on the horizon.

At this point, some political intrigue entered into the story. When the crew returned to Winnipeg late that night, their cameraman filed for overtime pay, frustrated because in his view he had been on a wild goose chase. So, the next morning, when the news director received the formal request for overtime, he was upset at the extravagance that resulted in no worthwhile footage. He then forbade all cameramen from going to film any UFOs unless they went on their own time.

This complication and directive resulted in Kendricks booking off on his own time. On May 13, he and film lab technician Allen Kerr took a spare TV camera and met with a crowd of UFO watchers a few miles north of Carman to wait for Charlie to appear. They were well rewarded for their persistence. Around 11:30 p.m. a light appeared on the western horizon. It rose above the trees, moved slowly south, then flashed brilliantly and abruptly shot "straight up at incredible speed." It went so fast that only two of the many witnesses who had gathered actually saw the manoeuvre.

The game was afoot. Everyone piled into their cars and trucks, splitting into three separate groups in order to corner the elusive Charlie. The first group consisted of newspaper editor Howard Bennett, Kerry McIntyre, and Red Storey. They drove northwest and stationed themselves a few miles east and north of the road Charlie seemed to favour.

They believed the crowd's action had "scared it into flight" and were convinced they would be able to get extremely close to Charlie.

Bennett noted, "I could see this big glow behind some trees less than half a mile away off to the right and ahead of us.... It was smoky red, a hazy glow, and to me the thing was higher than the trees, maybe 50 feet tall. It was about 20 feet thick and was sitting at an angle of about 45 degrees. The edges were fuzzy and not sharply defined. It was much like seeing a drive-in movie screen from the side."

Later, Bennett led investigators to the area where he believed the object had landed. Convinced that some evidence of its presence should still remain, they took readings with a radiation survey meter, but the energy detected was only normal background effects. However, they did find several hot spots about eighty-five yards apart, each with a radius of approximately twenty-five feet. The readings from these areas were not much higher than the normal background level, and it was thought they could have been due to equipment malfunction or inadequate operation of the device.

The second group of UFO chasers was made up of Bob and Elaine Diemert and Bill Kendricks and his wife, who was eager to tag along on the expedition. From the original starting point, they drove south one mile and then went west to approach from the exact opposite direction of the first group. To them, Charlie seemed to them to be "rising and falling like a blood red moon through the trees." The group tried to get closer, but Charlie suddenly "popped into the air, hovered ... and then took off straight for the CBC tower [to the east]."

It was the third group that had the most success that night. Allen Kerr and his troop took up a position near the CBC tower and watched as the other two groups gave chase. With camera rolling, Kerr captured the object on film as it "jumped into the sky." He panned with the object as it approached and flew overhead, moving the camera from about 45 to 90 degrees, held the camera steady for a few seconds, and then followed it again to about 120 or 150 degrees. The result was three and a half seconds of film showing the stationary light on the ground, then a few seconds of the light moving swiftly across the field of view. The object on the ground appeared to increase slightly in size and then jump up to the top of the frame after a flash of light illuminated the horizon.

A close examination of the film, frame by frame, showed that in one frame, the light was simultaneously at the top and in the middle of the view, an impossibility if it actually moved between the two positions. One camera expert suggested that this "flash frame" was a defect caused by an erratic exciter lamp inside the camera mechanism itself. However, this idea was rejected by most of the individuals involved with the sighting, even though none of them had seen any such flash of light themselves.

A second sequence showed a red, pulsing light following a snakelike up-and-down motion in its flight across the frames, with a series of echoes following it across the film. UFOROM studied the film at length, enlarging the images and checking the film for other clues as to what may have been seen. Dr. J. Allen Hynek, director of the Center for UFO Studies in Illinois, visited Winnipeg that year and was put on the spot by CKY when he was asked on camera what he thought of the UFO film. He replied, quite diplomatically, that it was "the best film of a nocturnal light" he had ever seen. He was quite right; the film offers no proof of aliens invading Canada, or of anything else significant for that matter. It's just a small light in a sea of blackness on some movie film. Certainly not high-grade *X-Files* material, to say the least.

Yet, three widely separated groups of witnesses saw what appears to have been the same object at the same time, proving that something was moving in the skies near Carman that night. The Diemerts insisted that it was not an aircraft, given their considerable knowledge of the appearance of such things at night. Furthermore, the light was uniformly red, not displaying the accompanying green light that an airplane would have had. And no noise of a propeller was heard, either, which should have been audible if the object was flying as low as had been calculated.

Charlie Redstar continued to put on a show for observers all summer; UFO-watching became a favourite pastime for Carman residents, and once the CKY film made the evening news, many Winnipeggers joined the fray. Carloads of curious people came each night to try to see their own UFO bobbing through the night sky. The media made a mockery of the hysteria, both in print and on the airwaves. Ads in local newspapers urged readers to "Shop where Charlie Redstar shops!" A *National Enquirer* reporter arrived to interview witnesses and put Carman on the map. A circus-like atmosphere evolved; cars lined the dirt roads along favourite hot spots, and traffic jams occurred as Charlie flew by and drivers scrambled to be first in the chase. During these chases, speeds of eighty or ninety miles per hour were not uncommon, and it was perhaps only luck that no serious accidents happened. UFO-watching parties took place throughout the region, lasting in many cases through the night and into the dawn. It is no wonder, then, that literally hundreds of sightings of Charlie Redstar and his friends were made during that summer.

One of the strangest reports during the Carman wave could have been an *X-Files* episode in its own right. At about 2:00 a.m. on May 16, west of Carman near the town of Stephenfield, three youths were at a large beach party on the north shore of Boyne River Lake. Since it was a well-known place for teenagers to have drinking parties, all three later readily admitted they had been imbibing. They said that at one point, they had wandered away from the party and found themselves on the south side of the lake near a small dock. One of them looked skyward and called to the others when he saw a bright, moon-sized red light that was stationary only about five hundred to one thousand feet above the dam at the eastern end of the lake. They all watched it for ten minutes as it hovered motionless but were amazed when it suddenly shone a "solid" searchlight-like beam of white light down onto the lake near them, between two buoys only about one hundred feet from the shore.

This *Star Trek*–like opaque stream of light moved upon the surface of the lake, and then a strange glowing object appeared just below the surface of the water, underneath the moving patch of illumination. As they watched, this unidentified underwater object (UUO) began to move toward the trio on the dock, its own light bright enough that the bottom of the lake was visible. It moved in their direction, small ripples appearing on the surface of the water as it drew nearer. When the UUO had approached to within twenty feet of the witnesses, one of them bravely grabbed a rock and threw it towards the light. He apparently hit it, and it broke into four sections that reversed direction and returned one by one "like a conveyor belt" to the patch of light on the surface from the solid beam. The light from the hovering object dissolved and the glow underneath the water went out. The object over the dam then broke into two half-moons, which then flew away in opposite directions.

Admittedly, this is a rather bizarre story, but it is indicative of the richness of the stories surrounding the visit of Charlie Redstar in southern Manitoba in the seventies. Factoring in the effects of alcohol, it is still rather odd that all three would imagine the same experience. They were hesitant to speak with investigators but eventually complied and independently supported one another's testimony. They had nothing to gain by publicity of the event and probably more to lose in terms of standing within the community.

During the afternoon of June 4, 1975, a man was just north of the town of St. Claude, northwest of Carman, in a pasture attending to his farmyard duties. As he worked, he looked up to see a large, disc-shaped object only about twenty-five feet away from his truck, flying over some trees. He described the craft as two domes lip to lip with a middle section that seemed composed of "clear material that resembled glass." The top was silver and the bottom was milky white, "like the belly of a fish." This unnerved him so much that he immediately tried to take flight but found that his truck wouldn't start. He was forced to sit and watch as the object flew slowly eastward and disappeared behind the trees.

Another sighting, only a month later, also gave some witnesses a disturbingly good view of a strange flying object. Three people were about one mile west of the town of Roland on July 1 when they saw an object in the sky moving towards them in an up-and-down bobbing motion. As it went by, the UFO passed over a grain elevator, shining its light down upon it so brightly that "you could actually see the nails in the elevator." The object was described as about eighty-five feet in diameter and perfectly circular. It, too, was shaped like two saucers or domes lip to lip but was close enough that the witnesses could see that the two halves were rotating in opposite directions. The centre section didn't move and had what looked like several oval windows. As they watched, the object descended and appeared to land in a nearby field. Somewhat braver that the lone witness in St. Claude, the three turned and gave pursuit, driving their four-wheel-drive truck across the field, but the object took off before they reached it.

One significant characteristic of the wave of Charlie sightings was the diversity and complexity of the cases. During the many months of reports throughout the area, many landing rings were found, which seemed to suggest that the UFOs had a tendency to come down to Earth as well as fly through the skies. On July 2, a farmer living near Halbstadt, a hamlet about sixty miles south of Winnipeg, discovered an unusual oval barren patch in his otherwise healthy field of sugar beets. This landing site measured exactly thirty by thirty-nine feet and was two hundred yards from a dirt road. Vegetation within the oval was apparently dehydrated, crumbling to bits when crushed in the hand. The plants outside this patch were healthy and unaffected except for an area immediately to the west, where the condition of the plants progressively became less withered over a trailed swath of about fifty feet. The implication was that something swooped over the field from the west, spewing radiation before landing on top of the foot-high plants.

What was most remarkable about the site were the "tripod marks" inside the oval patch. These impressions in the dry, hard soil were bowl-shaped, about eighteen inches across and three inches deep, with small rectangular holes in their centers. It was as if something like a lunar module with three legs had hovered over the field and landed, its nuclear engines heating the plants and soil to the point where desiccation occurred. Yet, it should be noted that no one in the area had reported seeing a UFO at any time before the site was discovered. This was a UFO case without any UFO involved.

Although UFO sightings dwindled in number throughout the fall and winter, reports continued to be made, even in the cold months of January and February 1976. Once the snow began to disappear from the fields, UFO watchers returned to the highways and farm roads in the Carman area to try to catch another glimpse of Charlie. Few were disappointed, as the familiar bobbing red light returned to entertain onlookers.

One of the most determined and dedicated UFO spotters at the time was Grant Cameron, now a well-respected ufologist who specializes in archival research and retrieving government documents related to UFOs. In 1975, he spent night after night parked along roads and byways hoping to get photographs and close-up views of UFOs in the Carman area. He would typically work through each day then drive to Carman and spend all evening and part of the night looking for Charlie, then drive home to catch a few hours of sleep before starting the cycle over again. As a result of his persistence, Cameron managed to view Charlie and his cousin "Little Charlie" on several occasions. ("Little Charlie" was the name given to a smaller version of the original UFO, a LATER that commonly sat at the end of farm roads, winking on and off, tantalizing and teasing observers.)

One of Cameron's most memorable and dramatic encounters with Little Charlie was on April 3, 1976, when he and a friend staked out a UFO hunting spot near the town of Sperling, just east of Carman. Around 8:00 that evening, they saw an orange ball of light appear suddenly over a small bridge. Cameron noted in his diary that the light seemed to be about five feet in diameter, compared to the size of the bridge, although the glow from the object made the actual size difficult to estimate. They got out of their car and walked to within approximately one hundred feet of the light, which seemed precariously perched on the side of the bridge. Cameron casually looked back towards their car and was surprised to see a second orange ball of light "sitting right on top of the car." On impulse, they both turned and ran towards the car, thinking they could finally catch the object, but then as they ran they turned back to see what the object on the bridge was doing. To their continued surprise, it had disappeared, and as might be expected, when they again turned back in the direction of the car, they saw that the object there was receding, "going down the road a ways, where he turned off his lights." When they finally reached the car, they looked toward the bridge and found that the object there had magically reappeared. Cameron admitted they both were "quite shaken by the whole affair." In his diary, he speculated that the second object had acted as a ruse to draw them away from reaching the first one on the bridge. There was no question in their minds that the lights were guided by some intelligence that had chosen to torment them with a unique game of cat and mouse.

Charlie and his cousin were seen numerous times throughout 1976, making the Carman wave one of the longest of any on record, lasting about sixteen months. Photos of lights in the sky were snapped, landing traces were found, and literally hundreds of area residents claimed UFO experiences. To these and others, Charlie was real — the personification of a playful and mischievous alien who vacationed on the Canadian prairies in the mid-seventies.

TRANSITION YEARS

CHAPTER TWENTY

INTO THE EIGHTIES

GEOFF DITTMAN

The eighties brought significant change to ufology. Prior to that point, people's ideas of UFOs were largely restricted to flying saucers in the distant sky. Contact with any occupants of such vehicles was not considered likely. Now there certainly had been numerous incidents of beings observed; for example, there were large numbers of alleged encounters with aliens in France, Italy, and South America in 1954. But these cases were largely ignored in North America, even by investigators, who eyed such cases with great suspicion. For years the only American investigative group that paid any attention to close encounters of the third kind was the Aerial Phenomenon Research Organization (APRO). Other organizations, such as the National Investigations Committee on Aerial Phenomena (NICAP), felt that publicizing such encounter cases would only bring further ridicule to ufology.

But more and more cases involving close encounters of the third kind, or "occupant" sightings, began to appear, and they became harder and harder for investigators to ignore. There were waves of sightings of not only UFOs but also occupants in the U.S.A. in 1951, the mid-sixties, and then again in 1973. Not only were craft being seen in the skies over North America, but they were seemingly landing on the ground, too. Strange beings were even seen walking around the landed objects. Despite the large number of sightings, however, the alien archetype wasn't ingrained within the popular UFO mythology. The aliens seen were varied, and the waves were too short. In fact, sightings began to decline after the 1973 wave.

It took a well-known horror writer to really popularize the idea of up close and personal contact with alien beings. Whitley Strieber, author of numerous popular works of horror and science fiction, published a book describing his abduction by aliens. Suddenly the public saw the idea of close encounters as plausible. His book, *Communion*, became a bestseller, and many other people began to claim that they too had been abducted.

To be fair, the idea of alien abduction had been around for a while. A Brazilian by the name of Antonio Villas-Boas claimed to have been abducted back in the fifties, but his tale received little widespread attention. The abduction of an American couple (Betty and Barney Hill) in 1961 did receive a lot of attention but was largely seen as a one-of-a-kind unusual event. A New York artist named Budd Hopkins was among the first to study abductions on a larger scale, publishing a book on the subject in 1982. His work, however, was mostly ignored until after Strieber published his own account.

But with the release of Strieber's book, talk of alien abduction was everywhere. The cover of the book featured a pointy-faced, large-eyed alien that seemed to resonate with many people. Many other abductees came out of the woodwork, and the alien abduction phenomenon was presented everywhere from daytime talk shows to the Sunday funnies.

While the media was bombarding us with tales of alien abduction, reality was a little different. The majority of UFO reports was still the old-fashioned kind — primarily lights in the sky — and only rarely was a structured object seen. An example of a typical sighting occurred early in the new decade on January 28, 1980. At around 9:30 p.m., a man looking out of a window of his Winnipeg home saw a strange red light off in the distance. The man and his son went outside, where they observed the light almost directly above them. For about five minutes the two watched the light seemingly give off sparks, which fell to the ground.[1]

UFO reports dropped off for a period in the eighties, and for the most part, those reported were much more mundane than what was starting to get widespread coverage in the popular media.

CHAPTER TWENTY-ONE
ANGEL HAIR

GEOFF DITTMAN

While most cases were garden-variety sightings, some more unusual cases were nonetheless reported. One such event happened on October 8, 1980, in Selkirk, Manitoba, where a woman and her two children observed a phenomenon known as "angel hair."

First the family observed "something misty and metallic-looking, gaining in size and emitting sparks, like firecrackers."[1] As well, the three could see a weightless "cottony substance" falling to the ground. It was coming down both in clumps and in large strands, landing primarily in their yard and their neighbours' property. There was a slight smell to it, reminding the mother of camphor. Whatever the substance was, it disappeared rapidly, shrinking until it vanished from sight. "We could not hold any of it for more than a minute or so," she reported, "because it just held its shape as it grew smaller and smaller and just vanished without a trace.... We didn't call the police or anyone because it kept disappearing and we didn't want to appear foolish."[2] Most of it was gone in a matter of minutes.

This substance, nicknamed "angel hair" by investigators, has been found off and on, with most of the cases occurring in the fifties. Unfortunately, much like the Selkirk case, the substance always disappears quite rapidly, so no detailed analysis has ever been performed on this unknown substance. There have been many attempts to explain the phenomenon. The most often heard explanation is that it is simply spiderwebs. Some spiders, particularly newborns, fly to new habitats by ballooning. The spider draws out a web, which the wind eventually lifts up and carries the spider away, much like a balloon. Spiders can travel surprisingly far by ballooning, with some spiders even being found by ships at sea.[3] Some have even been found at great heights, even as high as sixteen thousand feet.[4]

Could angel hair be nothing more than the leftover silk of a large number of ballooning spiders? Perhaps in some cases it very well could be. But the description of the angel hair in many cases is not consistent with what we know about spider silk.

The biggest inconsistency is the strength of spider silk. While there are different kinds of spider silk with many different purposes, what they all have in common is strength.[5] Weight for weight, spider silk is considerably stronger than steel and is extraordinarily elastic. It is waterproof and durable at temperatures down to -40 degrees Celsius.[6] It is for these reasons that spider silk is being examined to improve such things as bulletproof vests and bridge suspension cables.[7]

A key factor in many angel hair cases, at least those also involving UFO sightings, is that the substance falling to the ground rapidly disintegrates. One of the pieces of angel hair in the Selkirk case was five feet long, and it disappeared in minutes. Similarly, in a famous case from France in 1952, schoolteachers watched in amazement in their schoolyard as the substance disappeared before their eyes. A science teacher watched one strand, about forty feet long, disappear before he could properly analyze it.[8]

Would a substance like spider silk, incredibly durable for its weight, disappear into nothing in a couple of minutes? It seems unlikely. As French UFO researcher Aime Michel noted, "Spiders would not be able to spin their alleged skeins: like new Penelopes, they would never have time to finish their work, constantly spinning at one end while the other evaporated in the air."[9] How would the ballooning spiders manage to travel any distance (and survive) if the silk was that fragile? Certainly evolution would have selected against ballooning. While perhaps spider silk would explain some, it seems an unlikely explanation for many angel hair cases. Whatever was responsible for the cottony substance that rained down on Selkirk back in 1980, it wasn't spiders.

CHAPTER TWENTY-TWO
THE MEN IN BLACK

GEOFF DITTMAN

UFO cases even stranger than angel hair were yet to occur in the eighties. One such case, investigated by researcher Dr. P. Edwards, occurred in October 1981.[1] The story began in Victoria, British Columbia, around 9:30 p.m. on October 2. The principal witness was a young man named Grant Breiland. Breiland, his mother, and his sister were outside chatting, his sister preparing to go home. During this time Grant saw up in the sky a brilliant white light. Grant's mother and sister, as well as a paperboy, were unable to see anything. Wanting to find someone else who could see the strange light, Breiland got on his CB radio, where he in fact was able to talk to another witness: a man identified in the literature only as "N.B.," who was located about three miles away. Breiland then grabbed a camera (equipped with a 400-mm zoom lens) and was able to examine the object briefly before it flew off. What he saw looked somewhat like a stereotypical flying saucer. Hours after the sighting, in the early morning hours of October 3, both witnesses began to suffer from severe headaches.[2]

Nothing too unusual at this point, at least as far as UFO sightings go. What happened a few days later on October 5, however, belongs more in an *X-Files* episode than in the real world. Or at least in a Will Smith movie, for the two witnesses were seemingly visited by real-life "men in black."

Popularized by an early UFO researcher by the name of Gray Barker, men in black, or MIBs, were, according to some people, government agents out to intimidate UFO witnesses into silence.[3] Others felt the MIB were not government agents but aliens out to cover their tracks. Whatever the case, Barker's book *They Knew Too Much About Flying Saucers* popularized the legend of the men in black, even if it was full of dubious stories.[4]

Never too common, there have nonetheless been various cases over the years where these mysterious men approached witnesses. While the cases occurred all over the world, many had one thing in common: utterly bizarre behaviour on the part of the men in black. The MIBs' behaviour and appearance are typically so bizarre as to draw undue attention to themselves. The case involving Breiland and N.B. was to fit this pattern.

N.B. was the first of the two to be paid a visit. He was working at a gas station when he observed two men walk up to the station in a mechanical manner and ask for "petrol," as opposed to the more colloquial term "gas." The men wore dark suits and seemed to have unusually pale skin (also common in MIB stories). They drew attention to themselves by refusing to give their names when N.B. asked, for purposes of the receipt. The men then grossly overpaid for the gas and marvelled at the change that was given to them. Some fifteen minutes later, the men returned, giving the jerry can back to N.B. He was startled to discover that the can was still full![5]

Some three hours later, Breiland was himself visited by the men in black. While at the local K-Mart, Breiland used an outdoor payphone to call a friend. He began to experience what in ufology is known as the "Oz Factor." Jenny Randles, who coined the phrase, described it in her book *UFO Reality* as the "sensation of being isolated or transported from the real world into a different environmental framework."[6] Streets normally teeming with people seemingly become empty. No noise can be heard. The experiencer seems to partially suffer from sensory deprivation. While rare, the Oz Factor has turned up in some UFO cases, particularly those involving alien abduction.

In Breiland's case, the normally busy shopping mall parking lot became empty of people. Empty except for two strange-looking men standing outside of the phone booth. They were well-tanned and had no eyebrows or fingernails.[7] They stared at Breiland for several moments, with one man finally speaking to him in a monotone voice while seemingly not moving his lips.[8] The man asked Breiland for his name, address, and phone number. Naturally Breiland refused to provide the men with the information. With that the two men turned around, as if they were joined at the hip, and stiffly walked away. Breiland watched the strange sight, turning away only after hearing someone call his name repeatedly.[9] Seeing no one, he again turned his attention back to the two men but discovered they had disappeared! He walked into the muddy field where he had last seen them, but not even footprints were visible.

Later that night, Breiland had a dream that his encounter hadn't ended as it seemed. In the dream, he was abducted and questioned by the men in black. Furthermore, they ordered him to forget the encounter. Adding to the mystery, Breiland awoke the next morning and found a strange welt on his thigh.[10]

The skies over British Columbia must have been quite busy back then, as only a few days later there was another significant UFO sighting. Mrs. Hannah McRoberts was taking photographs of the mountains by Vancouver Island. With her were her husband and young daughter. Nothing out of the ordinary was seen that day. When they had the negatives developed, however, what should appear on one of the photographs but a flying saucer! The object was in focus and just to the right of one of the mountains that was the subject of the photo. It was a classic flying saucer, with some people suggesting it was a similar object to what Breiland saw a few days earlier.[11]

The photograph received extensive scrutiny from Dr. Richard Haines, a former employee of NASA. He found nothing in his investigation that was indicative of a hoax. The camera was not capable of double exposure and nothing was found to suggest the object was being suspended in the air by a line or that it was something like a Frisbee thrown in the air and photographed.[12]

CHAPTER TWENTY-THREE
THE STRANGENESS CONTINUES

GEOFF DITTMAN

The strangeness continued in Canada, though fewer cases were reported on an annual basis for some time. In July 1982, outside of Laval, Quebec, four young people had too close an encounter with a strange object and its occupant early one morning.[1] The four witnesses (three aged sixteen, the fourth aged twenty-five) were camping in a tent when at around 2:00 a.m. their attention was drawn to an object moving silently through the air. With an estimated altitude of only two hundred feet, the helicopter-sized craft gave off a white light powerful enough to light up the ground. After a short time, the object went behind some buildings and out of sight of the witnesses.

But they were not to be alone for long. Hearing a strange noise, they peered out of their tent and saw a bizarre being, roughly the size of a human but with orange eyes and a huge head. The youths became enveloped in a whirlwind of dust and, experiencing terrible stomach pains, they ran into a nearby house. No more was seen of either the craft or the being.

By the end of the decade, things began to pick up again. In 1989 there were numerous interesting cases from around the country, ranging all over the spectrum, from relatively boring nocturnal lights seen by lone witnesses to cases involving multiple independent observers and trace evidence.

One such interesting case occurred on January 4, 1989, around Wesleyville, Newfoundland.[2] Four of the witnesses were driving toward the town of Wesleyville at around 11:30 p.m. One man pointed out an unusually bright light in the sky ahead of them. They debated the source of the light, suggesting a star, meteor, or plane. They continued to watch the object for a while as they drove to their destination. At one point they estimated the light was no more than one hundred feet away from the town's water tank. They figured it was also no more than five hundred feet above the ground. They could see two flashing red lights. One woman said she could see a door or window underneath the object. For most of the sighting they couldn't hear any sound, though at one point they did hear something resembling a jet engine. Eventually the object flew out of their sight.

At the same time, a short distance away, a young man and his girlfriend were driving along a nearby highway when they noticed a bright light a couple of miles away. It approached their car, eventually flying over it at an estimated altitude of only three hundred feet. The bright lights on the object shut off while it passed over the car. No noise could be heard. They took some pictures with a 35-mm camera, but none of the pictures came out.

The witnesses reported the sighting to the RCMP. A check with the nearby Gander airport and a military base suggested there were no aircraft in the vicinity at the time of the sighting.

Strange lights continued to be seen over Canada that year. On October 26, 1989, a lone adult male was standing beside some railroad tracks in Calgary, Alberta. At approximately 8:45 p.m., he saw a puzzling sight in the sky in front of him. Between eight and ten lights of various colours were moving slowly above the ground. He estimated they were only 300 to 350 feet above the ground. No sound was heard during the approximately ten minutes of observation.[3]

Another case comes from Hall Beach in the Northwest Territories on November 4, 1989.[4] A couple, "Joshua" and "Ruth, " along with their two children, aged eight and five, were sitting in front of a large living room window, watching television. It was approximately 5:30 p.m., and it was already quite dark out in this northern town. The family dog began barking; Joshua assumed the object of the dog's attention was nothing more than a polar bear along the shore. At this time, he heard a jetlike sound that lasted for a brief second. Ignoring this noise too, Joshua went back to watching television.

Suddenly Joshua's attention was drawn away from the TV to a strange object in the sky. He walked over to the window to get a better look. His family, having seen it too, joined him. What they saw was an object somewhat resembling an upside-down cup and saucer. The bottom portion — the cup — was rounded and had a red light in the centre. In the middle of the object were what appeared to be three windows, which emanated bright white light. The top portion of the craft — the saucer — was round and had alternating red and blue lights along the side.

After only a couple of seconds from when the family reached the window, the object departed, seemingly straight up, disappearing from sight extraordinarily quickly. Joshua estimated it was gone from sight in one to two seconds. The entire sighting lasted not much more than five seconds.

The witnesses were reluctant to estimate the altitude, distance away, or size of the object, acknowledging they had no accurate way to make such an estimate. Joshua did say the object was over the ocean, at about a forty-five-degree angle from the horizon.

At 9:00 p.m. the RCMP were notified of the incident. They received the initial report not from the primary witnesses of the case but rather from an employee of the Department of Public Works. After about an hour, the police were able to locate the witnesses, who were able to confirm the sighting and elaborate on the details.

The RCMP contacted a local DEW station.[5] The police were advised that no one was monitoring the radar locally and that they would have to contact the Canadian NORAD headquarters at North Bay, Ontario. They did say, however, that there were no known flights at the time of the sighting.

The police tried to find other witnesses but gave up after several days with no success. The RCMP filed a report with the National Research Council and closed the file. The police didn't come to a conclusion, but they did indicate the following: "It should be noted that there was no liquor, drugs, etc. involved in this report on the part of [the witnesses]. The matter appears to be completely above board. What was seen is not known, however, the reliability of the witnesses, as far as the writer is aware, and as a result of public opinion, is very reliable."[6]

CHAPTER TWENTY-FOUR
ELECTROMAGNETIC EFFECTS CASES

GEOFF DITTMAN

As has been pointed out elsewhere in this book, the majority of UFO reports are simply lights seen in the night sky. An investigator is at the mercy of people's poor perceptive skills to determine if something really was out there. Some cases, however, provide us with evidence that something really was there, that the object interacted with the environment in some way, shape, or form. For example, an encounter might have electromagnetic (EM) effects. While relatively rare, there has been an impressive number of such cases over the decades.[1] Many of these cases involve car stoppings, where automobiles cease to function in the presence of a UFO. Others involve interference with radios or televisions. A handful of cases even tell of large-scale power failures.[2]

What causes the EM effects? Obviously no one knows for sure, but some speculate that microwave radiation from the UFOs results in ionization of the local atmosphere.[3] Is such interference intentional? Again no one knows for sure, but the consensus is that it is purely accidental — the unfortunate result of UFOs getting too close to our electrical equipment. It is interesting to note that while there have been numerous cases of planes' radios and navigational equipment failing in the presence of UFOs, there has not been a documented case of any aircraft's engines shutting down, unlike cars, which tend to suffer widespread interference. This is suggestive of at least some control on the part of whatever is causing the interference, as in the fictional movie

The Day the Earth Stood Still, where the Earth's electrical systems were shut down entirely except for aircraft in flight and hospitals.

The majority of EM cases are small-scale: a car's engine is shut down or a radio's reception is interfered with. Only occasionally does such interference occur over a larger area. One such incident took place in northwestern Ontario around Kenora in 1989. It began on November 19, at about 9:30 p.m. Kurt Rosentreter was on the Trans-Canada Highway, headed east from Winnipeg to his home in Kenora. While near West Hawk Lake he saw a bright flashing light just above the woods to the east of him. In an interview with the (Kenora) *Daily Miner*, he stated: "I noticed it change direction, move parallel to my car and then toward me, and then it was gone after 20 minutes. It couldn't have been an airplane because it was flashing too inconsistently and could change directions too suddenly."[4] He estimated it to be about sixty yards off the ground.

Things were to get considerably stranger as the night continued. At about 11:30 p.m., people all around Kenora began to experience unusual phenomena. Joanne Leonard woke up in her home southeast of Kenora to the sound of her phone ringing. Upon answering it all she could hear was a strange buzzing sound. She hung up the phone, but it rang again. Mrs. Leonard looked out a window and observed the streetlights turning on and off. To the northwest, she could see a red-orange glow in the sky. The light was pulsating, and her ringing phone and the streetlights seemed to be in sync with the pulsation.[5] Her television, which hadn't been used in several hours, began to glow.[6]

Mrs. Leonard was hardly alone. Mrs. Robin Rowe lived northeast of town. She awoke to find her bathroom light turning on and off repeatedly. Looking out her window Rowe thought she could see an object, approximately one hundred feet in diameter. She could also see a red light reflecting off the clouds. She said the light was pulsating and that the lights in the valley below her home were going on and off with the pulsation.[7] Mrs. Rowe's porch lights were going on and off as well. Rowe tried to phone her friends, but she could only hear a buzzing sound from the phone. Finally, after a few minutes, the light in the sky faded and the power in her house returned to normal.

"Mike," who lived northeast of town, saw a bright light coming from Kenora at about 11:30 p.m. Like the other witnesses, he described it as reddish in colour, but unlike the others he said it wasn't pulsating. Curious as to the source of the light he got in his car and drove towards Kenora. Before he could get to town, however, the light went out.

Clayton Riehl, a teenager at the time, observed what he thought was a revolving object over the vicinity of Kenora. It was giving off an orange light, and he saw it just above the trees for about fifteen seconds around 11:30 p.m.[8]

The region's emergency services were affected by the strange goings-on as well. The Kenora police received at least three calls about the incidents. The Ontario Provincial Police received at least six calls. In addition, the OPP's Crimestoppers line was affected by the same ringing and buzzing sound as other phones in the area. The Kenora fire department told the press that its "switchboard lit up and the alarms sounded."[9] At least one emergency responder, an OPP officer, actually observed the red lights in the sky.

Is there a natural explanation that could reasonably account for the various unusual phenomena observed over Kenora in 1989?

At any given time the sun typically has several sunspots visible on its surface, or photosphere. These sunspots are basically giant magnetic fields. The fields are incredibly strong, considerably stronger than the Earth's own magnetic field.[10] The sunspots give off solar flares, which are massive releases of solar energy and radiation. This energy is blasted out into space, and some of the radiation can hit the Earth. If not for the fact that the Earth is protected by its own magnetic field, such massive doses of radiation would wipe out all life on the planet.[11]

While life on earth is relatively protected from solar flares, that is not to say flares don't have any impact. When the electrically charged particles from the sun hit the Earth's atmosphere, the atoms in the atmosphere absorb some of the radiation and become ionized (lose electrons). Particles begin colliding with one another, resulting in further ionization.[12] These active atoms create light, resulting in aurora borealis, or the northern lights. These lights are incredible waves in the sky that appear at night over the northern hemisphere.

Could the northern lights be a source of the Kenora UFO reports? A qualified "yes" is the answer. Ionized particles are capable of interfering with anything electrical.[13] Blackouts and problems with radio and telephone communications are certainly possible. In fact, such a problem caused by solar flares occurred in Quebec some eight months before the Kenora sightings in November 1989. Power went out northeast of Kenora, and Ontario Hydro wasn't able to explain the cause. Bell Canada suggested the phone problems were due to a power surge.[14]

It appears that solar flares and aurora could be the cause of the strange electrical problems. Then of course there are the lights. What several of the witnesses saw (a pulsating glow in the sky) is not inconsistent with the northern lights. One would, however, have to explain the claim that the light was seemingly bouncing off the clouds. In other words, the source of the light appeared to be below the clouds. Also, according to Environment Canada, the sky was overcast over Kenora that night, which should have obscured the northern lights. Was there a break in the cloud cover that could have allowed the witnesses to glimpse the aurora? In fact, one witness did indicate that the sky was clear when the sighting concluded.

Sunspot activity increases and decreases in an eleven-year cycle. In the early years of the cycle, activity is low. As time goes on, activity increases, reaching its peak at the end of the eleven years. With the increase in sunspots, there is an increase in solar flare activity. This in turn results in an increase in aurora activity, with the peak in aurora activity about two years after the peak of the sunspot cycle.[15] It should be noted that 1989 was near the peak of a sunspot cycle. While aurora activity would therefore not be quite at its peak, it would nonetheless be increased at this time. In fact, there was quite spectacular aurora seen over Kenora in the weeks around the November 19 sightings. Investigators from the private UFO research group UFOROM witnessed a brilliant display on November 27 while investigating the earlier sightings.

Whether or not the aurora could explain the lights is another question. Not only does the cloud cover cause problems, but the behaviour and description of the lights cast suspicion on the aurora hypothesis. The teenager's mysterious revolving object and Rosentreter's ball of light don't sound like the northern lights. There are other possible explanations, however. Perhaps what Rosentreter saw was a plane. He was travelling on a winding highway through a forest at the time of the sighting. The apparent repeated change in direction of the object could have been due to the witness's own movement. The intermittent flashing might simply have been due to the light being temporarily obscured by the trees.

Finally, it should be noted that the UFO reports around Kenora didn't end on November 19. Four nights later, on November 23, three more events were reported. The first sighting occurred around 7:00 p.m. The witness observed multiple flashing lights darting around at high speed over Blindfold Lake, southeast of Kenora. The witness claimed it was just over the treetops. Responding to the witness's phone call, members of the OPP positioned themselves nearby but saw only an airplane and some meteors.[16] The second sighting occurred about fifteen minutes after the first. At 7:15 p.m., a witness observed an object travelling from one end of Longbow Lake to the other.[17] (Longbow Lake is northwest of Blindfold, approximately halfway to Kenora.) Then, at 7:42 p.m., an eyewitness on a flight from Winnipeg to Kenora saw a flashing blue light. The plane was approximately ten miles south of Kenora airport (which is northwest of the city), at about twenty-one thousand feet.[18] It should be noted that there is a flashing blue light on a ham radio tower in the area, but given that there were other sightings in the area at the time, one should not so quickly dismiss this sighting.

RCMP files tell of another UFO case involving electromagnetic effects that occurred in 1989. About three weeks after the Kenora incidents, a resident of Regina, Saskatchewan, had his own disturbing close encounter on December 14, 1989. It was about 7:00 p.m., just south of Punnichy, Saskatchewan, and the witness had just left his father-in-law's house. Lights suddenly appeared overhead, and his car promptly died, with the engine, headlights, and radio all shutting off. Gravel hit the car, presumably debris kicked up by the power source of the object.

After a period of time, the flying object departed the scene, moving away to the north. The man promptly returned to his father-in-law's home, all shook up from the encounter. The two then returned to the scene of the sighting. While they didn't get an up-close look at anything strange, the men did see two bright lights off in the sky.

There was one potentially collaborating witness to the event. An RCMP officer reported seeing a bright light at the approximate location of the encounter.[19]

CHAPTER TWENTY-FIVE
A UFO LANDS IN QUEBEC

GEOFF DITTMAN

While no evidence was left behind for the police to examine in the last case, occasionally investigators are left with something a little more tangible to look at. One example is the Marieville, Quebec, encounter of 1989. In this case, the RCMP, along with civilian researchers Christian Page and Francois Bourbeau, were left with a circular trace on the ground to study.

It began at about 5:30 a.m. on November 20, 1989, when several people in a rural neighbourhood of Marieville (also known as Ste-Marie-de-Monnoir) heard and saw something strange going on over the town.[1]

"Mr. Jean Prigent" and his spouse, "Camille," awoke to the sight of a strong blue light shining through their curtains. They could hear a noise similar to an electric generator and could also feel a vibration. Looking outside however, they were unable to ascertain the source of the light and noise.[2]

At the same time, about three hundred yards down the road, neighbour "Alain Rondeaux" also was awakened by the bright light. He, however, could see the source: four blue balls over Prigent's house. Rondeaux too described hearing a sound similar to a generator and feeling vibrations. He described the lights as being somewhat intermittent. They seemed to go out and shortly thereafter come back on, doing this at least four times during the sighting. When the lights would reappear, they would show up in a different location, but not straying more than a kilometre away. At one instance, Rondeaux noticed that the streetlights along Highway 112 weakened, seemingly the result of interference from the lights when they got too close.[3]

He couldn't see if there was any structure behind the lights. Between the bright light, the early morning darkness, and the poor weather (fog with light snow/rain), his sight was too hampered. Rondeaux did estimate that the lights were approximately thirty feet off the ground.[4]

At the same time there was another witness to the lights. "Chantal Nahon" was already up at 5:30 a.m., as her husband had to get an early morning start to go to work. Chantal was in her kitchen when she observed a bright blue light through the kitchen window. She too heard a noise resembling an electric generator. At one point she saw sparks fly when the light got too close to a power line.[5]

At 6:00 a.m. one final person saw the strange lights. "Adrienne Gachignard" was in her kitchen when she saw the bright light through her kitchen window. She described it as being like a bright white ball of fire that appeared and disappeared three times. Each time it reappeared, it seemed to interfere with the power, as the electricity in her home would decrease. The final time the light appeared her power fully went out for ten minutes. Ms. Gachignard wasn't able to see if there was any structure behind the light, given its intensity.[6]

Some two days after the sighting, a strange pattern was found outside of the Prigent residence. In the backyard, about 150 feet from the house, was a perfectly round circle, sixty-five feet in diameter. The grass was flattened on the inside and upright like normal on the outside. Somewhat unusual for an alleged UFO landing site, the grass was not burned but was actually greener within the circle than it was without.[7]

The RCMP was called, and officers were sent to the scene on November 23. There was still some snow on the ground, but it was noted that there was less snow inside the circle than outside it. RCMP visited the site again some five days later. It had been raining for two days at that point and all the snow was gone. The difference in the colour of the grass between inside and outside the circle was quite obvious.[8]

The RCMP did some investigating to see if they could come up with an explanation. The police verified that there was no search and rescue or other air operation conducted that day. They also contacted Hydro-Quebec to inquire about any electrical problems on the day of the sighting. Hydro-Quebec indicated that no repairs were carried out in the vicinity on that day, nor was there any known power failure.[9] The source of the lights and the strange ground markings is still unknown.

TOWARDS THE MILLENNIUM

CHAPTER TWENTY-SIX
THE CARP CASE
CHRIS RUTKOWSKI AND GEOFF DITTMAN

In late 1989, several UFO investigators and researchers in Canada and the United States received a package of documents sent anonymously through the mail. The documents described the crash of a UFO that had occurred outside Carleton Place, near Ottawa. A photocopied photograph of what was said to be an alien was also included.

The documents read:

> Canadian and American Security Agencies are engaged in a conspiracy of silence, to withhold from the world the alien vessel seized in the swamps of Corkery Road, Carp, in 1989.
>
> UFO sightings in the Ontario region had intensified in the 1980's, specifically, around nuclear power generating stations. On Nov. 4, 1989 at 20:00 hrs Canadian Defense Dept. radars picked up a globe shaped object travelling at phenomenal speed over Carp, Ontario. The UFO abruptly stopped, and dropped like a stone.
>
> Canadian and American Security Agencies were immediately notified of the landing. Monitoring satellites traced the movements of the aliens to a triangular area (see aerial map) off Almonte and Corkery Roads.
>
> The ship had landed in deep swamp near Corkery Road. Two AH-64 Apaches and a UH-60 Blackhawk

headed for the area the following night. The helicopters carried full weapon loads. They were part of a covert American unit that specialized in the recovery of alien craft.

Flying low over Ontario pine trees the Apache attack choppers soon spotted a glowing, blue, 20 metre in diameter sphere. As targeting lasers locked-on, both gunships unleashed their full weapon loads of 8 missiles each. All 16 were exploded in proximity bursts 10 metres downwind from the ship.

The missiles were carrying VEXXON, a deadly neuroactive gas which kills on contact. Exposed to air the gas breaks down quickly into inert components. Immediately after having completed their mission the gunships turned around, and headed back across the border.

Now the Blackhawk landed, as men exploded from its open doors. In seconds the six man strike team had entered the UFO through a 7 metre hatchless, oval portal. No resistance was encountered. At the controls, 3 dead crewman were found.

With the ship captured, the US Airforce, Pentagon, and Office of Naval Intelligence were notified. Through the night a special team of technicians had shut-down and disassembled the sphere. Early the next morning Nov. 6, 1989 construction equipment and trucks were brought into the swamp. The UFO parts were transported to a secret facility in Kanata, Ontario.

As a cover story the locals were informed that a road was being built through the swamp. No smokescreen was needed for the military activity as Canadian forces regularly train in the Carp region. Officially nothing unusual was reported in the area. Although someone anonymously turned in a 35mm roll of film. It was received by the National Research Council of Canada, in Ottawa. The film contained several clear shots of an entity holding a light. (see photo) At this time the photographer is still unidentified.

The humanoids were packed in ice and sent to an isolation chamber at the Univ. of Ottawa. CIA physiologists performed the autopsies. The reptilian, fetus-headed beings, were listed as CLASS 1 NTE's (Non Terrestrial Entities). Like others recovered in previous operations, they were muscular, grey-white skinned, humanoids.

The ship was partially reassembled at the underground facility in Kanata. Unlike previous recoveries this one is pure military. Built as a "Starfighter" it is heavily armed and armored. In design no rivets, bolts, or welds were used in fastening, yet when reconstructed there are no seams. The UFO itself is made up of a matrixed dielectric magnesium alloy. It is driven by pulsed electromagnetic fields generated by a cold fusion reactor. All offensive capabilities utilize independently targeting electronic beam weapons. In the cargo hold were found ordnance racks containing fifty Soviet nuclear warheads. Their purpose was revealed by advanced tactical/combat computers located in the flight deck.

Threatened by recent East-West relations, and the revolutionary movements within itself, Red China is preparing for the final ideological war. The aliens have agreed to defend China from the free world's combined military and nuclear forces.

At this time China is arming the Middle East with their own nuclear arsenals, in order that they can successfully take on Israel. Unifying the Arabs under one Chinese command was simple, especially with Israel's recent "iron fist" attitude toward occupied territories.

The Soviet warheads found in the UFO were destined for Syria. CIA operatives in the Middle East have noticed huge movements of Chinese "technicians" and "advisors". China is also supplying the Arabs with bacteriological agents, Migs, Hind gunships, tanks, and missile launchers. The use of "Soviet" instead of "Chinese" nukes is part of a disinformation campaign to break up East-West relations after the annihilation of Israel. The Warheads were hijacked from Soviet subs in the Dragon's Triangle. A section of alien controlled Pacific once frequented by Russian subs. After losing some 900 high yield warheads and 13 vessels, commanders were ordered to steer clear of the area.

The most important alien-tech find were the 2 millimeter, spheroid, brain implants. Surgically inserted through the nasal orifice the individual can be fully monitored and controlled. The CIA and Canadian Govt have actively supported mind-slave experiments for years. Currently the Univ. of Ottawa is involved in ELF wave mind control programs. A continuation of the CIA psychological warfare project known as MKULTRA, started at the Allen Memorial Institute in Montreal.

Using ELF signals transmitted at the same wavelength the human brain uses, the researchers could subliminally control the test subject. The alien implants utilize the same principles except that the whole unit is subminiaturized and contained in the brain. Fortunately the implants can be detected by magnetic resolution scanning technology. All individuals implanted by the aliens are classified as ZOMBIES.

The ZOMBIES have been programmed to help overthrow Mankind in the near future. When China finishes with Israel it will invade Europe. At the same time Chinese spacebased bacteriological weapons will be launched at the Arctic. The winds will carry the diseases into Russia and North America. In days 100's of millions will be dead, survivors will have to deal with Chinese, aliens, and the ZOMBIES.

The aliens want all out war so that human resistance would be minimal, when they invade. They tried this same tactic once before with Nazi Germany. Most of the scientific advances we have today came from German science which was based on alien technology. Had Hitler won the war, the earth would have become a concentration camp in order to depopulate the continents for the aliens.

Data aboard the sphere explained why the aliens are so comfortable on our world. They preceded man on the evolutionary scale by millions of years; created

> with the dinosaurs. Some 675 million years ago an interdimensional war destroyed most of their civilization, and forced them to leave the earth. Now they have chosen to reclaim what was once theirs.
>
> The alien forces with their Chinese and Arab allies will attack within the next 5 years. Waiting longer than that would make it impossible even for the aliens to reverse the ecological damage inflicted on the Earth by Man.[1]

The absurdity of the information contained in the material made it particularly easy to dismiss as nonsense. It included snippets of rumours about secret military operations, splicing together stories about underground bases, clandestine laboratories, and advanced technological weaponry. The political commentary was very much like the paranoid "New World Order" missives issued by civilian militia groups that spawned such events as the Oklahoma City bombing.

Tom Theofanous, a Mutual UFO Network (MUFON) field representative in Toronto who was one of the people to receive the material, believed the package was part of a hoax, but contacted his colleagues and began an investigation. A resident of the Carleton area, Graham Lightfoot, was asked to check into the matter. He was able to locate the supposed crash site near Manon Corners and also found some apparent witnesses.[2]

One such witness was a woman named "Diane Weston." (Several of the names in this case have been changed. Where done so, the name is initially presented in quotation marks.) She indicated that on the night of November 4, 1989, she observed an incredibly bright light fly over her house. She also saw searchlight-equipped helicopters seemingly scanning the area.[3] Other unusual events that were noted that weekend included a woman frightened by an intense light shining through her bathroom window and cattle escaping from their pasture. Many others questioned by Lightfoot, however, including a couple of amateur astronomers who had been busy stargazing, could not remember anything unusual occurring that night.[4]

Lightfoot examined the field behind Westons' home but could not find any sign of a massive recovery effort with the heavy equipment that would be needed to retrieve a crashed flying saucer. His report to Theofanous noted, "I could find nothing conclusive to support or disprove any of the witnesses claims."[5]

Other UFO investigators began to show interest in the story. MUFON representative Clive Nadin and Quebec UFO director Christian Page visited the area and interviewed the witnesses. Much like Lightfoot, Nadin and Page felt there was nothing substantive to support the documents and that the case was likely a hoax.[6]

Then, almost two years later, the Carp case resurfaced with even more bizarre twists. In the fall of 1991, UFO investigators began receiving more "leaked" documents through the mail, all postmarked in Ottawa. First, a large envelope arrived with some "censored" documents. The documents were partially blacked out in an apparent attempt to make them look like legitimate government documents released to researchers like Stanton Friedman.[7] The documents, photocopied on plain white paper, described how "Red China was preparing for the final ideological war," assisted by aliens in an attempt to rid the Earth of inferior species. The alliance would attack with nuclear and "moisture-breeding biological weapons" to genetically destroy "specific ethnic populations." The document writer boasted, "America will be crippled; power grids, tanks, missiles, cars, antennas, phone lines will stop." The documents offered some good news, however, in that the "ELITE will survive WW3" in "installations under mile-thick Canadian-shield granite." They also noted that "huge facilities run by joint AMERICAN/CANADIAN military corporations" operate in the Carp area, with secret research done at the University of Ottawa and Carleton.

This "war" is sociological and cultural as well, since:

> ALIENS [blacked out] BLOND types. [blacked out] infiltrate the artistic centres of Canada. It appears that they need artists to get the message out.
>
> The GOVERNMENT is attempting to fight back by cutting funding/freedom of expression to filmmakers, writers, & visual artists. There is a secret list for the elimination, imprisonment [blacked out] artists in CANADA.[8]

The package also included a map and sketch of alien activity near Ottawa between 1970 and 1991, with sketches of Masonic symbols and guides to identify UFOs in flight. There was also a black and white photograph of a white-faced alien standing in what appears to be a field of tall grass. Some packages also included a Polaroid photograph of a bright UFO over a gravel road.

Some investigators received another package that contained a VHS videotape. On the label was a thumbprint and the name "Guardian."[9] Researchers also received playing cards that "Guardian" had inscribed handwritten notes on.[10]

The video showed what Guardian alleged was an alien craft resting in a field. During part of the video, lights like road flares could be seen to the left of the object. One scene, possibly included accidentally or as an afterthought, was only three frames long and was a close-up of a pair of windshield wipers extended across a truck or car front windshield. The entire video was only a few minutes in length; the only sound that could be heard was the distant barking of a dog. At least one researcher, however, received a copy with no sound at all.[11]

Debate over the nature of the documents and video raged throughout the winter. Incredibly, some UFO investigators thought there might be a genuine crash event or UFO encounter as the basis of the material. However, it was decided to wait until spring before an intense ground investigation could be undertaken.

In March 1992, American MUFON investigator Bob Oechsler in Maryland contacted Canadian ufologists and set up a meeting in the Carleton area to begin on-site investigations. He had also received a video and documents from Guardian, although his video apparently had an additional close-up shot of the UFO, a few minutes of the windshield, and several still shots of the alien. His version of the videotape had no audio.

Oechsler had shown the tape to UFO photographic analyst Bruce Maccabee. Impressed by the tape, he felt the investigation deserved to continue. The Americans made plans to meet with not only Lightfoot but also other researchers from Ottawa and Toronto. In May 1992, Oechsler and his son met with Lightfoot, Tom and Lise Theofanous, Victor Lourenco, Vaughn Killin, Drew Williamson, Harry Tokarz, and Wayne St. John at a motel near Ottawa.

Using Guardian's map as a guide, the group left the motel in search of the landing site. While near the Westons' home, the group came upon a series of bizarre signs on private property. "DND Killing Fields" and "Do Not Enter" were written on two of the signs, along with drawings of tanks and weapons. The researchers looked at the surrounding terrain, comparing it to the map, and began to suspect that they had found the site where the Guardian video was shot. They could even hear a dog barking nearby.[12] The group followed a path along the Westons' property but gave up when it began to get dark.

The next day, some of the group went back to talk with Diane Weston. She vaguely recalled seeing the light in the field back in 1989, but then told them about an event in August 1991. At around 10:00 p.m., barking dogs had caused her to look outside to see what was the matter. Looking out a bedroom window, she could see flames and smoke coming from the field behind her house. The smoke and flames might have been caused by flares, she thought. Then she saw a strange-looking ship land close to the flames. She said the object was silver in colour with a zigzag pattern on it.[13] The object rested on three legs. The craft as described by Weston strongly resembled a drawing that was in one of the Guardian letters. Investigators were puzzled as to how Weston was able to see in the dark more than seven hundred yards away. Even the video was not able to pick up the kinds of details Weston claimed to see, and Guardian was closer to the object than Weston.[14]

Diane wasn't the only Weston to claim to have seen a UFO. Apparently, on February 17, 1993, Diane's mother saw an object hovering not more than fifty feet from the house. And Diane's husband had also seen a UFO over the backyard on at least one occasion.[15]

Helicopters were also showing some interest in the Weston home. The Westons claimed to have been repeatedly bothered by low-flying choppers, some apparently flying low enough to blow shingles off the roof of the house. Talk of mysterious unmarked helicopters is quite common in UFO stories, with conspiracy theorists believing that the helicopters belong to a super-secret government project investigating UFOs.

It was this helicopter activity that caused the RCMP to begin an investigation into the goings-on around the Weston home. The Westons filed a complaint, arguing that the helicopters were flying well below the five-hundred-foot floor demanded by Canadian law. However, Diane told UFO investigators that her family was being harassed in turn by the RCMP. She claimed the Mounties had shown up at the house insisting what she had seen in 1991 was nothing but a helicopter and trying to get Diane to sign a confession to that effect.[16]

A slightly sanitized copy of the RCMP report on the case was obtained by Christian Page of MUFON Quebec. The Westons' complaint, filed with the RCMP on February 10, 1993, read:

A. To ascertain if sufficient evidence was available to support a prosecution under the Aeronautics Act, Section 534 (2) (b) for flying below 500 feet.

B. To ascertain if in fact the object observed was an aircraft.
C. To ascertain if the craft observed is a UFO.[17]

On February 15, 1993, the RCMP began the investigation. The RCMP interviewed many people in the area, looking for other witnesses to the low-flying helicopters. While many people admitted to seeing helicopters, only one individual mentioned in the report described the helicopters as flying low.[17] Many of the witnesses simply mentioned seeing the local air ambulance helicopter that regularly flies over the area.

The RCMP contacted the military in an attempt to eliminate them as a source of the helicopters. While admitting that military helicopters do regularly fly in the area, the spokesperson indicated that flying below the five-hundred-foot minimum usually isn't permitted, although helicopters do occasionally land in farmers' fields. At that time the military denied there were any helicopter exercises in the area.[18]

The RCMP contacted the Department of Transport (DOT) to see what could be learned from them. According to DOT officials, the military had in fact been flying over the general area.[19] Upon examining the video, however, they suggested that what was on the tape was not a Canadian military helicopter but rather a Sikorsky manufactured chopper, either a commercial S-76 Eagle or a U.S. Air Force UH-60 Blackhawk. The pattern of lights visible on the object was reasonably consistent with a helicopter, and the DOT officials also felt they could pick out pieces of a helicopter, such as the main rotor and tail bottom assembly.[20] As for what a U.S. Air Force helicopter might be doing in Canada, the DOT informed the RCMP that "it is not uncommon to see the U.S. military making unscheduled or unspecified flights into Canadian Air Space, without alerting Canadian authorities."[21]

While the investigation continued, the Westons saw more helicopter activity, namely six separate incidents involving low-flying white helicopters over a ten-day period in February. They also recorded video but the quality was too poor to make positive identification possible.[22] The RCMP again contacted the military and the Department of Transport to inform them of the activity. The military indicated two of the helicopters were United Nations aircraft.[23] The DOT suggested the helicopters belonged to the RCMP's (now disbanded) counter-terrorism Special Emergency Response Team.

The RCMP took the video to more experts for their opinions. Employees of a local aviation company viewed the tape. Much like the DOT, they felt that the object was a Sikorsky UH-60 Blackhawk.[24] The

RCMP Video Analysis Department also decided the object shown on the tape was likely a helicopter.

In conclusion, the RCMP felt the object in the video was most likely a helicopter. With regards to the Westons' complaints of low-flying helicopters, they felt there wasn't enough evidence for a successful prosecution.[25]

After the RCMP investigation, Bob Oechsler located another witness to the landing on the Weston farm. This person, known only as "Susan Gill," said that one night she heard her dog barking and she got up to see what was the matter. She could see red lights through the trees in the Westons' field. Her first impression was that they were fireworks. But as she watched, other lights lifted off the ground, flew up over the treetops, and vanished. Gill went outside to try to get a better view. Outside she saw an object over her own house. Later she told investigators of her memories of being taken aboard the UFO and communicating telepathically with the "oriental" aliens inside.[26]

MUFON investigators were skeptical of Gill's story, noting that it was inconsistent and that the details changed over time.[27] But MUFON investigators were not only suspicious of Gill's story, however. Through the course of the investigation, it was learned that a local man named "Bobby Davidson" was an avid UFO buff and had referred to himself as "Guardian" on many occasions. Diane Weston admitted knowing Davidson well and that she and Bobby were good friends. Had the Westons conspired with Davidson to hoax a UFO video? To add further suspicion, Weston had told investigators that she knew nothing about UFOs nor was she interesting in talking about them. Yet, when a crew from NBC's *Unsolved Mysteries* visited her home, many UFO books were seen on bookshelves.

Eventually, MUFON Ontario came to some conclusions regarding the Carp case. In a fascinating essay describing the investigation, Tom Theofanous and Errol Bruce-Knapp wrote in the MUFON Ontario newsletter that:

- the Westons, along with Davidson and possibly others, hoaxed the video of the object;
- the object was likely either a pickup truck or a helicopter; and
- Susan Gill's abduction, if it actually occurred, likely occurred at a different time from the Weston event.[28]

Despite the MUFON investigators' formal publication of their full and detailed report and conclusions, the Carp case has continued to be debated and discussed in ufological circles and other forums, and the video has been promoted as "one of the best" UFO videos on record. The image on the video has been shown on TV programs about UFOs and described as showing a hovering saucer with lights or some kind of helicopter that may have been "buzzing" the Westons' farm.

An exposé of the hoax has been offered to the UFO community on many occasions. For example, the UFO Updates discussion list had a discussion on the Carp case as late as 2003. One researcher suggested that the video depicted an emergency landing of a Comanche helicopter gunship, flown out of the Boeing plant not far from Ottawa. Others felt the object was nothing that unusual. Some believe it was a pickup truck. MUFON Ontario had noticed that a relative of Diane Weston's owned a pickup truck that bore a similarity to the object in the video. A subscriber to UFO Updates described MUFON Ontario's findings thusly:

> The Carp video is clearly not that of an aerial craft. It's true that some investigators reported seeing helicopters near Carp, but this is likely unrelated to the Carp case. … The video *seems* to show an aerial object because it is positioned in a black sky with no reference points. However, diligent investigation and analysis shows that the object is actually a much more "down to Earth" pickup truck parked on the ground, surrounded by bright sources of light. This illusion is easily deconstructed by looking at stills from the video, found on MUFON Ontario's Carp web page: http://www.virtuallystrange.net/ufo/mufonontario/archive/carp. html
> The truck is facing the camera, rotated about 45 degrees clockwise to the left of the observer. The cab and windshield can be clearly seen partly illuminated by the bright sources of light beside and to the front of the truck. It's an interesting trick, because when the camera is panned up and down and around in a black sky, the bright lights make it nearly impossible to see the truck and make it appear as if there is an object moving about in the air.[29]

So it would appear that the video shows not a flying saucer but a much more mundane truck. The Carp case is another unfortunate attempt to fool researchers with a hoax. Investigators have a hard enough time interpreting evidence brought forward by sincere witnesses without having to worry about insincere ones.

CHAPTER TWENTY-SEVEN
BUT "THEY" KNOW EVERYTHING

CHRIS RUTKOWSKI

In 1994, I made a trip to Ottawa to visit the National Research Council office that housed recent UFO reports received from the Canadian public. I arrived in the city around midnight on February 17 and was met by George Kriger, a long-time friend and occasional UFOROM associate. The next morning at the crack of dawn, we went to the NRC and began poring through documents and studying UFO case data for the past year. It took an entire day to read through the hundreds of pages of documents, copying down the data needed for analysis. We celebrated our hard work by going to sleep by 8:00 p.m. (Ufologists cannot always be party animals.) My flight out wasn't for another few days, so I had time to check out bookstores and various other attractions in the nation's capital. There was a one-man band in the ByWard Market, and some good deals in the Glebe, as usual. The lineup for Beaver Tails was too long, so we opted for some fast food.

While at the NRC, I had seen a copy of an article from the *Ottawa Citizen* from just before the Guardian video was originally aired on *Unsolved Mysteries*. In the article, a local hot-air balloonist claimed that the video might have been of his own balloon during a night flight, since he flies with a strobe and light sticks. It sounded like a reasonable possibility, so I thought I'd check into it. I tried to track down the balloonist with no success, although a rival balloonist told me that the strobes on the balloons didn't match the ones in the Guardian video, confirming my own recollection of the last time I saw such lights on night flights. Later, as I was reading through a book about UFOs, I found the name of an individual in Ottawa who was listed as an investigator. This seemed the perfect opportunity to meet, so I called him. We discussed some recent cases and found we shared some common ground, so agreed to meet the next day. It turned out we disagreed about some issues, not the least of which was the abduction phenomenon.

On February 21, George Kriger and I visited this person at his office in the basement of his house. I asked him if I could be blunt with my questions, and he consented. As he had stated up front that he believed aliens were the cause of UFOs and were indeed abducting humans, I asked if he had any trouble with criticisms of his objectivity in treating abductees (whom he called "experiencers") given that he believes aliens are definitely involved. He was almost surprised. "No," he said. "They're definitely here."

He explained to me that a "select group of scientists" have physical evidence of alien intervention, including tissue samples from "extraterrestrial biological entities" (EBEs), pieces of crashed saucers, and various photographic evidence.

"Who?" I asked.

"I can't tell you."

"Why?"

"Because."

"Does Friedman know? Stringfield? Clark? Andrus?"

"They may or may not."

"Bullshit," noted Kriger.

And so it went. It seems that this "secret group" is keeping this information from the public "until the right time."

"When?" Kriger asked.

"Soon."

"How soon?"

"Sooner than you think."

The game continued.

He then turned on a VCR and television and began to show us some tapes of UFOs in flight. One of the first was the Guardian UFO.

He noted, "If you don't believe already then these videos won't convince you."

And they did not.

One of the last Guardian-related items I received was a small envelope containing a single sheet of paper that contained more ranting about aliens, the "Brotherhood," the Holy Grail, and attacks by Red China. I notified the RCMP, whose hate crime division was quite interested in the material. Upon investigation, it turned out that the envelope was mailed from the main post office on Parliament Hill, or nearby, in the central Ottawa/Hull region. In other words, "Guardian" mails his or her packages in Ottawa. I would have to concur with the Ontario researchers that a UFO buff in the Ottawa area, or one who has travelled to the area several times (because he or she knows the Kanata military base and can get good maps of the area), is responsible for the mailings. It is worth contemplating that given the current climate of zero tolerance for terrorist activity, if Guardian were to resurface, his missives and actions would be viewed in a much harsher light.

CHAPTER TWENTY-EIGHT
EBENEZER'S ICE CREAM CONE

CHRIS RUTKOWSKI

The evening of Wednesday, August 22, 1990, was clear and cool throughout all of Canada's Maritime provinces. At about 7:00, Walter Benoit of Bellefond, New Brunswick, saw a "very bright object, 4 to 5 feet long" and "clear in colour." He reported it to the RCMP, who sent a report to the National Research Council of Canada, which at the time was Canada's official repository for UFOs.[1]

At 7:15, Carmelle Morrissey in Morristown, Nova Scotia, happened to look up into the early evening sky. Morrissey saw a "very bright, circular object" moving in the sky for an estimated four to five minutes. The sighting was reported to CFB Greenwood, and the base commander filed the report with the Department of National Defence (DND). Copies of the report were sent in turn to an alphabet soup of official acronyms: RCCPJAC NDOC OTTAWA, RCWBOCA, ACOC WINNIPEG, RUWOKDB NORAD COC CHEYENNE MTN COMPLEX, DOFO, RCCBNVA FGCANCHQ NORTH BAY, SSO, NT, CCCEON, and NRCOTT OTTAWA"METEOR CENTRE."[2]

The rash of sightings continued that night. At 7:30, an anonymous caller in Iles-de-la-Madeleine, Quebec, notified the Department of Transport (probably through an airport control tower operator) that he or she had seen a "bright red ball followed by a tail." It was seen for only five seconds, which prompted the NRC to file the report with the annotation: "Identified as possible meteor."[3]

At the same time, Gerald Foster of Kingston was in Middleton,

Nova Scotia, and saw an "orange/yellow circular object" for about three to five seconds. He also reported it to DND, which identified it as a possible meteor.[4]

Also at 7:30 p.m., Anne Mazeralle of Chatham Head, Nova Scotia, saw a "bright, lime green, oval-shaped object" for a few seconds. She reported it to the RCMP, which also sent it to the NRC, and the report was also identified as a possible meteor. (This report was actually dated August 23 in the NRC files, but this may have been a mistake because it seems to have been part of the meteor activity of the day before.)[5]

Meanwhile, something odd was happening on Prince Edward Island.

From 7:50 p.m. to 9:15 p.m., Shirley Yeo of Ebenezer, P.E.I., was "eyewitness to [a] glowing white object which landed in woods." She and all her family watched the strange object, which they described as "like an ice cream cone." Remarkably, after it landed, the object was reported to be "still glowing at 0300Z," two hours later![6]

Helen Gallant, who lived with the Yeo family, reported that "it looked like a great big round ball of light through the trees."

While the glow was still visible, the group of witnesses watched as military helicopters and aircraft arrived and began circling the area. Although there is a civilian airport at Charlottetown, seven miles southeast of Ebenezer, and a military base at Summerside, twenty-eight miles southwest, witnesses were puzzled by the appearance of the aircraft because such activity seemed unnecessary if the UFO was really only a meteor.

Charlottetown RCMP confirmed that they had received more than a dozen calls about the Ebenezer object and had sent two constables to investigate. They noted that one officer "could see it in the distance, but then he just lost sight of it."

Meanwhile, Alexander Davis of Frenchvale, Cape Breton (Nova Scotia), said he had seen a "red-hot sheet of metal land 300 yards from him in woods." It was noted that "he swears he knows exactly where it can be found." At the time the NRC report was filed, the RCMP were planning to question him the next morning.

The report contains comments about the large number of reports that night, noting that the "phenomena [were] seen from Anticosti Island to Halifax, and from Newfoundland to Maine." Furthermore, "all colours of flares [were] reported as well as fireballs, flaming aircraft and burning boats," and reports were received over a period of ninety minutes. One note recorded that "RCMP detachments in [the] Maritimes have reported location of debris."[7]

Spurred by the possibility that the object was in fact a meteorite that may have fallen, a group of thirty amateur astronomers with the Charlottetown Astronomy Club searched the area the next morning but found nothing of interest.

Clive Perry, president of the club, was doubtful the UFO had been a meteor. "I wouldn't think it would be a meteorite when it glowed so long," he said. "It pretty well had to be space junk or parts of a satellite. That's about the only thing that could have come down unless you want to talk about little green men with buggy eyes."

Perry himself did some investigating, interviewing the witnesses and finding them to be honest and truthful. "They are very credible," he noted. "It would take a pretty good mind to make up a story like that."

Another astronomer, Paul Delaney of York University in Toronto, also offered his opinion to the media that because of the duration of the sighting, the UFO was probably not a meteor. He thought that the presence of the aircraft indicated the falling object was a satellite.

However, despite witnesses' reports and the negative findings of the astronomers, NORAD and CFB Halifax insisted the UFOs were ascribable to meteors. A newspaper report noted, "Neither military agency would say if anything struck the ground."[8]

Like the Shag Harbour case, the reports were filed away without further investigation because it seemed no new information was forthcoming. For lack of any other evidence, the sightings might as well have been due to meteors. After all, they did have some of those characteristics.

The case would have been dropped were it not for the fact that in 1997 "Kerri Thomas" began investigating UFOs. Thomas, an ex-military paramedic with rescue training, had left the Canadian Forces in the early nineties. A single mother living in Labrador, she started doing some writing for local newspapers and became intrigued by media stories about strange phenomena and personal accounts related to her by friends and associates.

In July 1997, she posted a message to an online UFO discussion group, asking for information about cases in Labrador and Newfoundland. I contacted her because previously there had been no active UFO investigators on the far eastern coast of Canada, and this seemed a good opportunity to foster Thomas's interest and help her gather information.[9]

In telephone conversations, Thomas mentioned to me that she had been based at CFB Summerside several years earlier when she and her rescue team had been scrambled to assist following a crash of some object near the base. Knowing of the P.E.I. case, I asked her for more details, and Thomas began to describe a very different scenario than had been publicly offered.

Thomas said that she and her medical team had been flown into the Ebenezer area on a Hercules transport after being told to prepare for a rescue mission. She says they were told to bring along their banana suits — protective yellow outfits for going into contaminated areas. However, once on the ground, she and her team were told by senior officers that they could not go near the crash site because of an unspecified security issue.

As they waited, Thomas said she watched as a flatbed transport arrived and then left the site with something covered by a tarpaulin. She says she was sure that whatever had crashed had been recovered and taken away on the truck.

Thomas said that she and her team were given strict orders not to talk to the media about the operation. However, she said she was concerned when her own family later asked her what had happened and related to her the media stories about the meteor. She did not tell them about her experiences that night, however, obeying her instructions.

She also related that one day in the mess hall, a group of American air force officers were sitting beside her discussing the recovery operation at Ebenezer. She said she casually asked them what had been recovered, and she was told outright that it had been a spaceship.

The question is, then, what do we do with Thomas's information? How can it be interpreted? While the original reports could be explained as meteors, the explanation of a spaceship would only work if we ignored some of the witnesses' observed details and assumed they were in error. Further, we could also reason that the military aircraft activity was part of a planned operation and unconnected to the UFO sightings.

Given that the American military has admitted using UFO reports as a subterfuge to conceal secret missions, UFO researchers might be justifiably suspicious of military explanations of UFO sightings. If we assume instead that the witnesses' observations were relatively accurate and that the military activity was a result of the observed object, it is possible that the fallen object was in fact a satellite of some kind as had been speculated.

In other words, without invoking the idea of aliens and crashed flying saucers, it is possible to attribute the events of that night in P.E.I. to an actual military rescue and recovery operation that was "covered-up" with a fictitious explanation given to the media for dissemination. Of course, why the crash of a satellite would need such elaborate security is not obvious.

In any event, even without Thomas's statements, the P.E.I. case is not explained to everyone's satisfaction. And if her version of events is taken into account, the incident becomes even more puzzling. Who knows? Perhaps it was even a contemporary UFO crash, rivalling Roswell, New Mexico.

CHAPTER TWENTY-NINE

GIANT UFO ALARMS MONTREAL

GEOFF DITTMAN

There is a common misconception that UFOs tend to be seen by lone individuals rather than large groups of people. This tends to reflect the belief that UFOs are natural or man-made phenomena that individuals with no one to bounce explanations off of can't explain. Had there been others present to witness the UFO, someone in the group would have come up with a decent explanation. In the past, some skeptics went one step further and argued that hallucinations and wild imaginations usually explained such single-witness sightings.

Reality, however, tends to be a little different. The authors have been analyzing UFO reports for years and found that UFOs typically have multiple witnesses.[1] Now, this isn't evidence of alien visitation. But it does suggest that something real is being seen and that there isn't always an obvious natural explanation.

While cases with two or three witnesses are common, sightings involving large numbers of people have always been rare. This is why in 1990 ufologists were excited to hear of a case in Montreal that involved upwards of seventy-five witnesses, including police officers from several different departments, as well as members of the media.

While presented widely in the French-language press, most English-language researchers were introduced to the case by researchers Richard F. Haines and Bernard Guenette when they published their essay "Details Surrounding a Large Stationary Object Above Montreal." Details of the case, taken from Haines and Guenette's essay, as well as from RCMP reports and the local press, are as follows.

November 7, 1990, was a Wednesday. While cold, many people were still out and about in the early evening. And with a heated swimming pool on the roof, many guests of the International Hilton Bonaventure Hotel took the opportunity to enjoy the outdoors. This provided them with a ringside seat to a strange event about to occur over downtown Montreal.

At 7:15 p.m., the first of what would be many more witnesses observed the strange sight. An American guest looked up to see an oval-shaped object in the sky. She promptly informed the lifeguard, who in turn contacted hotel security. Apparently feeling that dealing with unusual objects in the sky was not in his job description, the security officer contacted the local police department.[2] He also attempted to call Montreal's international airport but was unsuccessful in getting through. Next to be called was the Montreal newspaper *La Presse*, which sent a journalist to the scene.

The object seemed to be getting brighter during this time. The police were called again. Around 8:11 p.m., Francois Lippe, the first of several police officers, arrived. While approaching the rooftop the officer jokingly asked if he could open fire on the UFO.[3] The officer observed three stationary lights when he reached the rooftop.[4] The description of the object differed somewhat from person to person. Typically, however, witnesses described anywhere from three to nine lights, in either a circular or an oval pattern. The lights were usually described as white, though some referred to them as having yellow, blue, or reddish tints. Strange rays of light shone from the lights, seemingly ending suddenly, as opposed to fading out.

As luck would have it, a small private plane happened by. The plane was observed to fly beneath the cloud cover well below the object. *La Presse* journalist Marcel Laroche indicated the private plane was dwarfed by the UFO.[5]

At 8:30 p.m., Lippe's colleague, Sergeant Masson, arrived on the scene. He too was impressed with the sight, feeling the need to contact the RCMP. In turn the RCMP contacted the Department of National Defence to find out if there were any military operations being conducted that could explain the sighting. The answer was no.[6]

The witnesses were finally able to get through to Dorval Airport around 8:52 p.m. Dorval indicated that they had received other calls about the strange lights over Montreal, but they were not picking up anything on radar.[7] The airport suggested that perhaps what they were seeing was merely lights being reflected off the clouds.[8]

Around 9:00 p.m., more witnesses arrived on the scene. Another police officer, Denis Pare, the district director, and two more *La Presse* employees showed up.[9] The rooftop must have been getting quite crowded by this time.

One of the journalists, Laroche, having fetched a camera from the trunk of his car, began taking pictures.

Witnesses continued to arrive. Around 9:30 p.m., Inspector Luc Morin of the RCMP showed up on the roof. At 9:45 p.m., Officer O'Connor of the Montreal police arrived. At some point, an Air Canada pilot (apparently a guest at the hotel) also observed the lights, saying he didn't think they were from an aircraft.[10]

The object began to disappear, obscured by the lowering cloud cover.[11] It completely disappeared from view by 10:10 p.m. Shortly thereafter the police left the scene. The reporters had all left more than a half-hour earlier so that they could file their stories.

But the unusual events didn't end here. Shortly after 10:30 p.m., a young man observed a brightly lit boomerang-shaped object in the sky. He watched it seemingly hover near a Hydro-Quebec power station. Not long after this sighting, the military base that was fed by that station experienced a power failure.[12] This power failure apparently ended the night of unusual occurrences that affected so many Montrealers.

What was responsible for the strange sights over Montreal that night? Several different explanations were put forward. Astronomer Robert Lamontagne suggested that perhaps the lights were nothing but the aurora borealis.[13] Another suggestion was that it was the reflections of lights coming from a nearby construction site.[14]

Not surprisingly the witnesses themselves tried to come up with an explanation during the sighting. Morin considered the aurora borealis but dismissed it as unlikely. Considering the possibility that the lights were reflections from the ground, the Montreal police asked the neighbouring construction sites to shut off their lights. This had no effect on the lights in the sky.[15] Researchers Haines and Guenette did not come to any conclusion in their report as to what caused the light show. They frustratingly noted that even though the object in question was visible for as long as two and a half hours, no real evidence was obtained. Given this, Haines and Guenette asked, "how long an unusual aerial phenomena [sic] must remain stationary and in plain sight in order to evoke an adequate scientific and/or technical analysis response. This is yet another reason why traditional science has not become involved in UFO studies."[16]

CHAPTER THIRTY
RESOLUTE

CHRIS RUTKOWSKI

In early January 1998, a researcher stationed at Resolute Bay, Northwest Territories, reported to some colleagues via the Internet that he and other people stationed at Arctic scientific centres had been seeing unusual lights in the sky. News of these lights, which glowed, dimmed, hovered, and vanished, spread throughout northern communities.[1]

In one message, the researcher asked if any Chinese launches had taken place on January 6, 1998, as there had been a vivid sky display seen from a particularly High Arctic base at 74.43 N, 94.4 W. Because there is a U.S. military base in the area, an inquiry was made about the possibility of a drone aircraft of some kind, although the weather was too bad for helicopters and most other aircraft to be flying.

The researcher noted that he and other technicians and scientists at high Arctic stations live in extreme isolation. They tend to be quite media shy and were reluctant to discuss their UFO sightings with others, even colleagues at other bases. However, he said that enough sightings had been documented that it was felt some inquiries were in order.

The UFO sightings were characterized by the appearance of a light high in the dark sky, increasing in brightness to that of a full moon but usually appearing between visual magnitudes of -2 to -6, much brighter than any star or planet, and then fading away relatively slowly. These lights were stationary, a fact verified by aurora cameras and ruling out the possibility of meteors. Their colour was most often a subtle blue-green. Later, some of the lights were seen to move, as noted by some

Innu hunters and other observers. Duration of the sightings ranged from a few seconds to at least four minutes. The typical sighting consisted of an extremely bright stationary light appearing for approximately ten seconds, then a smaller light moving about a few minutes later. Calculations by ground observers suggested the lights were moving at an altitude less than four thousand feet.

The researcher suggested three possible explanations: a secret American aircraft flying from Sondestrom or Thule, an unusual natural phenomenon, or an extraterrestrial vehicle of some kind. The first option made little sense as it had certainly lost its "secret" status through numerous observations. The second was conceded as a remote possibility, but the Arctic correspondent favoured the third choice. Some Innu elders called them *Igniruyaqs*, the closest translation being "plasma balls." Tradition was that they had been seen by ancient Innu for millennia.

The first sighting was of a stationary object, seen by two witnesses driving to work in early November 1997 at about 1330Z. (The Z refers to what is known as "Zulu Time," an aeronautical reference to Greenwich Mean Time [GMT]. In Canada, GMT is six hours ahead of Central Standard Time [CST].) These luminous, stationary objects were frequently seen in November and December 1997. Then in late December and early January, the unusual lights were often seen on Cornwallis and Ellesmere islands. There were flashes and "plasma spheres" on Ellesmere Island in late December and in Resolute Bay in early January. Observers had the impression of "someone" monitoring or surveying the remote scientific stations. Scientists at first attempted to explain the stationary lights as meteor showers but soon realized that such phenomena would not appear stationary.

A significant sighting occurred on December 18, 1997, at 2349Z. An extremely bright light was seen in the sky near Ursa Major, the Big Dipper. A second light appeared and dimmed, and then a blue-green sphere of light moved away from the first. The first object was so bright it lit a darkened room from outside the window. On January 3, 1998, at 2100Z, hunters were nearing a village when they saw a green ball of light flying over them at an estimated height of only six hundred feet, heading directly towards them. They thought they were going to be hit by the descending light. In the village, the researcher saw a flash out the window and looked outside to see a "slow pure white sphere with tail" moving very slowly north. Dashing outside, he saw the same or a similar object heading south, at an estimated altitude of only four hundred feet.

Credit: Christian Page

Above: In the early hours of November 20, 1989, some people living in Marieville, Quebec, observed glimmering lights in the morning sky. When dawn broke, they found a circular area about sixty feet in diameter where the grassy field showed an unusual green coloration.

Below: A circular craterlike impression approximately eight feet in diameter, found in a field near Etzikom, Alberta, in April 2001.

Credit: Pano Karkanis

Credit: Chris Rutkowski

The St. Paul UFO Landing Pad and Museum.

"For Service Outta This World" window dressing typical of businesses in the town of St. Paul, Alberta, site of Canada's only UFO landing pad.

Credit: Chris Rutkowski

Credit: Chris Rutkowski

Above: Stanton Friedman, the "Elder Statesman of Canadian Ufology," in his home in Fredericton, New Brunswick.

Below: Some "Lights At The End of the Road," or LATERS, near Sperling, Manitoba, photographed in 1988.

Credit: Chris Rutkowski

Credit: Unknown

Alien with luminous face, allegedly photographed near Carp, Ontario, in 1991.

Credit: Unknown

Blurry Polaroid photograph of a UFO hovering over a road near Carp, Ontario, in about 1991.

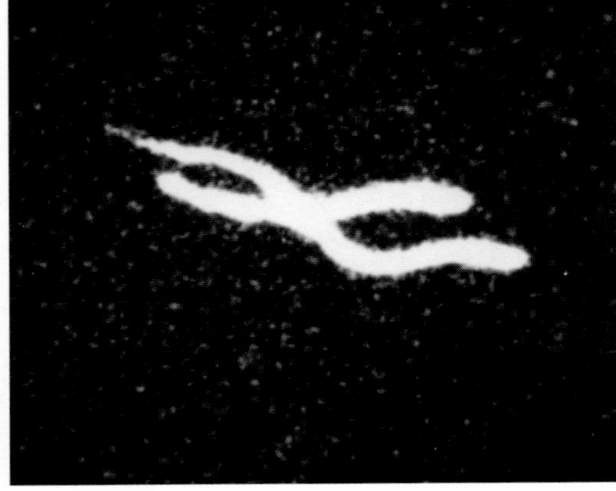

Credit: Grant Cameron

Twin UFOs with trails photographed near Carman, Manitoba, in 1975.

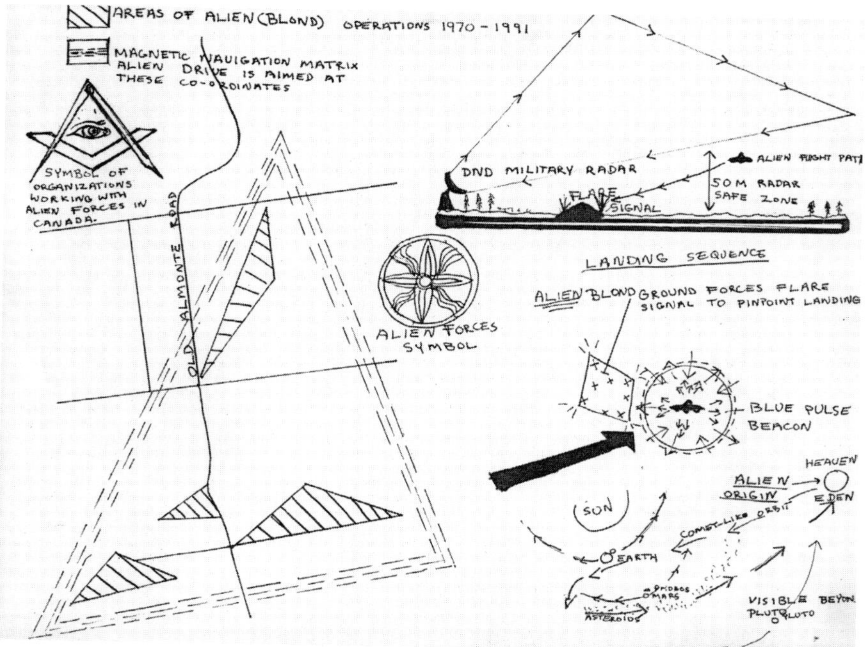

Map sent to UFO investigators by a person calling himself "Guardian" in 1991, showing areas where aliens were conducting "operations" near Carp, Ontario.

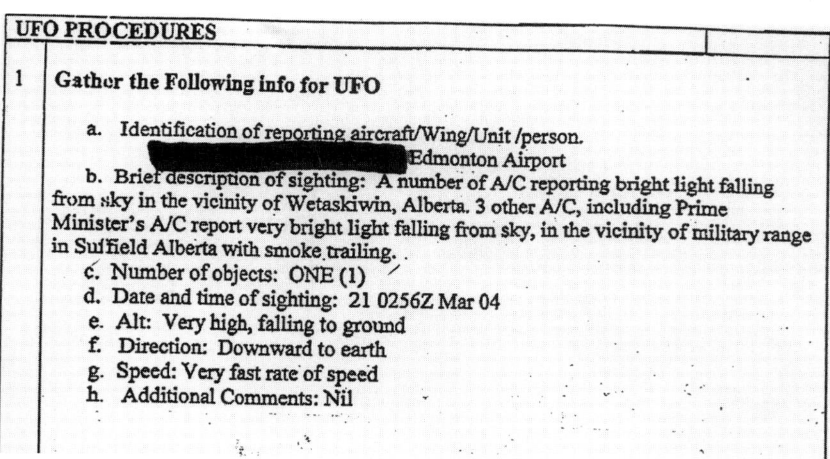

UFO PROCEDURES

1 **Gather the Following info for UFO**

a. Identification of reporting aircraft/Wing/Unit /person. [redacted] Edmonton Airport

b. Brief description of sighting: A number of A/C reporting bright light falling from sky in the vicinity of Wetaskiwin, Alberta. 3 other A/C, including Prime Minister's A/C report very bright light falling from sky, in the vicinity of military range in Suffield Alberta with smoke trailing.

c. Number of objects: ONE (1)

d. Date and time of sighting: 21 0256Z Mar 04

e. Alt: Very high, falling to ground

f. Direction: Downward to earth

g. Speed: Very fast rate of speed

h. Additional Comments: Nil

Credit: UFOROM

DND UFO Procedures document describing details of the sighting of a bright fireball over Alberta on March 20, 2004, witnessed by several pilots including the pilot of the prime minister's aircraft.

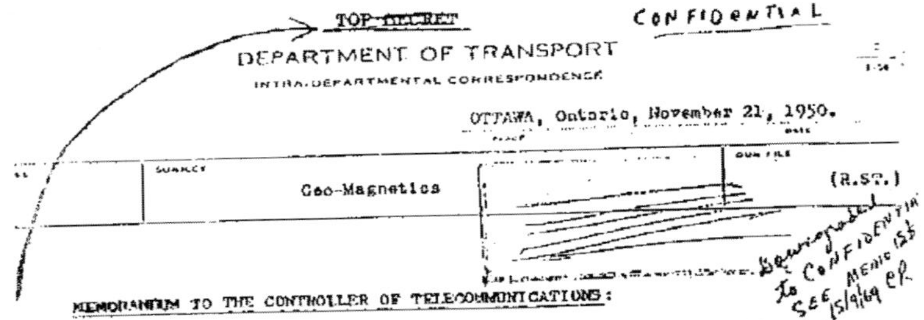

~~TOP SECRET~~ CONFIDENTIAL

DEPARTMENT OF TRANSPORT

INTRA-DEPARTMENTAL CORRESPONDENCE

OTTAWA, Ontario, November 21, 1950.

SUBJECT: Geo-Magnetics (R.S.T.)

Downgraded to CONFIDENTIAL SEE MEMO 15/9/69

MEMORANDUM TO THE CONTROLLER OF TELECOMMUNICATIONS:

For the past several years we have been engaged in the study of various aspects of radio wave propagation. The vagaries of this phenomenon have led us into the fields of aurora, cosmic radiation, atmospheric radio-activity and geo-magnetism. In the case of geo-magnetics our investigations have contributed little to our knowledge of radio wave propagation as yet, but nevertheless have indicated several avenues of investigation which may well be explored with profit. For example, we are on the track of a means whereby the potential energy of the earth's magnetic field may be abstracted and used.

On the basis of theoretical considerations a small and very crude experimental unit was constructed approximately a year ago and tested in our Standards Laboratory. The tests were essentially successful in that sufficient energy was abstracted from the earth's field to operate a voltmeter, approximately 50 milliwatts. Although this unit was far from being self-sustaining, it nevertheless demonstrated the soundness of the basic principles in a qualitative manner and provided useful data for the design of a better unit.

The design has now been completed for a unit which should be self-sustaining and in addition provide a small surplus of power. Such a unit, in addition to functioning as a 'pilot power plant' should be large enough to permit the study of the various reaction forces which are expected to develop.

We believe that we are on the track of something which may well prove to be the introduction to a new technology. The existence of a different technology is borne out by the investigations which are being carried on at the present time in relation to flying saucers.

While in Washington attending the NARB Conference, two books were released, one titled "Behind the Flying Saucer" by Frank Scully, and the other "The Flying Saucers are Real" by Donald Keyhoe. Both books dealt mostly with the sightings of unidentified objects and both books claim that flying objects were of extra-terrestrial origin and might well be space ships

Above: The infamous "Smith Document," in which Canadian engineer Wilbert B. Smith described his meeting with American military officials who shared information with him regarding the nature of investigations into flying saucers.

Below: The front page of the *Winnipeg Tribune* on July 8, 1947, carried a feature story on an "expedition" to probe "Flying Saucers."

Dr. Murray Scientific Expedition Probes "Flying Saucers"

Scientists are eager beavers. | "Bring on your saucers." | An explorer needs a nap, sometimes. | "Coo, there's a saucer!" | "Heavenly days! It's BIG!"

It Looks Like Pie in the Sky

By VICTOR V. MURRAY

The Winnipeg Tribune

FINAL EDITION

THE WEATHER

58th Year — WINNIPEG, TUESDAY, JULY 8, 1947 — 22 PAGES

Credit: University of Manitoba Libraries, Archives and Special Collections

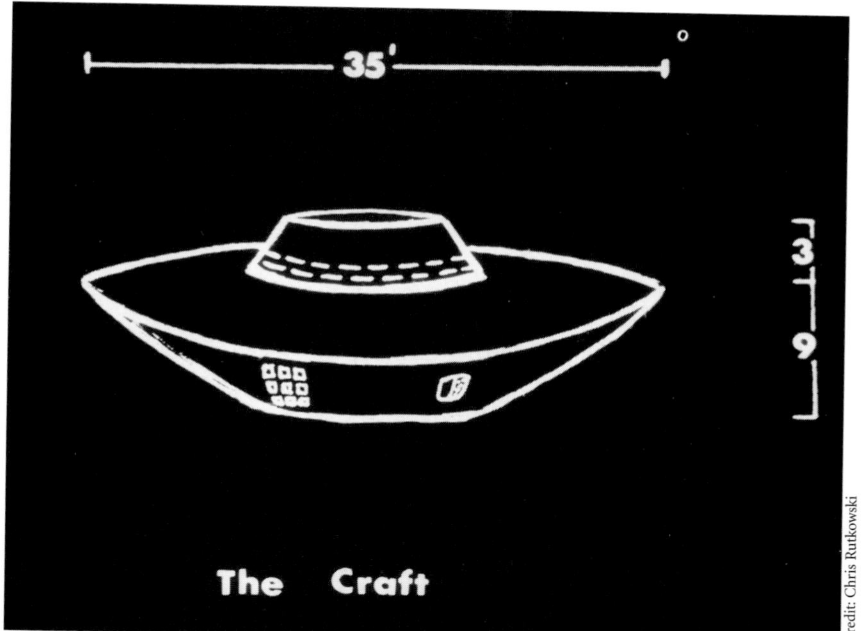

Credit: Chris Rutkowski

Artist's drawing of the saucer-shaped craft that burned Stefan Michalak near Falcon Lake, Manitoba, on May 21, 1967.

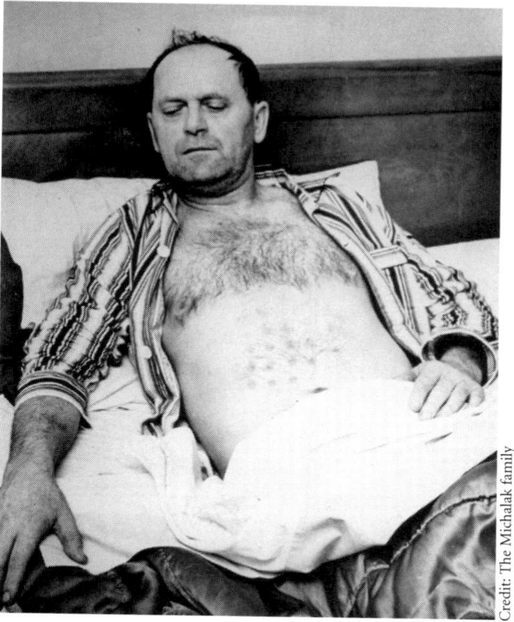

Credit: The Michalak family

Stefan Michalak ill in bed following his UFO encounter near Falcon Lake, Manitoba, in May 1967.

Credit: Unknown

Credit: Martin Jasek

Above left: Advertisement in a Canadian newspaper, c. 1896, using the image of an airship to sell White Star Baking Powder.

Top right: Artist's drawing of strange creature seen in a window by a witness in Joliette, Quebec, on November 21, 1973.

Lower right: Artist's conception of large object seen and reported by many witnesses over Fox Lake, Yukon, on December 11, 1996.

Thinking it may have been an earthquake light, he checked with the Geological Survey of Canada, but no seismic event had occurred around that time. However, NORAD noted that on January 6, 1998, at 1345Z, the Chinese rocket booster Long March II re-entered the Earth's atmosphere north of Baffin Island. Satellite trackers opined that a "Smart Dispenser" used in the launch of two "dummy" Iridium satellites on September 1, 1997, with the NORAD/USSPACECOM number 24927 and the International Designation 97- 48 C, according to the SatEvo Decay List #46 on January 17, 1998, decayed on January 6, 1998, at approximately 1312Z. If the Chinese booster rocket had remained in orbit for thirty minutes longer, which is very possible, it would have passed quite close to the observers.[2]

The only other re-entry on that date was that of a minor piece of debris from the exploded STEP-2 Pegasus rocket (USSPACECOM #24476 or 94- 29 TZ). It might have overflown the observers at about 0243Z on a northeasterly track and probably decayed within a few hours (plus or minus) of that time. Information about satellite decays can be found on the Internet, collected by dedicated observers.[3]

Later, the RCMP detachment at Grise Fjord reported that six individuals there had seen the rocket debris re-entering over Ellesmere Island. An unusual aerial object was sighted over Resolute Bay as well by four "reliable observers," flying north to south, contrary to the object sighted in Grise Fjord, which was seen moving to the southwest. This object, seen at 1343Z, was orange with a long tail and vanished with a bright flash after twenty seconds. Although the researcher believed it to be the *Aurora*, a pulse plane allegedly under development by the U.S. military that flies with bursts of energy rather than a continuous firing of its engines, the object seen from Resolute Bay matches the characteristics of a satellite re-entry.[4]

Scientists at high Arctic stations such as Eureka were said to be baffled by the unusual light displays. Some of them at an atmospheric observatory were there to study gravity waves, stratospheric ozone, and aurora. The lights in the sky were out of their fields of study. Witnesses included physicists, hunters, technicians, and civilians.

Early in the morning of December 31, 1997, a bright white light was seen moving northward at an estimated altitude of four hundred feet. The temperature was about –40 degrees F. An airline manager estimated its speed to be between four hundred and five hundred miles per hour. The researcher noted to UFOROM, "Nothing flies here at that speed, and especially not at 3:00 a.m. We live in a very small isolated community!" An all-sky camera at a nearby meteorological station did not record an object, suggesting that the object sighted was definitely flying below four thousand feet.

When contacted by UFOROM, the director of the Resolute Bay Observatory, which has an all-sky camera, insisted that nothing unusual has ever been photographed there. Despite this, sightings at Resolute Bay occurred on November 24 and 25, December 9, 18, 21, 26, and 27, 1997, and January 3, 5, and 6, 1998. Sightings were also reported from Eureka, Northwest Territories, specifically the appearance of an unidentified light recorded on an aurora camera at the station.

Date/Time	Duration	Intensity	Comment
1230/120550Z	10 seconds	4X Venus	Seen by tech and scientist
1225/012223Z	37 seconds	Full Moon	Seen by tech and scientist
1219/142143Z	7 minutes	4X Venus	No visual witnesses

No sighting in Resolute was recorded in Eureka at the same time. All stationary lights were starlike objects, without twinkling, each growing in size and intensity, reaching a luminosity peak and subsequently very slowly fading away. Witnesses reported that most lights were pure white but most had a blue tinge.

According to a news release from the European Space Agency on July 16, 2001, there is a Mars Arctic Research Station on Devon Island in Nunavut, not far from where these sightings occurred. The habitat, built by the Mars Society with privately raised funds, is at latitude seventy-five degrees north.[5]

The chilly terrain is snow-free in summer and is as close to the Martian surface as there exists on Earth. The dry, cold, rocky desert that is Devon Island, the world's largest uninhabited island, even has the Haughton meteor impact crater, a twenty-kilometre feature gouged out 23 million years ago. The similarities with Mars are striking. The high Arctic has been studied scientifically for many years, and observation satellites may have been orbiting over the area as part of the planning for the Mars habitat.

Furthermore, according to Environment Canada, in January 1993 the ARQX Arctic Stratospheric Ozone Observatory, a new scientific observatory to study the protective ozone layer over Canada's high Arctic, became fully operational on Ellesmere Island.[6]

The observatory allowed Canada to participate in a global network of highly sophisticated ozone-measuring stations, coordinated by the

World Meteorological Organization. It was developed to monitor the ozone layer during a time when significant climate change due to human activities is becoming apparent. Between 1993 and 2001, researchers manned the observatory, using an ozone spectrophotometer to measure changes in atmospheric composition. The observatory ceased operation in about 2003.

This is testimony to the scientific studies and observations that have been conducted in the north. It is possible that the unusual lights seen over the stations were military aircraft on classified missions, but most UFOs were likely just Iridium satellites flaring briefly in the jet black sky.

CHAPTER THIRTY-ONE
NEVER TOO COLD FOR UFOS

CHRIS RUTKOWSKI

It all started on November 13, 1995. That's when a Liidli Ke elder named Leo Norwegian saw what he thought was the stationary red light of a radio tower, visible just over the treetops. It was just after 5:00 p.m., and he and an eight-year-old boy were driving from Fort Simpson to a small subdivision outside of town. "But we could see the radio tower lights, and this one wasn't part of it," Norwegian said.

They watched as the light remained in place over the Mackenzie River and changed colours from red to blue to white to green and red again. After about a minute and a half, the light suddenly "sped away faster than any aircraft." It was "so fast, it left a trail of brilliant light behind it."

"At first, I thought it might be a plane or a helicopter, but then I knew it couldn't be because it went away so fast and because the colours of lights changed," Norwegian noted.

However, this UFO flap in the Northwest Territories didn't really begin with his sighting. Norwegian came forward with his story only after literally dozens of residents of Fort Resolution, Northwest Territories, reported seeing strange hovering lights during the first weeks of January 1996. After hearing so many others in the community relate their tales, Norwegian felt confident enough to come forward with his own report.

I first heard about the Fort Resolution sightings in late January 1996 on CBC Radio, on the program *As It Happens*. They were interviewing Euan Hunter, the mayor of Fort Resolution. The mayor described how essentially everyone in the community had noticed a bright, stationary light hanging just above the treetops in the southwestern sky. After a few hours, the light would drop lower to the horizon and be lost to sight. While in the sky, it flashed various colours and dazzled residents with its display.

The mayor said that the Department of National Defence had come up to investigate and took a video of the object back to their headquarters for analysis. The mayor also said that no one had an explanation for the object. As I listened to the radio interview, I mentally reconstructed what the mayor was describing and arrived at a few obvious explanations, one of them being the planet Venus, which was in the night sky around where the UFO had been observed night after night. I remember listening to this and wondering, "Why is everyone getting so excited about Venus — and why the heck is DND investigating?"

I went to my computer and used some astronomy software to plot out the night sky for the Fort Resolution area. It was simple enough to see that there were a number of bright objects about where the UFO had been seen. Venus was indeed bright even further south in the Winnipeg city sky, and I had fielded several inquiries about it. However, according to my plot, in Fort Resolution Venus would be *very* low on the horizon — perhaps too low to be seen that far north at the appropriate times.

To check this, I contacted Jay Anderson, a meteorologist with Environment Canada and an associate of mine from my council terms with the Royal Astronomical Society of Canada, Winnipeg Centre. He verified that Venus was probably the culprit and then told me about an article that had appeared in the newspaper that same day, announcing that Venus was identified as the Fort Resolution UFO.

The newspaper article was compiled from Canadian Press reports and said simply that astronomers had identified the UFO as Venus.[1] This was all well and good, except that I received a call from a Toronto TV talk show, wanting me to be on their show with Michael Strainic, MUFON's Canadian director, to discuss the Northwest Territories cases.

Strainic, for one, wasn't buying the Venus explanation. One Northwest Territories newspaper carried an article that read:

> Meanwhile, the Mutual UFO Network, an international alien-tracking agency, says it has reason to believe the secret behind what everyone is seeing may be more mysterious than expected. Michael Strainic, the net-

> work's Canadian director, said … "We have determined that some people have seen a bona fide UFO by definition. But what that UFO is, we don't know … I think what we're seeing here is the beginning of something much bigger."[2]

Strainic was also quoted about Canadian UFO activity in 1995 — that the Northwest Territories cases came "on the heels of a British Columbia summer strewn with daylight spaceship sightings and UFO abductions. 'We got buried alive with this sort of thing last summer, and so far it looks like there's going to be more of it in 1996.'"[3]

Strainic was also quoted as saying, "The things we are beginning to hear [about UFO sightings and abductions] are completely off the wall. They almost seem like they're staged events — that something is trying to send us a message through a dramatic display. The message may already be there for us to decipher, but we may not be mentally able to understand just what the message is yet."[4]

I wanted more facts about the cases so that I could get a better handle on what was happening up there. A new group, the Alberta UFO Research Association (AUFORA), also received media attention when it began investigating the Northwest Territories reports via the telephone. AUFORA director Cory Sine was justifiably reserved in his interview. He explained that a star or planet could indeed be the culprit, carefully detailing atmospheric refraction and how stationary objects can appear to bob, weave, and scintillate many colours. "What we'll do is collect as much data on the sightings as we possibly can. We'll look at all the possibilities and we'll forward that information to the witnesses," he said.[5]

One interesting point is that in its "AUFORA Update 02.06.96: The NWT UFO Sightings — Special Report," the UFOs are described as "an aerial bright light usually visible just above the treeline. The magnitude of these lights has been described as staring into the high beams of a car. The light shifts color between blue, red, green and white before leaving by accelerating straight up at an incredible speed. The sightings usually last for 1 to 6 minutes."

This directly contradicted the UFOs' characteristics as described by the mayor of Fort Resolution, who said on the CBC Radio interview that the objects remained visible for several *hours*, not minutes. Furthermore, only a few sightings had the UFO zip away quickly. In others, the objects remained motionless in the sky for long periods of time.

One of the speedier objects reported was a bright fireball observed on January 17, 1996, near Hay River. In that case, the object was described as a bright white light leaving a red trail as it descended quickly over the town. It looked like a flare and looked like it was falling apart. This one had all the characteristics of a fireball and was easily classified as a bolide.

Yet, through all of the media frenzy and hype about the Northwest Territories UFOs, I had not seen any actual case reports. I still had no real data about how many cases were involved and if any (besides Norwegian's) were more unusual than a stationary light in the sky.

Ufologist Blaine Wasylkiw of Yellowknife helped me greatly by posting the newspaper articles verbatim and answering other questions via email. His website had a great deal of information, including an interview with P. J. Harston, a newspaper reporter who wrote many of the UFO articles in the NWT.[6]

In one of his articles, Harston related that "a scientist who is linked with [MUFON] saw the [UFO] … and he doesn't know what the hell it is!" Also, Harston said that he was told "there's no record of a star or a planet being in that section" of the sky. This was odd, because simple star plots showed that both Venus and Saturn were in the southwest sky, as well as many bright stars. This was especially strange because, Harston said, "they've checked with observatories … nobody has a record of a renegade star or planet or anything being in that part of the sky."

The AUFORA report noted, "The military has ruled out the possibility of a planet, such as Venus, as being the cause of the lights because of the swift departure of the UFOs."[7]

In Harston's opinion, MUFON's most logical explanation was that "it could be the American military testing out some new gadget — which [MUFON says] has happened before and wouldn't necessarily be uncommon."

Nevertheless, I wanted some factual information about the sightings. I called Harston myself — and got a somewhat different picture of the NWT affair.

Harston told me that he had been deluged with calls from around North America, from media and self-styled UFO investigators. Indeed, the day I called him, I myself received a call from a UFO buff in Akron, Ohio, who wanted information about the NWT cases. I was glad Harston agreed to talk with me. (After all, I could have been another "UFO nut.")

Harston explained how the NWT flap had unfolded. It had evolved as a typical, textbook flap: beginning with a few reports, then more and more witnesses coming forward as the media barrage continued. First, a few people had seen the singular stationary object near Fort Resolution and had mentioned it to others in the town. Soon everyone else had seen it too, as word spread.

Among the witnesses were a group of Northern Rangers — members of the Canadian army reserves who were given "a rugged rifle and half a dozen rounds" to patrol the north against enemy attack. (It's an image that is a bit romantic and intuitively outdated, but that's how Harston described their original function.) Anyway, they had seen the object, too, and took the witnesses' statements. Since the NRC and DND don't officially investigate UFO sightings, one can only wonder where these reports were going. Harston didn't think they had shot the video, but they had looked at it. (AUFORA said it was a ranger who took the video.)

"But you really can't tell anything from it," Harston said. "It's only a light, bobbing and moving around on the screen, and you can't tell if it's the light that's moving or if it's the camera."

Harston said that when news of the original Fort Resolution reports spread, CBC Yellowknife did a story and it became big news across the North. People in widely separated areas began reporting their sightings to media representatives — along with the mayor of Fort Resolution. He seemed to be the authority figure whose testimony was beyond reproach.

It was about this time that Leo Norwegian came forward with his story. Even though it was viewed as a confirmation of the Fort Resolution sightings, his sighting had occurred much earlier and his UFO behaved much differently than the original Fort Resolution UFOs.

Sightings poured into radio stations and newspapers from Trout Lake, Yellowknife, and other NWT towns, and even Fort Chippewa, Alberta. Harston noted that all the reports seemed to come from about the same latitude.

On Friday, January 26, 1996, a Toronto TV talk show focused on the NWT cases. Among the guests were the mayor of Fort Resolution, a Canadian Press reporter who had done a story on UFOs in Canada, another media type who had "immersed" himself in the Canadian UFO subculture, and Michael Strainic. The mayor related how he had received reports from trappers who said that the UFO had been following their snowmobiles. Some, he claimed, had told him that occasionally the UFO would hover directly over their machines, cutting out the engines, which would mysteriously start again after the UFO had moved out of sight.

Yet even Harston pointed out that these stories were all just rumours and that no one had actually investigated the engine-stopping reports. He also noted that in –30-degree-Celsius weather, snowmobiles were pretty finicky machines at the best of times. Trappers often were stranded by their dead machines, even without the interference of UFOs.

Harston also elaborated on the investigations by DND. It seemed that a new commander in Yellowknife, Colonel LeBlanc, took the opportunity to "check into" the sighting reports as a way to meet others in the community, and so he flew across the lake to Fort Resolution. LeBlanc's public relations liaison was a Captain Gray, who arranged several interviews with reporters and witnesses. According to Harston, LeBlanc openly talked about "world change" and "major upheavals" in the context of the UFO sightings. Harston said LeBlanc was "less skeptical than I am," and that he told people that contact with aliens was "the next step in the evolution of the planet." One could wonder what approach he was taking in the evaluation of the UFO reports.

After all I had learned about the cases, the NWT sightings seemed much less mysterious and less substantiated than had been advertised. We had only unverified claims of UFO types more complex than simple nocturnal lights, which may or may not be ascribed to astronomical objects as explanations. Accurate descriptions of altitude, direction, times, and dates were still elusive.

I was eventually able to examine the reports and understand the dynamics of the NWT flap. One of the more important records was that of Mayor Hunter himself, in which he described his own sightings, which seemed to confirm what others had seen and give credence to the dozens of other witnesses. Hunter noted that on January 14, 1996, at about 5:00 p.m., he watched a bright light that looked like "2 or 3 stars all in one." At that time the object was "2 ft. on the left side of my power pole [but] at the end of the hour it had moved at least 8 ft. to the right of the power pole and quite visibly came down ... southwest of town." He then drove to the lakeshore and from 6:00 to 7:00 p.m. watched the "bright object very slowly move west and downwards." In other words, the light was low to the horizon and doing exactly what a star or planet would be doing: setting slowly in the west.[8]

The first sighting noted in official reports had been reported by a Fort Resolution resident who witnessed something strange on January 4, 1996, at 5:30 p.m.:

> My nephew came and told me that there was something above the lake and I should go check it. I grabbed my video [camera] and went to check. When I arrived there I saw a light above the lake so I started videoing it. I could see red and blue lights flashing which seemed to get dimmer then brighter. I videoed it for approximately four minutes then went home to tell my wife. I kept checking on it over the period of an hour and it seemed to get dimmer and dimmer then fade away.[9]

This object, too, matched the description of a star or planet.

Several other reports by different witnesses confirmed the object was really there. Another observer described a "very bright object … could see it without my glasses. Put on my binoculars [and] saw bright colours, red, blue, changing colours. It was out past the islands. It is nowhere near the beacon. It was a lot brighter than the stars. You could see it through the trees it was so bright."

Another noted, "Green, blue, yellow and red flickering lights. When the red light came on, it was really, really bright. It was sitting in one spot for awhile. It looked like it landed on the lake from where I was standing. It stayed there and I never seen it for awhile, it never came up again, so I went home."[10] As would a star or planet once it had set on the horizon.

One witness attempted to give chase in his truck, but to no avail. On that night, January 4, he was travelling from Fort Resolution to Little Buffalo River at about 6:00 p.m. and saw a bright light low on the horizon but over the trees.

> It wasn't an airplane or a helicopter and I shut my lights off and the lights [on the object] were changing colours. The top of whatever it was had bright white light on top and blue lights [in the] middle and red on [the] bottom. … I put my beacons on and this light started moving west from where I was watching from and I couldn't see it so I went on towards Buffalo Junction. … I came around [the] corner at KM64 at 6:25 p.m. and I seen this light again, this time it was just above the trees on [the] corner of KM62 and it started moving west again and again it left the road at KM56 at 6:30 p.m.[11]

The official DND report noted:

> UFO was sighted approx. 10-20 km southwest of Fort Resolution every night commencing 4 Jan. 96 and ending 7 Jan. 96. UFO sighted between 1730 and 190 hrs every night.
>
> UFO described as a bright white light that would change intensity fm dim to bright. Light would change in color fm white to red to blue and repeat the sequence continuously. Object would hover low on horizon, approx 500-600 feet AGL. The longest continuous observation of object was 30 minutes after which object flew off at a great speed and disappeared. A three minute video was taken of the object.... Approx. 20-30 people from Fort Resolution witnessed object.[12]

There was only one recorded witness's testimony (apart from Kennedy's, many weeks earlier) in which the object had moved quickly. He had reported, "I watched it for about 15 minutes, and it stayed above the trees. Then when I was leaving, it started going straight up real fast and all I seen was a red streak from the red light, and it disappeared."[13]

According to the official report, "the people reporting the sighting were credible, reliable witnesses."[14] There is no question that UFOs were indeed seen by many people in the Fort Resolution area during this time. It appears, however, that the mysterious object was only a star or planet setting on the horizon, visible each clear night in the same location.

CHAPTER THIRTY-TWO

UNIQUE YUKON UFO

CHRIS RUTKOWSKI

Unquestionably, the best-documented and well-investigated Canadian UFO incident of the past several decades was the multiple-witness event of December 11, 1996. The lead investigator who took on the case was Martin Jasek, a Yukon government employee who in his spare time devoted much effort and expense studying the UFO phenomenon in the North.

Jasek believed this particular case was of critical importance not only to ufologists but to all Canadians, because in the course of his diligent investigation he realized there did not seem to be a conventional explanation for what had been seen over the Yukon that night. He was so certain that the object must have been detected by military or government installations that he sent copies of his forty-five-page report to the federal government through his member of Parliament, to the provincial government, to the RCMP in Whitehorse, and to the Department of National Defence base in Yellowknife.

An interesting facet of the case is that the UFO sightings were not reported to military or government institutions at the time. Witnesses expressed to Jasek their fear of ridicule and lack of support if they were to make their sightings known. It was only through Jasek's consoling and compassionate approach that he managed to obtain detailed witnesses' testimony with the assurance of anonymity. Furthermore, the twenty-two witnesses were interviewed separately and at length and provided Jasek with a plethora of drawings of the object that were consistent with each other's observations. What emerged through his investigation was a complex and consistent series of observations of a remarkable object seen over two hundred miles during a puzzling journey north along the course of Fox Lake in central Yukon.

Around 7:00 p.m. on December 11, 1996, witness #C1 was in a car with three other people (witnesses #C2 through #C4) travelling north nearing the town of Carmacks when he saw a group of lights in the northwest above nearby hills. He didn't mention anything to the others until they too saw them about two miles further on, when they agreed to pull off the highway to get a better look. The lights now appeared to be on a larger unseen object moving across the sky. At first witness #C2 thought it was a trio of airplanes flying together but then realized there were several large orange lights in an oval pattern, with dozens of smaller white lights on the body of the craft. Witness #C1 saw only three large orange lights in a row with the other smaller lights to the right side. The object was very large, covering an estimated sixty to ninety degrees of sky, and moved ponderously across their view. Strangely, the arrangement of lights did not pass out of view but simply vanished suddenly after approximately ten minutes.

In the town of Carmacks, the brother of witness #C2 and his family were at home watching television at about this time, all facing a large window with an expansive view to the northeast. They all saw a row of lights that at first reminded them of a 747 jet airliner, but they heard no sound as the object slowly moved over trees to the northeast. Three children, the oldest of whom was only six years old, all watched with awe and believed that it was Santa Claus and his reindeer on their rounds. There were four large red and yellow lights in a row, with smaller orange and green lights trailing. Additionally, there seemed to be white sparkles dropping to the ground from the bottom of the object. The UFO was estimated to be at least one hundred feet across. As it made its way east, the lights went out one by one, as if the object was moving behind something. Finally, after about five minutes, nothing was left to be seen.

Driving north along the Klondike Highway from Whitehorse to Carmacks, witness #F1 was nearing the southern end of Fox Lake when he saw a bright white light to the north-northwest, apparently over the far end of the lake. He watched it casually during his ten-mile trip along the lake, noting that there were some cars parked at a campground halfway through the trip. When he reached the northern end of Fox Lake, he was closer to the light and could see that the light seemed to be on a larger object and was partly illuminating a curved surface. As he passed some oncoming traffic, he lost sight of the object in the bright headlights. He could not see the original object but soon was able to detect three rows of rectangular lights slowly moving over the crest of a hill on the east side of the highway away from the lake. He stopped his vehicle and got out to get a better look at the "windows." When they were out of sight, he continued north and stopped at Braeburn Lodge, twenty-one miles further along. He excitedly related his sighting to the lodge owner over a cup of coffee, even drawing what he had seen for the bewildered proprietor.

The only witnesses who went public with their sightings were the drivers of the two vehicles seen by witness #F1. These two people, witnesses #F2 and #F3, left witness #F3's home in Whitehorse at about 7:30 p.m. and headed for Carmacks along the Fox Lake road. Driving just ahead of witness #F3, witness #F2 was nearing the Fox Lake campground when he looked west and saw a large, football-shaped object with a rim of lights hovering over the lake. Astounded by what he was seeing, he pulled over to the side of the highway and waited as he watched witness #F3 (his cousin) also pull to the side of the road several hundred yards south because he too had seen the UFO. Witness #F2 watched as the large object moved towards the highway and soon found himself looking directly up at the underside of the craft, which was featureless except for a large bright white light in the centre. It continued to his right and passed over the mountains and out of sight. While watching the object, he tried to use his two-way radio but its band was filled with static.

Witness #F3 had been travelling about a mile or so behind his cousin when he saw the object over the lake. He stopped behind its path as he watched it move over the road ahead of him. Having a more oblique view, he saw that the large object was lighting up the surrounding countryside. His side view was spectacular, to say the least. The object was a domed, egg-shaped craft with two rows of rectangular lights along its midsection. Its upper and lower surfaces were outlined in small, diffused white lights, while two stacks of red rectangular lights were on either side of the smaller "windows." As he watched, he realized he had a camera packed in the back seat, so he began trying to find it. However, by the time he found it, the UFO had brightened and moved across the highway to the east or southeast and was quickly out of sight.

Witness #F3 looked at his watch and noted it was now 8:30 p.m. A few minutes later, he noted that a car drove past his position, heading south. He began walking towards his cousin up the road. They confirmed each other's sighting and agreed to get back in their vehicles and drive to the campground to discuss it. While they were there, another car pulled up and two people got out to ask if they had seen the UFO as well. After a while, they got back in their cars and drove north to the Braeburn Lodge where they, too, told the owner about their sighting. The next day, witness #F3 called the Whitehorse airport to ask about any unusual activity. He also called radio station CFON-FM and did an interview with the newsman there. This was the only public record of the sighting until Jasek did his investigation a few years later.

The two people who had met witnesses #F2 and #F3 at the campground were witnesses #F4 and #F5, a couple with their small child travelling north along the Fox Lake highway to their home in Pelly Crossing. Like witness #F1, they had first seen the object from the southern end of the lake, where it looked like a row of rectangular windows with flashing lights at either end and an additional searchlight beam on the right side rotating towards and away from the witnesses. They believed the object was quite large, judging it to be about four miles away near the campground. Witness #F4 thought he could also see several very dim white lights in the shape of an arc or dome above the windows. As they passed the campground, they noticed two vehicles and two people standing beside them. They stopped and spoke with witnesses #F2 and #F3, as mentioned previously. (The testimony of a sixth independent witness of the Fox Lake UFO was also obtained by investigators.)

After leaving the campground, witnesses #F4 and #F5 continued north to Braeburn Lodge where they spoke with the owner, who by this time had heard several versions of the story. Then they continued on home to Pelly Crossing, where the next day they discovered that many residents were excitedly talking with one another about unusual objects seen in the area the previous night.

One of these was witness #P1, who was working his trapline about nine miles east of the town. Around the same time as the Fox Lake sightings, he was looking west when he saw a row of lights moving over the hills in the distance. As they approached, he realized the object they were on was very large, as he finally had to move his head from side to side to look at its breadth. It stopped less than an estimated three hundred yards away, apparently attracted by the witness's flashlight, which he quickly covered. The huge object blocked out the stars across a wide expanse of sky, and he calculated the craft was three-quarters of a mile across and about 250 yards above the trees.

Witness #P1 noted the row of lights was composed of as many as one hundred individual rectangular windows, each approximately six by twenty feet in size. Above these and centred on the middle of the craft were seven larger rectangular lights, all white or yellowish white in colour. A beam of white light came from the bottom of the object and played upon the ground in front of him. The object made no discernable sound and was in view for about four minutes before moving behind some trees to the east, where it abruptly vanished.

Meanwhile, witnesses #P2 and #P3 were driving north along the Klondike Highway about ten miles away from witness #P1 and noticed what appeared to be a cluster of stars moving together through the sky. They saw the stars of the Big Dipper above this group of moving stars and reckoned that it had the same angular diameter as the well-known constellation. The cluster consisted of a middle row of lights surrounded by several others. The object moved slowly to the east over the hills and trees, turning off its lights as it vanished in the distance. The time was approximately between 8:30 p.m. and 9:00 p.m., and the object had been in view for approximately three or four minutes.

At about 8:30 p.m., four people (witnesses #P4 through #P7) were taking a break from classes at Yukon Community College in Pelly Crossing when one of them noticed some odd lights in the sky. She called it to the others' attention and they all watched a horizontal row of lights in the northwest moving to the northeast. The yellowish lights appeared to be on an object travelling slowly, making no noise, and about the same size as a large aircraft. Witness #P6 thought the object had square windows with larger ones at the leading side tapering to the rear, as if there was some differential perspective involved. Witness #P7 described the object as a large oval with rows of lights on either side. They all watched the object for about three minutes until it was lost to sight behind a hill in the north. An eighth witness, #P8, said he was walking across a bridge in the area when he saw the large UFO flying towards him. He was so frightened, he fell prostate on the ground as it passed only a short distance above the bridge. His agitated condition when he eventually got home was verified by a family member.

Almost sixty miles to the north, in Mayo, sometime after 9:00 p.m. a man saw an odd light in the sky and called it to the attention of four teenage boys playing hockey on an outdoor rink. As they watched, a second light appeared, then a third, all in a horizontal row. The trio of lights then moved away together at high speed. Three teenage girls and several guests at the Bedrock Hotel also saw a row of lights rise up from below the trees and then fly across the sky.

Jasek interviewed twenty-two witnesses and received second-hand information about scores of other witnesses across the Yukon and Northwest Territories that night. He sorted through the testimonies, calculated distances, directions, and a timeline to piece together what he believed happened that night. He then considered a dozen possible explanations, ranging from hoaxes and hallucinations to satellite re-entries and military aircraft. He rejected all of these, giving sensible and logical reasons for his judgement, showing that they "did not adequately explain the data." He concluded in his widely circulated report:

> Since present technology and [a] natural phenomenon [sic] have been shown to be unlikely, we are thus left with only one possible conclusion....
>
> The sightings of a giant UFO(s) in the Yukon Territory on December 11th, 1996 by at least 31 people were most likely a product of non-human intelligence and a technology far beyond current scientific knowledge reported by main stream science.[1]

Jasek sent his report to a host of officials, asking them to consider the subject of UFOs more seriously and, specifically, to take note of this particular case. He pointed out in a letter to the Right Honourable Louise Hardy, member of Parliament for the Yukon, that none of the witnesses was ever interviewed by an official investigator. He questioned that an event of such significance to the people of the Yukon was not considered important by the government or military.

Jasek called upon Hardy to initiate an inquiry into the matter and suggested several things that could be done to put an end to what is perceived as an "atmosphere of witness ridicule and government silence on the UFO topic." These were:

- Ask the Government of Canada to assess what was likely the cause of the sighting of a giant (at least 0.88 km long) UFO on December 11th, 1996 at Fox Lake, Carmacks, Pelly Crossing and Mayo, Yukon. Most importantly, they should make their conclusions public.

- Ask the Government of Canada what conclusions they have reached about the large quantity of other UFO data that they have collected and specifically the reports that are highly suggestive of non-human intelligence.
- Ask the Government of Canada what actions citizens should take if they are confronted with intelligently controlled vehicles of apparent non-human intelligence.
- Ask the Government of Canada to educate the public and civil servants about the potential seriousness of UFO sightings to encourage witnesses to report their sightings as well as feel free to discuss them openly.
- Explicitly list "Ridicule of Witnesses" as a form of discrimination.
- Encourage scientific study of the phenomena by sharing data that the Government of Canada has collected and conclusions (past and recent) it may have reached.
- Ask the Government of Canada to encourage and support universities and colleges to study the UFO issue/topic much the same way they support other scientific programs.
- Ask the Government of Canada to establish a government-sanctioned UFO study committee including both military and civilian investigators such as has been done by the Government of Chile.

Whether or not Jasek's recommendations were embraced by any department within the government of Canada, his noble effort to bring the subject of UFOs to the attention of politicians and Parliament is commendable. Jasek's outstandingly thorough investigation of a well-witnessed, well-documented UFO flap stands head and shoulders above nearly all other UFO case investigations. He has presented the evidence in a factual, objective manner; how his report will be considered by scientists and officials remains to be seen.

CHAPTER THIRTY-THREE
THE GYPSUMVILLE UFOS AND ENTITIES OF 1996

CHRIS RUTKOWSKI

At approximately 2:00 a.m. on October 25, 1996, several members of a family living near Gypsumville, Manitoba, saw an unusual object with flashing lights apparently hovering motionless over the lake near their home. Grabbing binoculars, they were able to see that it was shaped like an upside-down bowl and had five rectangular windows in a row on the side facing the witnesses.[1]

"The windows were lit up with different coloured lights, like Christmas lights," one witness said.

Calling a neighbour, the group watched as a beam of light shone down from one corner of the object towards the surface of the lake.

Two nights later, on October 27, the family again saw a flashing light moving high above the lake, so they got out the binoculars again and watched it for several minutes. They then drove to the home of a neighbour, who joined them outside to watch four objects "in formation, flying over the lake." As they watched, the two objects on the outer ends of the formation "changed direction suddenly and disappeared from view." The other two objects shone some beams of light at the surface of the lake again, and then disappeared by moving into some clouds.

On November 1, one of the witnesses telephoned a reporter for a local newspaper. The reporter contacted UFOROM, and associate investigators made arrangements to travel to the remote community. They learned that many residents of the area had seen UFOs during the past few weeks and that other sightings had occurred the past summer. On at least two occasions, a hexagon-shaped object had been seen hovering near the town.[2]

"We spend quite a bit of time outdoors," one witness said. "We know the sky. These things don't make any noise like planes or helicopters. And we've seen satellites and falling stars, but these are different."

CHAPTER THIRTY-FOUR
THE SURREY CORRIDOR

CHRIS RUTKOWSKI

In Canada, one UFO hot spot has been a region known as the Surrey Corridor. A suburb of Vancouver, Surrey is nestled in a valley between the Pacific Ocean and the rugged Rockies. It's also east of the main Vancouver airport, one of the busiest in the world, and just west of the foothills, which soon turn into the mountains. Nearly all air traffic flies directly over Surrey because of the lay of the land, and it seems reasonable to suggest that the numerous UFO sightings in the area are due to overflights of everything from 747s to a multitude of personal Cessnas. But are they all?

"We receive an incredible number of reports from this area," said Michael Strainic, who in 1995 was the Canadian national director of the Texas-based Mutual UFO Network (MUFON).[1]

The list of sightings in the Surrey Corridor is too long to include here, but a few representative cases will illustrate its reputation.

On three occasions during May and June of 1995, Bill Oliver of Surrey videotaped a brilliant white object zigzagging across the sky above his home. "It would change from a small intense dot to an acorn shape," he noted. "When we used a computer to invert the dot image into a negative, it looked just like a classic saucer with a black ring around it."[2]

Another witness described the UFO that followed the car in which he and four friends were sitting for more than ten minutes in the Sunshine Hills area as having a fluid nature. "It had no uniform shape.

It was changing all the time. Like kaleidoscope imaging, the lights kept moving and shifting."[3]

Malcolm Corey, a retired Canadian air force armament gunsight technician, said a large, glowing red ball flew over his White Rock home in early November 1995. "It was travelling quite slowly and varied its trajectory, wandering from side to side. There appeared to be black stubby protuberances on either side, but they weren't large enough in comparison to the ball itself to be wings."[4]

On May 21, 1999, a man ran into the Ocean Beach pub in White Rock at about 10:00 p.m. and excitedly told the patrons inside that he had just seen a huge ball of blue plasma flying over Semiahmoo Bay. The object lit up the surface of the ocean and seemed to fly as if it were under "intelligent control" as it moved over Kwomais Point and flew out of sight.[5]

At 10:00 p.m. the following night, three witnesses were at the McDonald's on Johnston Road when they saw a huge "boomerang-shaped object with eight lights on front." They watched it move "very, very slowly" for eight seconds before it suddenly took off and disappeared. One of the witnesses was so upset by her experience, she told investigators, that she slept with her light on the following two nights.

Just five minutes later, at 10:05 p.m., two women on the White Rock pier watched a wedge-shaped object flying slowly below the treeline for three or four minutes as it headed across the bay.

On May 23, 1999, at 10:15 p.m., a couple also saw a wedge-shaped object with blue and red flashing lights flying over Highway 99, near the Crescent Road turnoff. A second object appeared, which gave off an amber flash, like a flare.

Earlier in 1999, an Aldergrove witness saw what looked like two headlights blinking on and off just above a set of power lines. He said, "It sounded like a plane, like a turbine motor, but very, very quiet. It just slowly took off."

In the context of the Surrey Corridor, two points should be emphasized. First, as stated earlier, nearly all air traffic flying into the Vancouver area from the east will pass through the Fraser Valley directly over Surrey. A huge number of flights each night will be observable by people from Vancouver to Hope and often seen as lights flying over the tops of mountains, in and out of view as the aircraft move between mountain peaks. Second, the region is known to be seismically active, and this brings up another possibility for explaining some lights reported as UFOs.

A discussion of UFOs in Canada cannot be complete without mention of the work of Dr. Michael Persinger, a physiological psychologist at Laurentian University in Sudbury, Ontario. In the late seventies, he proposed a theory that seemed to explain many UFO sightings. His theory, called the Tectonic Strain Theory (TST), noted that rock under pressure deep within the Earth can produce electromagnetic discharges. The Earth's crust contains layers of rock that are compressing one another, causing the solid rock to bend and fracture, releasing electromagnetic energy. This energy is barely measurable, but seismologists believe that the frequency or timing of this energy may lead us to an understanding of earthquake prediction.[6]

Persinger suggested that this energy may somehow travel through the Earth's crust and burst through the surface, becoming visible as a moving spark or blob of light. Alternatively, the electromagnetic energy would be invisible but would affect the brain of an individual who would "see" a moving UFO or experience images and impressions that he or she was being abducted by aliens.

The evidence for this is mostly statistical. The numbers of UFO reports in a specific area and the number of local tremors seem to be statistically related. It's not that UFOs are caused by earthquakes or the other way around. What has been suggested is that there may exist a "strain field" that extends many miles across the Earth and deep underground. UFOs and earthquakes are simply phenomena that indicate such a field exists. According to the theory, an earthquake could occur far away and many days or months before or after a UFO is seen and still be related. It has been argued that a strain field may be transmitted great distances, even across continents. Intuitively, however, it makes more sense that UFOs would be seen nearer to where an earthquake occurs, where more energy is available to be released and not lost through dissipation along a particular route.

Earthquake prediction includes studies on how the ground swells and goes back down as stresses build up and decay. Another possible predictor is the emission of electromagnetic pulses or radio signals recorded before earthquakes. Since rocks and minerals under pressure produce energy, it makes sense that some of this energy could be visible as light. (This was how crystal radios worked.) We also know that energy fields can affect our minds directly, so it's possible that certain types of hallucinations can be induced through exposure to such energy. Weak magnetic fields have been shown to cause dizziness and irritation, whereas stronger fields may cause effects such as epilepsy.

The electromagnetic energy interferes with electrochemical signals within our brains and nerves.

Persinger also has suggested that electromagnetic fields may cause temporary paralysis and dreamlike states similar to out-of-body experiences and UFO abductions. Stimulation of the brain could also induce false memories of unreal events, making a person "remember" seeing an alien and being abducted by it.

While the TST seems to explain a variety of UFO phenomena, there is actually very little indisputable evidence for its function. A complex geophysical phenomenon may be able to explain some sightings of lights in the sky, but since investigators can demonstrate that a large percentage of UFO reports are already explainable as airplanes, stars, and meteors, why is the TST needed at all?

There is no question that some of the ideas involved in the TST are sound. Rock under strain can indeed give off electromagnetic energy, earthquake lights exist, and most UFOs are lights in the sky. But the observation of UFOs in geographical regions where there are no earthquakes seems to invalidate the TST. Even a seismically quiet area such as the American Midwest is apparently not immune to TST effects, according to the theory's advocates. Persinger linked the Carman, Manitoba, UFO wave of 1975–76 to a few minor earthquakes in southern Minnesota, hundreds of miles distant. Somehow, it is reasoned, the strain field extended between the two areas and the energy originally built up and generated in Minnesota travelled to Manitoba to be seen as odd lights dashing through the night sky. Again, why the UFOs would not be observed closer to the earthquake epicentre is a question still in need of a proper answer.[7]

Most serious UFO researchers recognize that the TST needs some decent evidence before it can be accepted as fact. It is perhaps because of science's need for a scientific-sounding explanation for UFOs that the TST has been embraced with more conviction by some researchers desperately trying to avoid the ET banner. On the surface, the TST has a definite appeal because of the plausibility of its components. It is easy to accept that there is ambient electromagnetic radiation in our environment and also that electrical and magnetic fields can affect the human brain. It seems to be a short step to link the two and suggest that natural radiation influences our perception and behaviour.

Surrey is in an earthquake-prone region situated near the Pacific Ring of Fire. This has led some to suggest that UFOs in and around Surrey are TST-related lights or kinds of earth lights, a phenomenon related to earthquake lights but of a more esoteric and ill-understood nature. The Surrey Corridor could therefore simply be a place where the gradual and endless waxing and waning of underground stress is creating visible luminous objects.

Witnesses from the Surrey area, however, describe more than just lights in the sky. Some have claimed daylight observations of shiny, metallic objects at relatively close range or black triangular objects with lights only at their corners.

In fact, one witness stated:

> I have seen at close range two classic flying saucers with shiny brushed aluminum-appearing surfaces that carried rotating lights. Many other people have seen structured objects that included windows and lights and aerials and vents and other paraphernalia. In such cases, I might as well call the commercial airlines I have seen landing at Skyharbour [Airport] earth lights. We can argue about the nature of luminescent orbs, but the UFO [phenomenon] includes structured flying craft.[8]

Proponents of the earth lights theory of UFOs countered that earth lights "can be as small as a few inches, or many metres across; they can be ovoid/discoid, square, rectangular, rod-shaped and simply slow flares of light. They can appear in daylight and artificial light as metallic — shiny or dull. They can last from seconds to an hour or more. They tend to haunt certain areas for days, weeks, months and — quite often — for generations."[9]

In other words, earth lights can be invoked as explanations for *all* UFO sightings. And as for exotic close encounters, there is no problem in interpolating a tectonic explanation. For example, the physical effects of the noted Falcon Lake close encounter case could have been due to a spaceship or a secret military device but also perhaps an earth light that is claimed to be able to appear as a "diamond of fire" and take on the appearance of dull aluminum.

Regardless, the Surrey Corridor continues to be regarded by many people as mysterious.

... AND BEYOND

CHAPTER THIRTY-FIVE
A HOLE IN THE GROUND

CHRIS RUTKOWSKI

It began as what may have been construed by some as an April Fool's Day joke but evolved into something much more unusual. On April 1, 2001, at 10:30 p.m., farm manager George Hofer and several children from the Rosedale Hutterite Brethren Colony near Etzikom, Alberta, saw something remarkable in the sky. They were startled to see a brilliant fireball falling straight down and appearing to impact the Earth only a few miles away. The incident was discussed briefly with others, then dismissed.[1]

On April 16, 2001, Ken Masson, who farmed thirteen miles south of Etzikom, was preparing his land for seeding when he discovered a circular, crater-like formation that he was certain had not been there before. Soon news spread throughout the community, as local newspapers carried stories about the two events that seemed connected. Many people visited the crater, and speculation flourished as to whether it was caused by aliens, a meteorite, or something else entirely.[2,3]

On April 30, 2001, a reporter from a local paper contacted Dr. Pano Karkanis of the department of geography at the University of Lethbridge and asked him to examine the crater and offer some opinion on what may have caused it. Karkanis visited the site on May 1, 2001, and conducted interviews with Masson, members of the Rosedale Hutterite Brethren Colony, and other people from Etzikom. Later, he also interviewed Hofer, the first witness of the fireball.[4]

Karkanis took photographs of the site, measured it carefully, and took soil samples. He found that the crater was a circle 6 inches lower than the surface of the field, with an inside diameter of 7.9 feet, surrounded by a mound of dirt 16 inches high and an outside circle diameter of 11.8 feet. He also noted four curious indentations inside the crater, which some had speculated were caused by landing gear of a UFO. The ground inside the circle was cracked and sere, very different from the smooth powdery nature of rest of the area. Finally, he found some odd reddish-brown particles of dirt on the mound surrounding the circle.

After completing his analysis, Karkanis published a report on the formation, in which he noted, "There was not any indication to suggest that the small circle is a formation caused by a landing of an extra-terrestrial vehicle. The four indentations in the middle of the circle … are not quite symmetrical which might indicate an object's leg-marks, these were probably formed by rain-water accumulation on softer soil spots inside the circle."[5]

Despite the physical appearance of the soil inside and outside the crater, Karkanis could not find any chemical or radioactive anomalies or any indication that the dirt was affected by intense heat.

He concluded that the crater was most likely caused by:

> a meteoroid, fragment of a meteorite, a small rock or metal solid object which plunged and fell into the earth from outer-space with great force, at SW 18-4-8 W4, with very high speed (probably 150 - 650 km/hr depending on the material of the meteoroid and height from which it fell) and extreme kinetic energy. An incandescent body accompanied by a fiery luminous phenomenon, which is caused by the substantial resistance of the dense atmosphere to the meteoroid motion (the light usually recognized at 100–150 km of the meteoroid height), near the end of its path, was observed by Mr. Hofer, who is a reliable eye-witness. The meteoroid's outer layer probably disintegrated a little, due to the high heat it was exposed to during its rapid flight through the atmosphere, scattering crusty thin and rusty fragments, as found around the crater.
>
> This fallen meteoroid object was not visible and could not be found on the surface of the ground at the investigation site, probably due to the great force by which it crashed on to the ground and eventually sank

> to a depth of approximately a metre (3 ft 4 in) or more, into the soft soil of the field (loamy texture). Therefore the meteoroid kind, shape, age and composition could not be recognized and its origin could not be identified whether it is of a chondrite, achondrite, iron meteorite or stony-iron meteorite origin. It is a future challenge, to excavate the site and retrieve the meteoroid for further study of the material.[6]

Once news of the Etzikom crater had reached ufologists, there was considerable speculation that this was a bona fide UFO case. What is most interesting is that it was investigated quite thoroughly by a number of scientists before the UFO community was even aware of it. Soil scientists, physicists, and geologists from two different institutions examined the site, and an official report was issued. I was called for my advice on the course of action early in the investigations by ufologists, and I consulted with a number of people as to the types of tests that might be useful.

Gord Kijek, founder of the Alberta UFO Research Group and one of the principal ufologists investigating the incident, examined the site in some detail and noted there was no explanation for the formation if it was not a meteor crater. He did not find any evidence that it was caused by a sinkhole, a lightning strike, or a natural gas explosion.[7,8]

However, if the Etzikom formation is a meteor crater, it is unique. Most geology textbooks illustrate meteor impact craters such as Crater Lake in Oregon, the Ungava Peninsula in Quebec, or the impressive Barringer Meteor Crater in Arizona, which is a major tourist attraction.

The Etzikom crater, albeit small compared with Barringer, may be the first significantly sized meteor crater discovered in Canada in modern times. Even the fireball that generated a huge wave of sightings across Eastern North America several years ago only made a bucket-sized crater in the soil. The Etzikom crater is about ten feet wide.

To further add to the puzzle, Dr. Alan Hildebrand of the University of Calgary, Canada's leading authority on impact craters, the scientist whose research received international attention when he concluded that dinosaurs died off after a major cataclysmic impact event, expressed his opinion to investigators that he did not think the Etzikom crater was made by a meteorite.[9]

But if it's not a meteor crater…

CHAPTER THIRTY-SIX
THE OKANAGAN ARCH

CHRIS RUTKOWSKI

On July 28, 2003, two very unusual objects were observed in the night sky by literally hundreds of witnesses in southern British Columbia, many of them in the Okanagan Valley.[1]

First, at approximately 12:45 a.m., a "moon-sized" object was seen flying over the region. The object travelled from the northwest to the southeast, changing direction in some cases to move over local mountains, and dropping into valleys. When it did this the object travelled briefly to the west and then made its turn back on course to the southeast. The object was reported by all witnesses as being "as large as a full moon" and extremely bright white in colour. Its movement was described by several witnesses as a zigzag. No sound was associated with the object. The weather conditions were clear, as it was a star-filled night.[2]

Shortly thereafter, a beam of white light appeared overhead, arching across the sky at about 1:00 a.m. and persisting until at least 2:00 a.m. This "Okanagan Arch" was observed from Kamloops to as far south and east as Jaffray, British Columbia. People who watched the strange and puzzling event said the white light looked "as bright as a fluorescent tube" and said it arched from horizon to horizon like a rainbow. The beam of light sat almost stationary in this position for approximately an hour before dissipating. Almost everyone who witnessed the beam of white light said they had never seen anything like it before. All said they had watched the northern lights many times but they insisted this was certainly not the aurora.[3]

The fact that hundreds of witnesses reported the two events is testament that something real was observed. In some cases, both phenomena were reported by the same observers.

The possibility of an astronomical cause was first considered, but this does not seem to be a viable explanation. If the arch was a meteor train, its hour-long persistence would be highly unlikely, especially one as bright as reported. As it turns out, there was a bright bolide reported near Omak, Washington, at 12:27 a.m. on July 28, 2003, fragmenting as it flew in the northwest sky. It lasted for two seconds. Although its location and direction would place it in the right area, it is very odd that none of the hundreds of witnesses of the arch reported seeing such a bright fireball.

Another factor that could be involved in the arch is the fire situation in the B.C. interior about that time. Forest fires ravaged much of the Okanagan Valley during the summer, especially where the arch was seen. This seems more than a coincidence. It is quite possible that the first object could have been, perhaps, a water bomber or a related firefighting aircraft. As for the arch itself, one can speculate that light from the fires reflected off their own clouds of smoke. One problem with this suggestion is that witnesses of the arch described it as brilliant white, whereas reflected firelight would likely be more red or orange in colour.

An astronomer at Penticton Observatory who was asked to comment on the arch noted:

> My recollection is that the fires had started before then so their effects are certainly something to consider. On the other hand, this summer I became aware of a phenomenon known as the "Okanagan Arch," a whitish band which crosses the sky, similar in form to an aurora but not an aurora colour, persists for hours, is seen in the Okanagan from time to time, and nobody knows what it is, in particular nobody at the observatory. One of these was reported in mid-August, and the descriptions for July 28 sound very similar.[4]

So, then, even astronomers were scratching their heads over this phenomenon.

Where does this leave us? A persistent aerial phenomenon that is not astronomical could therefore be atmospheric in nature. Noctilucent clouds, perhaps? But why suddenly, for an entire hour, so geometrically perfect, and so long after sunset?

Earthquake lights? Yet the description does not match most EQL reports. Further, the arch did not precede or follow any significant seismic activity in the region. There was a minor 3.2 magnitude earthquake on August 12, thirty-six miles west of Kelowna, but it would be difficult to connect such a low-energy event with such a phenomenal aerial display, especially since stronger events in the same area did not generate such arches. For example, a much stronger 4.6 magnitude earthquake in Wyoming on August 21 was not associated with any luminous aerial displays.[5]

Unfortunately, we are left with many reports of a well-witnessed luminous aerial phenomenon with no explanation.

CHAPTER THIRTY-SEVEN
THE 2004 FLAP IN NEW BRUNSWICK

CHRIS RUTKOWSKI

In early 2004, a curious UFO flap materialized in New Brunswick and Quebec. Some sightings were undoubtedly meteors, but others were not as simple to explain. Given that much of Canada was in the midst of a cold snap at the time, there might have been many more witnesses to the aerial objects had it not been too cold for most people to be outside, looking up.

The flap began with a group of fireball reports. On January 9, at about 9:30 p.m., at Lac-St-Charles, Quebec, a fast-moving light was seen zipping through the sky. About the same time, at St-Ambroise-de-Kildare, a bright fireball with a glowing trail was seen for three to four seconds.[1]

On January 17, at 7:45 p.m., a witness sixty miles north of Moncton at Bass River, New Brunswick, reported seeing a similar bright, fast-moving light as in the Quebec sightings. But at around 11:00 p.m., a couple near St-Louis-de-Kent, New Brunswick, watched two flashing lights low in the west. The lights descended rapidly then flew in front of the witnesses at tremendous speed. They then stopped and settled over the tops of some trees on the eastern horizon and disappeared. At the same time, a man in Caraquet, New Brunswick, was looking south and observed two objects, one on top of the other, flying west to east. They took five minutes to cross the entire sky. He was certain the objects were not airplanes. Meanwhile, in Moncton, yet another witness observed an object moving very steadily across the ocean towards the east. It was a single light, moving very fast. He was certain it did not look like an airplane. And in St. Paul, near Shediac, New Brunswick, a witness observed two lights heading towards the northwest. They made no sound and rotated around one another, hovered, and then left at high speed.

A few nights later, on January 19, at 5:15 p.m., two people were driving between Doldeau and Albanel, Quebec, when they saw an "asteroid shape," ten to twelve feet in diameter with a thirty-foot-long tail, coloured green, orange, and red. It was going north to east at high speed and was out of sight in five seconds. At about the same time, two people in Chicoutimi observed an intense light with a green tail streaking across the sky during a light snowfall. As well, an RCMP officer in Girardville observed a black ball with an orange and green exterior and a green tail flying across the sky at an estimated altitude of three thousand feet. The duration was two seconds.

One of the most curious cases was on January 21, near Sussex, New Brunswick. A man was driving on the Trans-Canada Highway ten miles north of Sussex, when off to his left he saw a blinking light that seemed to be hovering beside the road. As he got closer, he saw that the object was actually composed of two bright white lights that seemed to be attached to a larger structured object. It descended lower and seemed to remain over a field. The witness wanted to pull over and stop but couldn't because there was no place to do so on that stretch of highway. He passed it and it was soon lost to sight behind him.

On January 25, at 6:26 p.m. in Richibucto, New Brunswick, a woman and her son watched a strange object moving through the sky. They were facing west and noticed a triangular object with sparkling lights on top. It seemed to have a *V* shape on its underside. The object was going north. They had time to go inside and bring out a telescope. They resolved it to a large grey object, with what looked like a round door on the bottom. Lights were blinking along its edge. At first, the object moved very slowly, and then it suddenly sped up and disappeared in the distance.

There is no question that several of the sightings, such as those on January 9, were meteors or fireballs. Other cases where structured objects were seen over a longer period of time are somewhat puzzling and indicate that some unusual objects were being seen in the skies in Eastern Canada in the middle of winter in 2004.

CHAPTER THIRTY-EIGHT
THE PRIME MINISTER AND THE UFO

CHRIS RUTKOWSKI

A brilliant fireball was seen across Western Canada and east into Ontario on Sunday night, March 21, 2004. It was seen by witnesses on the ground and in the air, including by observers on the private jet carrying the Right Honourable Paul Martin, then prime minister of Canada.[1]

Ufology Research of Manitoba confirmed a report that the pilot of the prime minister's aircraft reported an unidentified bright object to air traffic controllers in Edmonton while flying near CFB Suffield on Sunday night, March 21, at 7:56 p.m. local time. It is not known if the prime minister was advised of the incident or in fact was also a witness to the event.

The report, made available to UFOROM through Transport Canada, noted that pilots of three aircraft, including an Air Canada flight, a Westjet flight, and the government jet, all reported seeing "a very bright light falling from the sky, with smoke trailing." In addition, pilots of several other aircraft flying near Wetaskiwin, Alberta, also reported seeing the object. One of these pilots was said to have described it as the brightest fireball he'd ever seen.

Astronomers and other researchers piecing together the events of that Saturday night believe that at least two separate fireballs were seen across Canada. There had been several earlier UFO reports received by investigators on Friday, March 19, from locations across Canada including Summerside, P.E.I., and Victoria, B.C. Those reports involved a bright source of light or a flash of light in the sky, moving from west to east at high speed.

On Saturday, March 21, 2004, around 7:30 p.m. CST, literally hundreds of people in Manitoba, including two RCMP officers, saw a comet-like blue-green object with a long tail fragmenting and flaring as it fell from the northwest to the southeast. One witness noted, "It was like Armageddon. A round ball of flames with a long tail headed straight east." It was thought that an aircraft had crashed, so emergency vehicles tried to respond to the reports, but to no avail. Across the border in Minnesota, witnesses near Minneapolis also saw "a blue light hurtling towards the ground" in the eastern sky around the same time.

Approximately an hour later, at about 9:30 p.m. EST, a witness in Quebec reported seeing a fast-moving object "shaped like two 'Xs'" flying quickly from the west to the east. Around the same time, a man and his son in their car near the Ottawa airport watched a bright blue-green fireball with a long tail falling into the southwest.

Another cluster of reports occurred in Alberta about the same time as the Quebec incidents, when hundreds more people watched a bright, bluish "comet" zip quickly through the night sky at about 7:30 p.m. MST, heading from the northwest to the southeast. Reports came from observers in Calgary and Edmonton and in other locations along Alberta Route 2. Some observers in Saskatchewan reported that the fireball flew from the east to the west, allowing meteor experts to pinpoint its impact site north of Kindersley. At least one all-sky meteor camera caught the fireball's terminal burst of light low in the sky northwest of Calgary at 7:33 p.m. MST. What makes the Alberta observations particularly significant is the fact that they included several reports from pilots, including that from the prime minister's aircraft.

Further complicating the investigations are reports of other sightings, such as the one that occurred at about 2:30 a.m. on Sunday morning in northern Alberta of another bright fireball falling into the east. Several reports were received in Manitoba of yet another fireball or bright meteor seen on Tuesday night, March 23. In almost all cases, the duration of the fireball was between five and ten seconds, considered quite long for a meteoric event. Some witnesses had time to call others to turn around and look at the object progressing through the night sky.

There was no question that some objects were witnessed by many observers across Canada on that weekend, but these were spectacular bolides (chunks of a comet) or perhaps a passing asteroid that entered the Earth's atmosphere at high speed and burned up, fragmenting as it zipped quickly across the sky. Many observers, including the prime minister's pilot, reported seeing this spectacular natural phenomenon. Perhaps the pilot would have thought the event remarkable enough to bring it to the attention of his most important passenger.

CHAPTER THIRTY-NINE

A CURIOUS CHRONOLOGICAL CLUSTER OF CONSECUTIVE CANADIAN CASES

CHRIS RUTKOWSKI

On April 7, 2004, I received an email from one of my Canadian colleagues informing me that he had been contacted by someone who works in an air traffic control tower at a major Canadian airport. He was told that three tower operators had observed a puzzling UFO while monitoring local flight activity, and provided me with some preliminary details. While the witnesses wished to remain anonymous, I made some inquiries and eventually was able to speak with all three.[1]

Their sighting began on March 28, 2004, at about 9:45 p.m. The three Transport Canada employees in the main tower at a major Canadian airport were performing their usual duties when one of them noticed a bright light low in the southwest. He brought it to the attention of his co-workers, who also observed the object. Each described it as a red light, similar to an aircraft light, but with no green or white navigational lights in evidence. It was also likened to a collision avoidance light on a radio tower, with respect to its brightness.

The object was first seen in the southwest, bearing 240 magnetic from the tower and only an estimated two degrees above the visible horizon. It was flying on an estimated heading of 130, moving west to east, with a constant brightness and flying level to the horizon. It was in view for approximately thirty seconds, although one witness thought the observation duration was only about twenty seconds. The UFO was last seen in the southwest bearing 210 degrees from the tower, disappearing as it slowly rose upward into the thick cloud ceiling of twenty-seven hundred feet. Based on their experience in judging distance and altitude, and comparing the object with another aircraft, they estimated the object was between five and eight miles away.

During the observation, the witnesses checked tower radar and found there was no radar paint nor aircraft transponder contact. The observers agreed that the object looked about twice as big as lights on a nearby Air Canada hanger as seen from the tower. The object left no trail and witnesses agreed that it was not a meteor, each having seen many meteors and fireballs on their shifts.

One witness used a pair of binoculars and said no structure was visible behind the object. He watched the object disappear "like a plane going up through the clouds." The witnesses also radioed the crew of a 737 in the area to check their radar and attempted to vector them visually to the object, but the 737 was above the cloud deck. There were no other aircraft in the area at the time. The object had the same apparent track as a later 737 that was below the clouds and came within the control area about thirty minutes later.

Another witness, who thought the object was only two miles away, said the object slightly resembled a road flare or fireworks but noted that the light would have to have been at least five times brighter than a typical flare to be seen at that estimated distance. Another witness disagreed, suggesting the object was the wrong colour for a flare and also did not behave as a flare would. He was experienced in working with and observing flares and was insistent that this was definitely not a flare. It had perfectly level flight and was a strong and steady light source.

The witnesses were certain that others must have seen the object, although no other reports were received. The witnesses questioned a nearby Canadian Forces Base Wing and were told there was no military traffic in the area at the time. In checking the UFOROM database, however, I found that there had been several other UFO sightings that night and within a day or so, although none was close to the location of the tower personnel sighting.

A review of the reports chronologically reveals some interesting things. At 8:30 p.m. on March 27, two witnesses near Rigaud, Quebec, saw "*une grosse boule lumineuse qui cachait quelque chose en arrire. On aurrait dit que le cercle tait une sorte de gaz.*" They watched the object with "something" behind it for about four hours, including some time with binoculars, and there is no question that they were observing a bright planet. At 10:45 p.m., a different witness in Montreal was observing the planetary procession and was startled to see two red balls of light flying together and crossing the sky from northwest to the southwest.[2]

In the wee hours of the morning of March 28, at 2:26, witnesses in Prince George, B.C., saw "two fiery orange balls hovering in the sky above [them], seemingly floating along. [They] watched the balls move for approximately a block and a half before one separated down towards the horizon. It was then [they] quickly got into the car to chase the other one, only to lose it." Later on during the day, a skywatcher took some photos of "chemtrails" over Newbury, Ontario, at about 2:00 p.m. The photos show only what appear to be regular jet contrails, which the photographer nevertheless considered unusual.

Five hours later, at 5:10 p.m. (taking into account the time zone difference), three witnesses were golfing in Calgary when they saw two daylight discs. One witness said:

> I was looking into the sky at the Confederation driving range watching a ball when I saw the first object moving across the sky at a high rate of speed. I was able to point it out to two friends I had there and they tracked it with me. As we watched it move across the sky, we noticed a second one in front of it. They were moving at such an incredible rate of speed that they simply vanished into the distance. The two objects were circular in shape and had a silver metallic color to them.

Later, at 7:20 p.m. EST, another witness in Montreal saw a light flashing red, blue, green, and yellow and moving slowly during the five minutes it was observed. "It was to the right of the moon and [faded out] to the left of the moon." It made no noise and had a very smooth trajectory. This object was very likely an aircraft.

Later that evening, the air traffic controllers had their sighting. An hour later, at 8:45 PST, a witness in Victoria, B.C., reported "a strange object between Venus and the moon." It was a bright white light that seemed to have an odd pattern of flight and faded after ten seconds of observation. Finally, at about 4:30 a.m. on March 29, a witness in Regina, Saskatchewan, reported:

> … a light about the size of Venus moving from north to south. I initially thought it was a satellite on a polar orbit as I believe the altitude was that high. It then

> maneuvered into a long 'S' shaped arc with the initial turn to the west and continued this arc until it had turned 180 degrees to the east and then once again turned to the west and then once again turned this time leaving my field of vision to the southeast. It seems to me it descended with this maneuver as it seemed at a lower altitude at the end of the 'S' maneuver. No sound was heard by me at anytime. It was not an airplane. I have been an aviation enthusiast all my life and know what to look for and none of it was there.

So, in the span of about forty-eight hours there were nine separate UFO sightings reported, almost from sea to sea. None were identical in description, and it does not appear that any of the witnesses saw the same objects. Some have possible explanations, while at least one may qualify as a high-quality unknown.

Since the air traffic controllers insisted on anonymity, the geographical location of their sighting is not given here. I asked them if they were going to file an official report with Transport Canada, and they replied they would *not* be doing so. This begs the question of how many other sightings by ATC operators go unreported.

UFOs IN CANADIAN CULTURE

CHAPTER FORTY
GOVERNMENT UFO INVESTIGATION

GEOFF DITTMAN

A staple belief of ufology today is the idea that the government knows more than they are telling us. Governments have been secretly studying the situation for decades, knowing full well that aliens are here — or so the theory goes. Some people even believe that the U.S. government is in possession of not only crashed flying saucers but their occupants as well![1] Stanton Friedman, a well-respected researcher who used to work on secret government projects, has come to label the conspiracy a "Cosmic Watergate."[2]

Ever since the original Watergate conspiracy of the seventies, suspicion of government has increased, with the belief of a UFO-related conspiracy increasing along with it. One of the more popular television shows of the nineties, *The X-Files*, is a testament to this. Public opinion polls suggest that the population believes many such government conspiracies exist. But is there any evidence of such conspiracies? What do we know about the Canadian government's studies of the UFO question?

Many people became interested in UFOs in June of 1947 after Kenneth Arnold's sighting over Washington State touched off the modern UFO era. Arnold, a private pilot participating in a search and rescue operation, observed a large number of crescent-shaped objects moving at an extremely high velocity. Speaking to the media after the sighting, he described the objects as behaving "like a saucer skipping across water."[3] Thus was born the concept of flying saucers. With the attention the Arnold sighting got in the press, the American government naturally became interested in what was going on in the skies over the United States.[4]

The U.S. Air Force started its first UFO investigation, known as Project Sign. The mood of Sign's staff was "a state of near panic"[5] in the early days, according to a former U.S. Air Force officer involved in the investigation. The press was giving the UFO sightings a fair amount of coverage, and the U.S. government was being pressed for answers.

The Canadian government began their research into the UFO question almost simultaneously. Little is known about this early period, however. What is known is that only a few days after Kenneth Arnold's sighting over Washington state, a UFO sighting occurred in Ottawa, Ontario. Probably this sighting, and likely the attention being paid to the problem in the U.S., prompted the Canadian military to begin a series of investigations.[6]

In the early years, attempts were made by the Royal Canadian Air Force to intercept UFOs. These attempts were apparently unsuccessful. Changing tactics somewhat, the military felt they would try something new: they encouraged UFOs to come to them! In the early fifties, the Defence Research Board (a group responsible for research and development for the military) set up a no-fly zone near Suffield, Alberta. The hope was to lure UFOs to the area using searchlights, radio signals, and other means.[7] The story officially came to light in 1967, when the defence minister admitted to the presumably unsuccessful program. The military had earlier claimed no such program ever existed.

In 1950, attempts were made to better organize the investigation. In his book *The UFO Files*, Palmiro Campagna describes such attempts at standardization.[8] Honourable Brooke Claxton, the defence minister at the time, indicated to Dr. Omond Solandt, chairman of the Defence Research Board, that Ottawa desired better coordination between the various branches of the military when it came to reporting UFOs. The problem was addressed during a Joint Intelligence Committee[9] meeting. During the meeting it was decided to prepare a unified reporting format for sightings investigated by the military and RCMP. The director of Air Intelligence was deemed ultimately responsible for investigating UFO reports, and the director of Scientific Intelligence was deemed responsible for reviewing the reports.[10] Despite the misgivings of the director of Air Intelligence, who felt that, given the conclusions reached by the personnel of Project Sign,[11] collecting UFO reports was unnecessary, a questionnaire was completed and released in October of 1950.[12] The Canadian government was beginning to get organized in its study of UFOs.

It was around this time that one of the more interesting characters in Canadian ufology first hit the scene. Wilbert Brockhouse Smith was a prominent electrical engineer with the Department of Transport. Smith was born in Lethbridge, Alberta, and obtained a Master of Science degree from the University of British Columbia in 1934. He first went to work for the DOT in 1939. During the Second World War, he was involved in signals intelligence. Shortly after the war, Smith was responsible for the creation of a chain of ionospheric measurement stations in Canada.[13] Smith, though an expert in radio waves, eventually became interested in geomagnetism. He became convinced that the Earth's magnetic field could be harnessed and used as some form of propulsion system.[14] It was because of this belief that Smith's interest turned to UFOs.

In 1950, Smith travelled to Washington, D.C., on business, where he stumbled upon two popular books on UFOs: *Behind the Flying Saucers* by Frank Scully and *The Flying Saucers Are Real* by Donald Keyhoe. According to Scully and Keyhoe, UFOs were alien spacecraft and the government was involved in some sort of cover-up of the truth. The UFOs' method of propulsion was apparently based on magnetic principles.[15] This caught Smith's attention, given his work on geomagnetics, and he became interested enough to want to find out more.

This interest led him to contact the Canadian embassy in Washington. Smith and the defence attaché at the embassy, a Lieutenant-Colonel Bremner, were able to set up a meeting with Dr. Robert Sarbacher. Dr. Sarbacher was the former dean of Georgia Tech's graduate school and had been a consultant to the U.S. government.[16] Arthur Bray, a respected Canadian ufologist, was able to obtain the notes made by Smith after the meeting. According to the notes, Sarbacher confirmed that Scully's book was essentially correct and that the UFO problem was being taken very seriously by the U.S. government:

SMITH: Then the saucers do exist?
SARBACHER: Yes, they exist.
SMITH: Do they operate as Scully suggests, on magnetic principles?
SARBACHER: We have not been able to duplicate their performance.

SMITH:	Do they come from some other planet?
SARBACHER:	All we know is, we didn't make them, and it's pretty certain they didn't originate on the earth.
SMITH:	I understand the whole subject of saucers is classified.
SARBACHER:	Yes, it is classified two points higher even than the H-bomb. In fact it is the most highly classified subject in the U.S. government at the present time.[17]

Attempts were made to confirm the accuracy of the notes. An investigator named William Steinman, among others, was able to ask Sarbacher about the accuracy of the memo. Sarbacher essentially confirmed the memo's contents, though he could not give any specific details of the crashes. He indicated that he was only peripherally involved in the investigation, participating in some discussions and reading some memos. Sarbacher did, however, tell Steinman that the "materials reported to have come from flying saucer crashes were extremely light and very tough,"[18] a claim that would come up again and again in UFO crash investigations. While Sarbacher did not provide any hard evidence of a cover-up, his verification of the accuracy of the memo and his continued support of the claims made do offer some food for thought.

The Sarbacher interview seemed to convince Smith that UFOs did exist and that there was an opportunity for him to further his research in geomagnetism and its use as a power source. In November 1950, Smith sent a memo to the controller of telecommunications at the Department of Transport: "For the past several years we have been engaged in the study of various aspects of radio wave propagation. The vagaries of this phenomenon have led us into the fields of aurora, cosmic radiation, atmospheric radioactivity and geo-magnetism … we are on the track of a means whereby the potential energy of the earth's magnetic field may be abstracted and used."[19]

Smith then went on to connect his work with UFO investigations:

> We believe that we are on the track of something which may well prove to be the introduction to a new technology. The existence of a different technology is borne out by the investigations which are being carried out at

> the present time in relation to flying saucers. ... It appeared to me that our own work in geo-magnetics might well be the linkage between our technology and the technology by which the saucers are designed and operated. ... If it is assumed that our geo-magnetic investigations are in the right direction, the theory of operation of the saucers becomes quite straightforward, with all observed features explained qualitatively and quantitatively.[20]

Smith then summarized the information on UFOs obtained in the meeting with Sarbacher:

- The matter is the most highly classified subject in the United States Government, rating higher even than the H-bomb.
- Flying saucers exist.
- Their modus operandi is unknown but concentrated effort is being made by a small group headed by Doctor Vannevar Bush.[21]
- The entire matter is considered by the United States authorities to be of tremendous significance.[22]

Apparently, the Department of Transport took Smith seriously. In November of 1950, Project Magnet was created by the deputy minister of Transport for Air Services, Commander C.F. Edwards.[23] The DOT's Telecommunications Division was given the project, with staff assigned to the project being made up of Smith, three other engineers, and two technicians.[24] However, based on the size of the staff, one could hardly describe the project as a serious attempt by the government to investigate the UFO phenomenon.

In fact, at least in the beginning, the UFO side of the project was downplayed, with the focus being geomagnetic research. But because of unforeseen problems, much of this work was cut back.[25] The group's attention then turned to UFO sightings, probably because it was believed the sighting reports could result in a breakthrough in geomagnetic research. The plan was first to collect data and analyze it to see what could be gained. The second part of the project involved "a systematic questioning of all our basic concepts in the hope of turning up a discrepancy which might prove to be the key to a new technology."[26]

Project Magnet was being carried out at least partially behind closed doors and was classified as "secret."[27] The reasons behind the classification were several. The department wished to ensure the project would be able to work with other classified projects, such as parallel American operations, as necessary. Furthermore, Smith felt that "in the event that a new technology should be uncovered, its implications would have to be carefully assessed before pertinent information could be made public."[28] While unmentioned, another concern was likely to limit any embarrassment the Department of Transport would experience should the public become aware of the investigation.

Early in 1952, the Canadian government decided to increase the size of its UFO investigation somewhat. The Defence Research Board requested that a committee be formed to look into UFO reports.[29] This committee, classified as "confidential," held its first meeting on April 22, 1952. Initially it was to be called Project Theta, but that name had to be abandoned because of military naming regulations. Presumably as a nod to the political sensitivity of the topic, one alternative name suggested was "Hot Tomalley."[30] Eventually, however, the name Project Second Storey was adopted.

The committee was chaired by Dr. Peter Millman, an astrophysicist who at the time was with the Dominion Observatory. (Millman would at a later point in time become well known for debunking UFO reports.) Another prominent name on the committee was none other than Wilbert Smith. It is somewhat confusing why the government felt it necessary to set up a second project to study the UFO situation; one can only assume it was because the military felt the need to have a project of its own. Other members in the committee included representatives of Naval Intelligence, Military Operations and Planning, and the Defence Research Board.[31]

The purpose of the project was first to decide whether or not more time and effort should be spent on investigating UFOs.[32] The last public UFO investigation in the U.S. (at that time) deemed the situation not worthy of attention. Secretly, however, the U.S. created a third project, named Blue Book, to further look into the matter. But was there anything of interest to the Canadian government?

To analyze the situation, it was deemed necessary to better collect UFO reports. The committee decided to create a new standardized questionnaire for such reports, as well as uniform procedures for collecting and analyzing the information obtained in an investigation.[33] It was decided the military and police would prepare the reports, while Project Second Storey would help analyze the information collected.[34]

Two more meetings were held during the following months. In the April 24 meeting, the committee deemed it worthwhile to liaise with the U.S. government on UFO matters. Apparently, however, little came of it.[35] In the third meeting, in May of 1952, it became apparent that the secrecy of the project was essential: "The committee and all deliberations are classified as confidential and must be so treated. Contacts with the press or public are not to be made."[36]

As Campagna noted, this seems somewhat bizarre and counterproductive given that Project Second Storey had decided in an earlier meeting to collect their reports from external parties such as the police.[37]

While Project Second Storey was moving on, Project Magnet was certainly not stagnant either. On June 25, 1952, Smith wrote a memo that included the following: "If, as appears evident, the flying saucers are emissaries from some other civilization, and actually do operate on magnetic principles, we have before us the fact that we have missed something in magnetic theory but have a good indication of the direction in which to look for the missing quantities."[38]

It should be noted that Smith himself indicated that his statements on the likelihood of alien visitation reflected his personal opinion and not that of the department.[39] The department has tried to distance itself from Smith and Magnet over the years. In a 1964 letter to Wilfred Daniels, the director of Telecommunications and Electronics at DOT stated:

> [W]e would reiterate that at no time has the Department carried out research into the field of unidentified flying objects. … a small program of investigation in the field of geo-magnetics was carried out by the Telecommunications Division of this Department between 1950 and 1954. This minor investigation was for the purpose of studying magnetic phenomena. … This personal project was at no expense to the Department, nor did it have any Departmental sponsorship.[40]

At best, this was a half-truth, given that the focus of the project was apparently geomagnetics and support from the department was seemingly limited. Magnet's involvement in UFO research, however, is now undeniable.

One of Project Second Storey's tasks was to analyze sighting reports. As such, the committee needed to know how much reliance could be placed on eyewitness accounts. It has been argued that eyewitness testimony is unreliable, that witnesses are frequently wrong in what they think they see. So how much trust could Second Storey place in sighting reports? To help get a better understanding, Wilbert Smith performed an experiment: he, in effect, faked a UFO sighting! Late in the evening of September 8, 1952, Smith launched a weather balloon, complete with a light source to make it more easily seen, into the sky over Ottawa. The plan was to wait for reports to be sent in and analyze them for their accuracy. Were the reports consistent with a weather balloon, suggesting that witness testimony is at least somewhat reliable? Or were witness accounts totally off-the-wall? Unfortunately for Smith, no one reported seeing anything unusual in the sky that night. Perhaps witnesses were able to identify the object or didn't consider it unusual enough to warrant reporting. Whatever the case, the experiment was a failure.[41]

Another meeting of the Project Second Storey committee took place in March 1953. The committee felt that there was at that time no reason to implement a full-scale military investigation into the UFO situation. The committee concluded, however, in good bureaucratic fashion, that they should continue meeting.[42]

Meanwhile, Project Magnet was coming to a completely different conclusion. Five months after that Second Storey meeting, in August 1953, Smith wrote another interim memo for Project Magnet. In this memo he stated:

> It appears then, that we are faced with a substantial probability of the real existence of extra-terrestrial vehicles, regardless of whether or not they fit into our scheme of things. Such vehicles of necessity, must use a technology considerably in advance of what we have. It is therefore submitted that the next step in this investigation should be a substantial effort toward the acquisition of as much as possible of this technology, which would without doubt be of great value to us.[43]

To date, researchers have been unable to get hold of any memos or other documentation about Project Second Storey's evaluation of Smith's conclusions. It would be reasonable to believe the committee did examine Smith's findings, given that Smith was a member of the

Project Second Storey committee. Furthermore, Arthur Bray, a Canadian UFO researcher, was informed that the interim memo went as high up as the Prime Minister's Office! [44] It would appear that the minutes of some Project Second Storey meetings remain classified after all these years.

As part of Project Magnet, Smith's next experiment was something a little unusual. On November 12, 1953, a press release was sent out:

> In a few weeks, an observatory which, it is hoped, will elucidate the mystery of the flying saucers, will begin its work at Shirley's Bay, about twelve miles from Ottawa. The laboratory has been equipped with all the instruments now available for that purpose. It will be directed by Mr. Wilbert Smith, Chief Engineer of the Electronics Division of the Canadian Ministry of Transport. Mr. Smith has made the following statement: "There is a good chance that the flying saucers are real objects. The odds are sixty to a hundred that they are extra-terrestrial vehicles."[45]

Smith had, in fact, set up a UFO-detection station! This idea is somewhat reminiscent of the so-called Pentacle memo. In 1967, while going through the files of Dr. J. Allen Hynek, an astronomer who at the time was working on the United States Air Force's UFO project Blue Book, Dr. Jacques Vallee found a document recommending that the U.S. Air Force set up a network of observation posts to help find and track UFOs:

> We expect our analysis will show that certain areas in the United States have had an abnormally high number of reported incidents of unidentified flying objects. Assuming that, from our analysis, several definite areas productive of reports can be selected, we recommend that one or two of these areas be set up as experimental areas. This area, or areas, should have observation posts with complete visual skywatch, with radar and photographic coverage, plus all other instruments necessary or helpful in obtaining positive and reliable data on everything in the air over the area.[46]

This Pentacle memo was dated January 9, 1953, only eleven months before Smith announced the set-up of his own observation post. While there is no evidence that the recommendation of the Pentacle memo was ever carried out, is the Shirley's Bay observation post evidence that Smith was in some way in the know about the more secretive goings-on in the U.S. UFO investigation programs? Some researchers have suggested that Smith was connected to an underground American program, though there is no hard evidence that such an American underground program even existed.

Smith's observation post was nowhere near as sophisticated as what the Pentacle memo called for but still had its share of equipment, including a radio receiver, a magnetometer, a recording gravimeter, and a gamma ray counter.[47] Now all Project Magnet had to do was wait for anomalous activities.

Before the station could even get up and running, however, controversy began. Solandt publicly began to distance himself from the experiment, indicating that the station was not part of an official government project. The building and equipment were, in fact, only "on loan" to Mr. Smith.[48] Upset at the publicity the government was getting by being associated with the UFO experiment, Solandt took Smith to task about the press attention. Smith was nonetheless allowed to conduct the experiment.[49]

While Project Magnet was seemingly picking up steam, Project Second Storey came to an end shortly after the set-up of the UFO observatory. The final meeting of the committee occurred on February 25, 1954. The committee came to the same conclusion that many other researchers have over the years: UFOs cannot be studied satisfactorily using science. "The committee as a whole has felt that owing to the impossibility of checking independently the details of the majority of sightings, most of the observational material does not lend itself to a scientific method of investigation."[50]

Thus ended the only dedicated UFO project known to have been run by the Canadian government.

Project Magnet, on the other hand, carried on, but the end was near for it, too. The significant amount of press attention Smith had received (he had even begun to be mentioned in the UFO press) was becoming exceedingly embarrassing for the Department of Transport. The superintendent of radio regulations in April 1954 expressed his opinion on Magnet in an internal memo. The department didn't have resources to spare on such matters as flying saucers, he indicated. Project Magnet should be shut down.[51]

Smith did his best to defend the project. On June 10 he replied to his detractor. While admitting that Magnet did not belong in the telecommunications division, the DOT must continue to carry on the project, he argued. In fact, the project must be expanded! According to Smith there was enough evidence to suggest that UFOs were alien spacecraft.[52]

The higher-ups were not convinced that Smith's conclusions were accurate. Dr. Omond Solandt felt the evidence was not compelling enough to merit the existence of Magnet or any other government project. Ignoring Project Blue Book, Solandt argued that Canada's allies had stopped looking at UFOs, so Canada should too.[53] The end of Magnet drew near.

Around this time, however, the little UFO observatory outside of Ottawa apparently did what it was set up to do: detect UFOs. On August 8, 1954, after months of inactivity, the station's gravimeter came to life in an unusual manner not suggestive of a normal aircraft. "First it waved, drawing a thin dark line on the graph paper being used to measure the movements of the instruments. Without further warning the gravimeter went wild. All evidence indicated that a real unidentified flying object had flown within feet of the station."[54]

Running outside to see what was up there, Smith couldn't see anything through the dense fog and cloud cover that was over the region. Smith missed his last chance at weathering the political storm.

The media learned of the possible encounter, bringing down even more unwanted publicity on the already weary Department of Transport. Having had enough, the department officially ordered Smith to shut down the UFO observatory.[55] In the press release, the Department of Transport said, "Considerable data was collected and analysed and many attempts were made to fit these data in to some sort of pattern. However, it has not been possible to reach any definite conclusion, and since new data appear to be similar to data already studied, there seems to be little point in carrying the investigation any further on an official level."[56]

The release did indicate however that Smith was still unofficially collecting UFO reports. But as far as the government was concerned, Project Magnet had come to an end.

It has been more than fifty years since the end of projects Magnet and Second Storey. Even after all this time, the public has yet to see many of the files related to these projects. Milllman, the former chairman of Second Storey, considered whether or not the minutes of the

Second Storey meeting reviewing Project Magnet should be released. In an internal memo, the DOT indicated:

> Since the question of flying saucers is still attracting public attention and since this file covers documents relating to the studies behind project "Magnet" and, indeed, records much of the discussion in the Department of Transport surrounding project "Magnet" which is confidential in nature, it is recommended that this file be down classified at least to the confidential level. At no time should it be made available to the public.[57]

It doesn't look like the public can expect any more openness from the government any time soon.

Wilbert Smith's UFO studies didn't end with Magnet and Second Storey. He continued his research privately, becoming involved in several investigations that received a fair amount of publicity. Smith came to be associated with some pretty wild ideas — too wild for many. He began to abandon the more traditional studies involving sighting reports in favour of more unusual activities involving forms of communication with supposed beings from outer space. According to some, Smith began to become obsessed with the idea of extraterrestrials.[58]

One of the more famous cases Smith became involved in began not in Canada but in the United States. Smith allegedly came into possession of the first of two pieces of flying saucers. In 1952, over Washington, D.C., a U.S. Navy jet was sent up to intercept a UFO. Shots were fired, and a piece of the UFO fell off into a farmer's field. The fragment was recovered by the government shortly thereafter.[59] As described in a book by journalist Frank Edwards, U.S. Navy Commander Frank Thompson confirmed that the piece was recovered and that the navy was unable to determine its origin.[60]

Smith provided more details about the piece of flying saucer in a 1961 interview with two Americans, C.W. Fitch and George Pepovitch.

FITCH: In what way, if any, do they [the pieces of the UFO] differ from materials with which we are familiar?

SMITH: As a general thing, they differ only in that they are much harder than our materials…

FITCH: What did the analysis show?
SMITH: There was iron rust — the thing was in reality a matrix of magnesium orthosilicate. The matrix had great numbers — thousands — of 15-micron spheres scattered through it.
FITCH: You say that you had to return it — did you return it to the Air Force, Mr. Smith?
SMITH: Not the Air Force. Much higher than that.[61]

It would seem that Smith possibly had his hands on definitive proof of the existence of extraterrestrials and that a covert organization within the U.S. government was engaged not only in an investigation of UFO's but in a cover-up as well.

In ufology, however, things are rarely as they seem. As part of a U.S. government–sponsored investigation into UFOs, the University of Colorado's Condon Committee investigated the incident. According to the committee's final report:

> A thorough search of all Navy records available failed to reveal any account of a Navy jet fighter's encounter with an UFO in July 1952 or at any other time. Perhaps more significant, however, were the facts that Navy records of the year 1952 carried only one Frank Thompson, an individual who had retired from active duty several years before 1952 with the rank of lieutenant, not lieutenant commander.[62]

Who's telling the truth? Did Smith obtain a piece of a flying saucer or was he the victim of a hoax? If the piece existed, it is unclear why the U.S. military would loan it to an outside party like Dr. Smith. Surely the U.S. military, with all of its funding and access to many of the world's top scientists, would not risk exposing a cover-up by working with a small, underfunded project like Magnet and its head Wilbert Smith? It seems more likely that Smith fell victim to a hoax.[63]

Smith supposedly came into possession of other pieces of flying saucers as well. Smith was convinced that a three-thousand-pound chunk of slag was in fact part of a now lifeless spaceship floating through space. In June 1960 a Quebec newspaper reported on an apparent meteorite being seen and heard over the province.[64] Intrigued, the Ottawa Flying Saucer Club (later the Ottawa New Sciences Club — an organization at the time headed by Smith) set out to find the meteorite. The club was unable to find any witnesses but they did find a huge piece of metal in a shallow channel of the St. Lawrence River about twenty miles from Quebec City.[65]

The club brought the metal back to Ottawa for examination. Wilbert Smith concluded that the piece was a part of a derelict spacecraft adrift in outer space. Holes in the metal, of which there were several, were from tiny meteorites.[66] Smith felt he had in his possession evidence of extraterrestrial life.

Others who examined the physical evidence came to a different conclusion. According to the Condon Committee report, "The Canadian Arsenals Research and Development Establishment (CARDE) had examined the non-homogeneous material, and described it as high-manganese austenitic steel. CARDE personnel considered the material the normal product of a foundry, consisting of slag with semi-molten scrap imbedded in it."[67]

There was no evidence of impact. However it got there, it apparently didn't fall from the sky.

Roy Craig, an investigator with the University of Colorado's Condon Committee, visited Ottawa and took a look at the metal. By that time, Smith had passed away (Smith died on December 27, 1962, from cancer), but Craig did talk with a member of the Ottawa New Sciences Club, a colonel in the RCAF. The colonel admitted the metal appeared at first glance to be quite terrestrial, but he claimed that "when viewed in a wider framework, the interface of this dimension with other dimensions, which parallel the physical, it well may be part of a spaceship."[68]

Years later, the club had another analysis performed, this time by Dr. Eric Smith, chief of the Metal Physics Section of the Canadian Department of Energy, Mines, and Resources. At the time Craig spoke with him, Smith had yet to perform a scientific analysis of the sample. Smith did indicate, however, that from its physical appearance he suspected CARDE's conclusion was correct. He even had a suspect for the source of the scrap: Sorel Iron Foundries, in Sorel, Quebec. Smith indicated that the company regularly buried pieces of high-manganese steel that were not suitable for its needs.[69] It appears likely that the source of the metal was a foundry fifty miles from where the scrap was found, not some spaceship light years away. Despite the repeated conclusions that there was a natural source for the metal, the club, following Wilbert Smith's lead, clung to a more New Age view of reality.

As time passed, Wilbert Smith came to view ufology not so much as an attempt to find proof of alien visitation or the lack thereof but rather as a belief in the existence of extraterrestrials and an attempt to understand their philosophy. He seemed to adopt New Age views of aliens, believing that the visitors were here to help humanity and had regular contact with favoured individuals, so-called contactees. Smith said, "As is the case in any new and romantic field, there are those who exaggerate, but it is not too difficult to establish that the vast majority are honest and authentic. For instance when a dozen or so independent contacts … all tell the same message, even to the names and descriptions which tally perfected, one has little choice but to believe that they are telling the truth."[70]

The "boys from topside," as he sometimes called the aliens, were here to help us if only we would choose to listen. "The people from elsewhere are much concerned about the choice we will make, partly because it will have its repercussions on them and partly because we are their blood brothers and they are truly concerned with our welfare. … We will be able to learn from them and bring about the Golden Age all men everywhere desire deep within their hearts."[71]

Smith had come to believe the truth of UFOs would not be found in science and technology, for such a thing as true alien life would be beyond our comprehension. "So another approach was tried — the philosophical — and here the answer was found in all its grandeur," Smith insisted.[72] He suggested we should listen to and in some cases take to heart what the contactees are telling us. While most serious researchers had little faith in the reliability and honesty of contactees, Smith felt that the truth of UFOs would be at least partially revealed through the individuals claiming regular contact with aliens.

Smith's work with contactees brought him into contact yet again with the U.S. government when he heard of a woman in Maine who was allegedly communicating with aliens via automatic writing.[73] Apparently, the woman was impressive enough to convince Smith of her authenticity. Aware of Smith's interest, the Office of Naval Intelligence felt compelled to start its own investigation, and two agents were sent to interview the woman. One of the officers even tried to contact the aliens himself, but to no avail. While at CIA headquarters in Langley to report their findings, the officer again attempted to contact the aliens. He entered into a trancelike state, and this time he apparently had a little more luck. After being asked for proof that he was in fact in contact with aliens, the entranced officer stated that if they were to look outside, they would see a UFO. The witnesses, two CIA agents and a naval intelligence officer, did apparently see a UFO! The CIA, embarrassed by the events, punished those involved for getting into such a bizarre situation.[74]

Not much is known about the government's investigations into the UFO situation following the demise of Magnet and Second Storey. While the government did continue to investigate, the body responsible for the investigation changed quite frequently. It seems that UFO investigation was viewed as a hot potato, to be passed on at the first opportunity.

Initially, upon the conclusion of Magnet, the Air Office Commanding Air Defence Command was tasked with investigating UFOs.[75] It was during the fifties that Canada entered into an agreement with the United States known as the Canada–United States Communications Instructions for Reporting Vital Intelligence Sightings, or CIRVIS. The purpose of CIRVIS is to provide standardized reporting procedures when something unusual is sighted by military personnel or civilians that might be of vital importance to the national security of Canada or the United States. Reports are filed under Joint Army Navy Air Publication-146, or JANAP-146. JANAP-146 includes categories of sightings (which are deemed to be of vital interest by the witness) that are to be reported:

- Hostile or unidentified single aircraft or formations of aircraft which appear to be directed against the United States or Canada or their forces
- Missiles
- Unidentified Flying Objects
- Hostile or unidentified submarines
- Hostile or unidentified group or groups of military surface vessels
- Individual surface vessels, submarines, or aircraft of unconventional design, or engaged in suspicious activity or observed in a location or in a course which may be interpreted as constituting a threat to the United States, Canada, or their forces
- Any unexplained or unusual activity which may indicate a possible attack against or through Canada or the United States, including the presence of any unidentified or other suspicious ground parties in the Polar Region or other remote or sparsely populated areas.[76]

The million-dollar question is how to interpret the term "unidentified flying objects" in that list. One could quite understandably read it as simply meaning an unidentified aircraft or missile rather than the popular connotation of flying saucers and the like. This is how the Condon Committee in its report "The Scientific Study of Unidentified Flying Objects" interpreted the statement.[77] But such things as unknown aircraft and missiles are effectively covered in parts (a) and (b). And why use the popular term "UFOs" if the more traditional connotation is not intended? As Palmiro Campagna has pointed out, drawings of examples were included with each item in the list, and a drawing of a stereotypical flying saucer was included for unidentified flying objects.[78]

A significant provision of JANAP-146 was that it was made illegal to make public any CIRVIS/JANAP reports:

> Military and Civilian Transmission of CIRVIS reports are subject to the U.S. Communications Act of 1934, as amended, and the Canadian Radio Act of 1938, as amended. Any person who violates the provisions of these acts may be liable to prosecution thereunder. Any person who makes an unauthorized transmission or disclosure of such a report may be liable for prosecution. ... The purpose is to emphasize the necessity for the handling of such information within official channels only.[79]

The inclusion of such consequences for going public with a report likely has little or nothing to do with UFO reports but instead with more traditional threats to national security like the intrusions of a foreign power. But it does hinder the ability of UFO researchers to gather official reports.

In the sixties, Air Defence Command ended its investigation into UFOs, and the task was transferred to Canadian Forces headquarters. In turn, the headquarters transferred the role to the Directorate of Operations in March 1966.[80]

Shortly after obtaining the role, DOPS introduced new reporting procedures for UFO reports. JANAP-146 is concerned only with observations of vital interest, so in October 1966, Canadian Forces Administrative Order (CFAO) 71-6, "Reporting of Unidentified Flying Objects," was introduced. The purpose of the order was to make it easier for DOPS to obtain less important UFO sightings reports from the various military bases and police forces around the country.[81]

The military began to categorize the UFO reports they received. Each report was first analyzed to determine if the sighting was of a meteorite/fireball. If so, the report was forwarded on to the government's scientific body, the National Research Council. The non-meteoric sightings, on the other hand, were analyzed further. These reports were slotted into one of three categories: A (the report shows promise and needs to be reviewed further), B (unusual but no investigation will be performed), and C (effectively worthless reports). As could be expected, there were few reports categorized as Class A. For example, in 1967 there were nine Class A reports. According to Yurko Bondarchuk, a journalist who wrote a popular book on UFOs, only six Class A cases were deemed unexplainable.[82]

Its role as clearing house for UFO reports ended in 1968 when the Department of National Defence announced it was turning over that task to the National Research Council.[83] The official reason for the transfer was that the military could no longer afford the time and money required for UFO investigations.[84] Bondarchuk hypothesized that the real reason for the transfer was to eliminate the embarrassment the DND suffered from being unable to solve the UFO problem adequately.[85] With the transfer, the DND claimed to be out of the business of UFO research and investigations.[86]

The National Research Council's primary interest in UFO reports was as a possible source of information on meteorites; the reports could aid the NRC in recovering fallen meteorites. Reports that suggested a meteorite sighting were treated with relative importance; the rest of the reports were placed in a "Non-Meteoric Sightings" file and promptly forgotten.[87] Such non-meteoric sighting reports were kept only because of their interest to the public.

The NRC continued to collect but ignore UFO reports into the nineties. In 1995, however, they announced the cessation of the collection. The reason given was that the lack of funds and staff changes were hindering the study of meteorites.[88] It would seem the Canadian government has given up on UFOs altogether.[89]

But has it really? Ever since the early days of the modern UFO era in the forties, there have been claims of conspiracies and secret government investigations. Every time the U.S. government announced they had found no reason to continue investigating UFOs and were shutting down the investigation, there were cries of cover-up. Many would believe that the investigation was continuing — just underground and away from the media spotlight. In many cases, time proved the conspiracy theorists right when the air force's latest program was uncovered. The last U.S. government program known to have existed, Project Blue Book, was officially shut down after the publicly funded study by the University of Colorado (the Condon Committee) found no reason to continue the project.

As could be expected, many people believe the investigation continued. Even renowned astronomer and UFO debunker Carl Sagan, in one of his last books before his death, *The Demon-Haunted World*, concluded that it was likely that there was another more secretive investigation aside from Blue Book being carried out by the air force.[90] Kevin Randle, a well-known American investigator, came to the conclusion that the U.S. Air Force continued to investigate UFOs under the cover of Project Moon Dust, run by a unit known variously as the 4602nd Air Intelligence Service Squadron (AISS), the 1006th AISS, the 1127th Air Activities Group, and finally Detachment 4, 696th Air Intelligence Group. Moon Dust itself was shut down after the name was leaked to the press, but the project is likely continuing under a different name.[91]

Beginning in the eighties, there was talk of a much more sinister cover-up in the U.S. Stories of crashed flying saucers, originally told in the fifties, were reintroduced. Roswell became a household name, along with stories of aliens, both alive and dead, being kept at the U.S. government's top-secret base in Nevada known as Area 51. Around this was talk of a super-secret research project known as Majestic-12. This alleged organization was said to be the investigative group looking into UFOs and was the source of the UFO cover-up. While numerous books have been written on the subject, there has been no hard evidence found of a cover-up of Majestic-12 magnitude.

Talk of a giant cover-up has occurred in Canada as well, though not nearly to the extent of what is going on in the United States. For example, several Canadian researchers, including John Musgrave and Grant Cameron, have brought forward accounts of Wilbert Smith being allowed to view alien bodies that were in the possession of the U.S. government.[92]

Smith himself allegedly claimed to have personally met alien beings. In 1967, a colleague of astrophysicist Jacques Vallee met with a UFO investigator from Illinois by the name of Achzener. Achzener told a story involving himself and Smith. At the suggestion of Smith, the two drove to a coffee shop. "At one point, Smith made a peculiar signal, which Achzener says could only have been seen by three other people: an old man, the waitress, and a short fellow about four feet tall who immediately got up and drove off in an old car with California licence plates. 'I wanted you to see this person.' Smith said. 'That's why we came here. He's an extra-terrestrial.'"[93]

Such a bizarre encounter is vaguely reminiscent of meetings with the so-called men in black, where UFO researchers or investigators meet up with individuals who stand out from the crowd in some fashion and frequently drive old cars. Typically, however, such MIBs try to frighten people away from investigating UFOs or reporting their sightings. While more commonly reported in the United States, there have been a handful of reports in Canada. In October 1967, a B.C. resident, a woman who regularly observed UFOs, was visited twice by strangely behaving men who falsely claimed to work for the hydro company.[94] In 1979 in Toronto, a girl and others with her experienced several UFO encounters. The girl during a lunch hour at school was followed and interrogated by a tall, strange-looking man with greyish skin, slanted eyes, and wearing a black suit.[95]

While there are stories such as the men in black and government possession of alien bodies that might suggest the Canadian government is involved in a grand cover-up, it is more likely that Ottawa is just as perplexed as the rest of us when it comes to UFOs. The behaviour of the government over the years is more suggestive of people frustrated by their inability to either conclusively solve the UFO question or make it go away than of a group trying to hide the truth. There seemed to be no real game plan being followed; instead, the government seemed to be groping around trying to find its way through the darkness. Whether or not there is a secret conspiracy in the United States is unclear; what is clear is that the Canadian government doesn't have a clue, and that is hardly a secret.

CHAPTER FORTY-ONE
LITTLE PAD ON THE PRAIRIE

CHRIS RUTKOWSKI

In 1967, the town of St. Paul, Alberta, decided to do something special to honour Canada's hundredth birthday. Many communities across the country embarked on symbolic or unique centennial projects, such as giant birthday cakes, local community publications, and of course fireworks. The wife of a St. Paul council member, Margo Lagassé of St. Paul, suggested only half-jokingly that they should build a UFO landing platform as a goodwill gesture to our extraterrestrial neighbours. At the time, UFOs were very much in the news, and it seemed like a surefire way to attract attention to their small community. The site was to be designated as a safe area for aliens to land so that they could make formal, peaceful contact with Earth.[1]

"We were just going to make an ordinary park," said Jules Van Brabert, mayor of St. Paul at the time, "but I started having a few beers with some committee members, and we got to thinking that we wanted something really different. Well, someone had just watched something on TV about flying saucers, and laughed that we should make the park into a UFO landing pad. It seemed like a great idea at the time."[2]

The pad didn't cost the town much money, only about $11,000. Materials were donated by local businesses, and the publicity of its inauguration made it a tourist attraction. On June 3, 1967, the Hon. Paul Hellyer, minister of defense, flew in by helicopter to officially "open" the pad.[3]

The site received national attention when it was built, but over the years it fell into disrepair. No saucer ever landed on it, and it had started to become a bit of an embarrassment to some local townspeople. The World's First UFO Landing Pad was used only for civic events and welcoming ceremonies for politicians and visiting rock stars. The recession added to the site's disrepair.

In 1982, the town decided to mark the International Year of the Child by contributing to the charitable organization led by Mother Theresa of Calcutta. A multifamily dwelling was built with donations of labour and materials and auctioned off. The proceeds were matched by government funds and the amount was donated to the charity. On June 25, 1982, Mother Theresa herself visited the town, and a ceremony was held on the landing pad to present her with nearly $1 million. Before her arrival, the pad and grounds were spruced up with new paint and significant repairs. During her speech thanking the town for its generosity, Mother Theresa noted the significance of the landing pad and said, "If there is sickness in outer space we would go there too."[4]

During the next decade, the site remained rarely used (even by humans). But in the mid-nineties, someone on town council realized that with the growing interest in UFOs, perhaps it was time to build upon the popularity of the subject. The town managed to obtain the travelling UFO exhibit from Center for UFO Studies historian and marketer John Timmerman when he decided to retire from public talks as he roved throughout North America. The town used the exhibit as a basis for a permanent UFO museum at the base of the platform. In effect, a unique tourist attraction was created long before the celebrated UFO museums in Roswell were built.

In addition to the exhibit, the town council installed a toll-free telephone line that allowed people to report their UFO sightings. The line was staffed by employees of the municipal office with little or no experience or knowledge of UFOs. They took down basic information and witnesses' descriptions of UFOs, typed them up, and posted a notice of the incident on public display in the museum. Visitors could browse recent cases while looking at the CUFOS display and also purchase t-shirts, key chains, and baseball caps featuring images of aliens. In terms of UFO research, the St. Paul museum was a source of first-hand UFO sighting reports, and the staff were helpful in providing case data to researchers.

In 1998, the first of a series of UFO conferences was held in St. Paul. While admittedly an effort to boost tourism to the town, the two-day event attracted hundreds of UFO buffs, serious investigators, and curiosity seekers.

"This is our first try at this, so if anything goes wrong, you can't blame us for it, because we're just learning," said Paul Pelletier, organizer for the UFO Conference in St. Paul, Alberta, Canada, on July 10–11, 1998. Paul had nothing to worry about. The conference was an outstanding success, according to the throng of attendees. Almost five hundred people registered for the event, most travelling more than two and a half hours one way from Edmonton, although many came from Calgary, Saskatchewan, Manitoba, and British Columbia. The museum's guest book filled with signatures of people from places such as Las Vegas, Billings, Whitehorse, Winnipeg, and Boise.[5]

The program featured noted ufologist Stanton Friedman lecturing about why "Flying Saucers Are Real," Gord Kijek of the Alberta UFO Study Group talking on an outstanding case involving triangular UFOs, crop circle investigator Gord Sobczak showing some of the striking shots of recent British crop circles, and Fern Belzil, an Alberta cattle rancher and mutilation investigator. His years of experience in raising cattle gives him a definite edge when it comes to interpreting mute evidence. (His illustrated talk was, unfortunately, immediately after lunch.)

John Timmerman of CUFOS both gave a history of ufology and commented on its future, describing the underappreciated work of physicist James McDonald and others, and how there are so many avenues for future research. Clinical psychologist Helen Neufeld described her work with abductees, in particular "Sharon," who appeared in person and agreed to share the podium and answer questions.

I gave details on other UFO sightings across Canada and spoke about trends in the cases across the country. The conference ended with a presentation by Martin Jasek, a UFO investigator from the Yukon and affiliated with UFOBC.

Outside the Polaris Conference Centre, the entire town got into the spirit of the festivities during the conference. "Welcome to our 'Pad'," announced an alien on a sign outside a Radio Shack outlet. "E.T. PHONE SMITTY'S," invited the sign outside a pancake restaurant. The local bingo hall had a saucer on its sign, and the shopping mall had a mural depicting the Roswell crash at its main entrance. After the formal presentations, speakers and attendees went for a bite to eat at, where else, "UFO Pizza." The restaurant was open late, had great pizza and pasta, and the decor featured UFOs in paintings, murals, and hand-painted signs on the front window. Naturally, there were "UFO Coolers" to drink. (At 6.9 percent alcohol, they sneaked up on you.)

Adjoining the conference auditorium was a dealers' room, where vendors were selling T-shirts, caps, pins, rings, and necklaces. The most popular item was a green alien head filled with $1 "alien pops." One artisan was selling her huge selection of ceramic alien heads and flying saucers, including some that had lights and made weird noises. There were "UFO guns" that shot foam saucers, alien key fobs, a UFO Pizza cap, and other assorted goodies.

The St. Paul Chamber of Commerce said they thought the conference brought in many more dollars into the town's economy than they spent on speakers and publicity.[6]

A big part of the display was set up by the Edmonton Space Sciences Centre. Director Frank Florian was there demonstrating simple gee-whiz science experiments to the kids and even had a Starlab planetarium inflated in one corner of the hall. The Fort McMurray astronomy club had a display, and that night they had a star party for the attendees, having set up their telescopes outside.

Media were everywhere: every network, every Alberta newspaper, and most radio stations were represented. Speakers were being interviewed in all corners of the hall.

Two years later, in July 2000, the second conference was held. Visitors could still tour the Polaris Arena, stay overnight at the Galaxy Motel, or grab a slice of pie at the Flying Saucer Diner. Speakers included Fern Belzil again and Ted Phillips, an investigator of ground markings and traces left by UFOs in some close encounter cases.

St. Paul remains a tourist attraction for those looking for destinations slightly quirkier than the typical historical or scenic sites in Canada. It remains to be seen if its landing pad will ever be used for what it was designed for.

CHAPTER FORTY-TWO
SCIENCE VERSUS THE FLYING SAUCERS

CHRIS RUTKOWSKI

If you were to ask the average scientist what he or she thought about UFOs, you would probably receive a cool response. The most typical reaction would be disdain. (How dare you ask such questions and waste the time of a respectable scientist?) But if you seemed to be sincere and in need of some enlightenment, you might receive a patient response.

More than likely, you would be told that UFOs don't exist and that people who report them are either mistaken or deluded.

If you were to take your query one step further and ask that same scientist how he or she acquired that bit of factual information, you'd be pressing your luck.

"Because there's no proof that they're alien spaceships" might be the reply.

And you'd be stuck.

There is, of course, no incontrovertible proof that UFOs are alien spaceships. No chunks of crashed flying saucers are on display at the Smithsonian; none of the supposed "implants" removed from abductees' bodies look like anything other than glass slivers and metal shavings; channelled messages from Ashtar or Semjase or any other "Space Brothers" are vague "love one another and stop all wars" godlike clichés and do not contain any useful information that might lead to a cure for cancer, AIDS, diabetes, or even the common cold; no contactee or abductee has ever returned from a nighttime saucer ride with as much as an ashtray or bath towel from the Zeta Reticuli Hilton.

However, there is some circumstantial evidence that aliens might be visiting us. The possibility of life elsewhere in the universe is strong, and if such life is carbon and water based, any advanced civilization might in fact have an interest in us, if only to want our planet as in the movie *Independence Day*. Furthermore, trained observers have made some good-quality UFO reports of vehicles that don't resemble conventional crafts.

Nevertheless, a good scientist would tell you that the proof of any claim that UFOs are alien spaceships rests with you, not him or her. If you want to argue that flying saucers are real, come up with some hard evidence, not just speculation and some fuzzy pictures of lights in the sky. There's no point in waving popular UFO magazines in anyone's face or playing tape recordings of abductees' narrative accounts of their sexual violations at the hands of grey-skinned aliens. Proof is what's needed, and there is precious little of that commodity offered by the general ufological community.

It's no wonder that the scientific community has a hard time with the subject of UFOs. Can you blame them? The tabloid media and the Internet are full of stories about alien spaceships following comets, photos of greys in various stages of vivisection, and claim after claim of mile-wide spacecraft hovering over densely populated cities.

Naturally, when such things are mentioned at the water coolers in the hallways of JPL, Harvard, and MIT, it is usually with a bit of derision. There are no regular discussions about UFOs in the pages of the *Annals of the New York Academy of Science*, *Scientific American*, or *Physical Review*. Physics textbooks are devoid of any mention of UFOs, and even the topic of the possibility of extraterrestrial life usually is given no more than a page or two in even the most liberal astronomy texts.

It might come as quite a shock to many scientists, then, that there is an existing and growing body of literature and material written by scientists regarding the serious study of UFOs. Some researchers address the problem of extraterrestrial visitation, some analyze UFO abductions, and some describe UFOs as a heretofore-undiscovered natural phenomenon.

In effect, some scientists are using scientific methodology to study UFOs. This is not to say that ufology itself is a science, but only that one can look at the subject rationally and objectively through a variety of scientific disciplines such as statistics, psychology, sociology, geophysics, and medicine.

Even though the first large-scale scientific study of UFOs, the Condon Report, declared that nothing of value would be gained through any further scientific studies of UFOs, subsequent examinations of the phenomenon have suggested that the reverse may be true. Indeed, later re-examinations of the Condon Report found evidence to suggest it may not have been as unbiased as needed and that many of its researchers and investigators thought some UFO reports were puzzling.

Regardless of the outcome of the Condon controversy, some inarguable facts remain concerning the UFO phenomenon that imply that science has been remiss by not paying more attention. Various surveys and polls have shown that a significant percentage of the population has seen UFOs. A recent poll of Canadians found that nearly 10 percent of those surveyed said they had seen a UFO.[1] Nationally, this value represents as much as 3 million UFO witnesses. Polls have shown the percentage is similar in the United States; European countries are thought to have identical numbers. What is most interesting is that although the percentage has waxed and waned over the last fifty years, it's never gone away entirely. Either there is a real physical phenomenon being observed by tens of thousands of people each year or there is something causing people to *think* they have seen UFOs.

If UFOs are not a physical phenomenon, then they are at the very least a psychological or sociological phenomenon. In either case, they obviously are deserving of scientific study. People *do* report seeing unusual objects in the sky. People *are* claiming they have been abducted by aliens.

It does not matter that science rejects such stories. What is important is that UFOs are continually being reported by sincere individuals. There are still many legitimate scientific questions that could be asked. Why do people see UFOs? How prevalent is the belief in their existence? Who holds it? Is it affecting families, causing trauma, job loss, and stress? Are there geographical areas more prone to the phenomenon than others? Are there environmental factors that may make you hallucinate a UFO experience? Is it possible that some UFO reports are of extraterrestrial craft? Why haven't UFO reports simply gone away?

CHAPTER FORTY-THREE
UFOS AND ALIEN ABDUCTIONS

CHRIS RUTKOWSKI

Many books and articles have been published since the late eighties regarding the alleged abduction of people by space aliens. The abduction "phenomenon" began with the appearance of early books such as *Communion* by Whitley Strieber and *Intruders* by Budd Hopkins. After these were published, both writers were on television talk shows discussing their theories, and *OMNI* magazine even conducted a readers' survey to find out how many people have had their own such experiences. There is some evidence to indicate that many hundreds of people believe that they have had abduction experiences, with stories ranging from visitations in witnesses' homes to the actual transporting of witnesses to places that are literally "out of this world."

The first alleged UFO abduction studied in great detail occurred in 1961. Barney and Betty Hill were driving home from a vacation in Canada and were travelling through the White Mountains of New Hampshire when they saw a strange light in the sky. Barney stopped the car to observe it better, and as they looked at it he thought he could see details on the object hovering in the sky. They continued on homeward, but at one point they both heard an odd beeping sound. Shortly, they realized that it had taken them longer than expected to reach their destination and were missing about two hours from their journey.

Later, Betty started having nightmares and dreams about the experience, and she shared her memories of the dreams with her husband.

Eventually they sought marital counselling for their disturbed sleep and the stress that accompanied the intense dreams. They were interviewed and hypnotized by Dr. Benjamin Simon, who conducted several independent sessions with each of them. Through hypnosis, an incredible story of their abduction aboard a strange craft and their examination by grey-skinned aliens was revealed. Although it has never been fully resolved whether their experience was real or was simply a series of very vivid dreams, the publication of a book about the case sparked an interest in the possibility that extraterrestrials are studying humans as "guinea pigs."[1]

Since then, many other abduction stories have been brought to public attention. In 1975, Travis Walton was working on a logging crew in Northern Arizona when he and several of his co-workers saw a disc-shaped craft hovering over some trees at the side of a road. Travis went over to the object to get a better look and was "zapped" by a strange beam of light emanating from it. His frightened companions drove off in their haste to escape but came back a short while later to retrieve Travis. However, he and the strange object were nowhere to be found. He was missing for several days and finally showed up in a dazed state not far from where he was last seen. His memories were fragmented, but he eventually "remembered" a bizarre encounter after waking up on board a large spacecraft and confronting small creatures with bulbous heads.[2]

A different kind of creature was blamed for an incident in Pascagoula, Mississippi, in 1973. Charles Hickson and Calvin Parker were out fishing very late at night when a large UFO appeared behind them. Out of it came what appeared to be silver robots that floated towards the two men, grabbed them with pincer-like hands, and took them on board the saucer. The men were examined with unusual mechanical devices, then released.[3]

A little closer to home, Mrs. Sandra Larson, her daughter, and a friend were driving to Bismarck, North Dakota, one morning in 1975 and had a classic abduction experience. After seeing a UFO approach their car, they all had apparent memory lapses and suddenly found themselves sitting in their car off the road. Under hypnosis, a detailed story of Sandra's abduction by alien creatures and her medical probing on an alien operating table inside the UFO was described.[4]

These are only a few of the many cases that have been written up in books and magazines over the past few decades. In several volumes, Whitley Strieber described his own series of abduction experiences, and his work and that of others has served to popularize the phenomenon with an alarming effect on the populace.[5]

Hundreds of people have come forward with claims of their own abductions, and investigators are trying to deal with this new aspect of ufology as best they can. Although some psychologists are convinced that abductions are a psychological reaction to personal problems, others, especially those who have studied a large number of such cases, do not believe that the abduction phenomenon can be so easily resolved.

There is no consensus about what causes these memories of abduction experiences. Some researchers insist that witnesses are actually encountering alien beings, while others suggest that the abduction experiences are nothing more than very vivid dreams. But even if they are dreams, the traumas associated with these experiences seem to indicate that the witnesses/victims are having particularly strange psychological reactions to something in their lives or their environment. And, since most abductees are declared otherwise normal by psychologists, then what mental process could be at work?[6]

Regardless of the reality of abduction experiences, it is obvious that something unusual is being reported and should be studied in detail. A number of decades ago, UFO investigators would often ignore reports of creatures associated with sightings of flying saucers. This was because the observation of aliens was deemed too bizarre, even for UFO enthusiasts, already facing a negative image or stigma from biased news stories that poked fun at UFO witnesses. Over the years, however, the acceptance of entities associated with UFOs has become the norm, and more attention is given to such cases. Statistically, very few UFO reports have associated entities, although when considering the hundreds of thousands of UFO cases now on record, the number of entity cases is not insignificant. Even in Canada, creatures have occasionally been reported with UFOs, though such cases are definitely rare.

Over the past few years, there has been a strong interest in abduction stories, perhaps the next step beyond mere contact with aliens. In general, if we are under observation by extraterrestrials, then the infrequent examination of a "guinea pig" is not a totally implausible scenario. Unfortunately, there has never been any incontestable physical evidence to support claims of such contact, leading to the basic problem of the acceptance of UFOs by the scientific community. No one has emerged from an abduction experience with an alien artifact: a Martian fountain pen, a Rigelian cookbook, or a Tritonian thumbtack. At least, nothing that has stood up under intense scrutiny.

Until such time as verifiable proof of alien visitation is accepted by the populace we are left with a volume of cases that are suggestive of space entities in our midst and with a fascinating body of stories that are said to be true tales of alien encounters. Skeptics insist that they are imaginary events, but to those who are witnesses or victims of the strange phenomena, they are as real as anything else in life.

Canadian UFO Abduction Stories

Many Canadian UFO cases have some elements of the abduction phenomenon, enough that they can be considered candidates for inclusion in this broad category. However, we must make a distinction between abductees and contactees. The former are UFO witnesses who believe they have had a contact experience with alien beings, though their recall of the event may be partially obscured. Sometimes hypnosis is used to enhance recall of the event, though its use in abduction regressions is being contested by skeptics. Contactees, in slight contrast, believe that not only have they had a contact experience, they feel compelled to tell the world of their meeting with aliens. Often, contactees say they were instructed by the aliens to warn us Earthlings of the consequences of our ignorant habits such as war, pollution, and secularity. Abductees generally do not have such missions and in fact shy away from public exposure to the point that they request anonymity at all costs.

One of the first popularized Canadian abductions was that of the Armstrong family of Ontario. Ufology author David Haisell painstakingly detailed his investigation of their case in a 1978 book that received wide circulation.[7] Gerry Armstrong mysteriously lost seven hours of his life while in his native England, and during the course of twenty-five years he and his family were the focus of many unusual experiences on two continents. Gerry and his wife were periodically subjected to strange beams of light from UFOs, strange noises and apparitions, and even encounters with their doppelgangers. On one occasion, Gerry found himself in Niagara Falls without knowing how he got there and on another drove 150 miles home in less than one hour. Haisell had been doing a radio talk show about UFOs, and Armstrong's call for help sent Haisell into a year-long investigative journey that led him to Jackson's Point, Don Mills, and other Ontario locations.

One of the most celebrated Manitoba UFO witnesses was Stefan Michalak. He was given a barrage of psychological tests at the prestigious Mayo Clinic in the United States and was found to be in excellent psychological health, despite his claims of contact with a physical craft of unknown origin and of hearing strange voices emanating from within. Michalak was neither a contactee nor an abductee, as he did not claim any direct contact with aliens. His opinion, in fact, was that he was a victim of an accident during a test of an American secret aircraft design.

But a contactee group called Mark Age claimed it had additional knowledge about Michalak's experience. Very similar to the groups that today receive channelled messages as part of their so-called New Age teachings, Mark Age's purpose is to warn mankind of the coming end time, and to encourage the spiritual "tuning-in" of our civilization (if that were possible). The group publishes books and newsletters relating information channelled to its members from the "Space Brothers," commenting on everything from politics to scientific developments.

In a 1968 book discussing UFOs titled *Visitors From Other Planets*, an alien emissary named Tukari described what really happened to Steve Michalak: "He came into contact with one of the scout ships, remotely controlled for the 'Operation Show Man' project. It was not the intention for him to be burned. It was not exposed purposely for his sighting. We were in the process of distilling some minerals in that area for future works in healing and contact work on the physical apparatus of mankind..."[8]

And as for Michalak's physical welfare, Tukari wrote that "he must get assistance ... to counteract the radiation exposure. First of all, he should burn or bury all clothing and metal objects which he had when in contact with the ship, and within a radius of four kilometers then. These retain the vibrational force emitted from the ship at the time of departure; which was an emergency plan, and not our usual exhaust."[9]

Operation Show Man was one of many projects Mark Age claimed are undertaken by the Space Brothers to make us aware of their presence through spiritual preparation. As powerful and omniscient as the aliens appear to be, their accidental injuring of Stefan Michalak shows that they are not infallible. (For the record, Michalak's burns were determined to be chemical in nature and not from radiation, and the possibility of tampering with the site by persons unknown has not been totally ruled out. Michalak's sincerity appears to suggest that a very unusual event occurred that afternoon at Falcon Lake, but we are still at a loss to fully explain what happened.)

An example of a contactee is a woman I shall call "V." In 1977 I was interviewed on a local television show about a series of UFO reports I had investigated in southern Manitoba. That evening, I received a telephone call from a woman in a northern Manitoba community. This person, V, explained that she had intimate knowledge of aliens and their spacecraft and that she spoke to the Space Brothers twice a week. She wanted to know if my associates and I would be interesting in having her lecture to us on her experiences. At the time, UFOROM was in its infancy, and although the members of the group were not yet fully defined, I was in touch with many people who were seriously interested in UFOs. I thought the group would be interested in hearing from V, regardless of what she had to say, so I agreed that she could come and talk to us. In fact, she said she was so anxious to speak with us that she would leave the next morning on the long journey south to Winnipeg.

I quickly called my friends, and about twenty of us gathered the next day in my small apartment. Finally, she arrived with her husband, and they brought in pamphlets, books, photographs, and a small movie projector. Her husband elected to sit on the steps of the apartment block rather than go inside (because he had heard it all before, he said). And V began her soliloquy: "I died when I was six years old, but I rose up again on the third day. I soon found that I could talk to the insects and animals."[10]

V went on to describe how she felt she was psychically gifted, and she began her contact with benevolent space beings at an early age. The Space Brothers took her to other planets and even inside the Earth through holes in the North and South Poles. Her station wagon was "teleported" while she was on a long road trip, and she proudly showed off the burn marks on her car (though they looked remarkably like rust). She lived part of the year in the Maritimes, where she had a large, church-like congregation of followers. She would often hold religious ceremonies in fields where scout ships had landed, encouraging others to tune in to the spiritual guidance of the Space Brothers. Her group built a pyramid in the middle of a field in Nova Scotia and would sit inside so that spiritual energy could be better focused upon themselves in meditation. At one point, V told us that she had been given a vision by these entities that she should hit the ground with a rod at a certain location (with a definite resemblance to a Biblical story) and a well would be created. According to her testimony, she did so, and water did spring forth; this water was used by her to heal the sick, to cause the blind to see and the lame to walk.

At the same time, it was easy to see the undercurrents of emotional reaction to her "teachings." V told us that she and some others had watched a scout ship land on a hilltop near their residence in Nova Scotia, and the next morning, a cross-shaped patch of burned grass was visible. She declared the site "holy," and it was immediately roped off. Soon religious pilgrimages were made to the venerated landing pad. But some local residents thought the whole thing rather silly and tried to use a bulldozer to get the worshippers off the site. V's group protested by lying in front of the bulldozer, and the attempt was halted. V told us that a few days later, however, the bodies of those trying to demolish the sacred site were found in a lake, as evidence that one must not tamper with the will of the Space Brothers.

In 1978, John Musgrave, a UFO researcher in Alberta, corresponded with a woman from a small town in southern Manitoba. She had been referred to him through the Center for UFO Studies in Illinois, which she had originally contacted, and they had sent her letter on to John, who was then their most active Canadian contact. But after some consideration of her case, John realized that the distance separating them was too great to be practical, so when he came to Winnipeg on a visit he passed on her letters to the most active Manitoban investigator — namely, me.

Mrs. W, as I choose to call her, had a very unusual series of contact experiences over the previous several years. She claimed that she could nearly always see dozens of spacecraft over her house, and what is more, she could see the planets that they were flying to and from throughout the night. She drew many charts of the courses of the spacecraft, with large round circles representing either the UFOs or the planets (I could never tell which). She felt obligated to pass on her observations to UFO investigators and was immensely relieved to learn of a researcher here in her own province. She wrote me several times, inviting me to come to her house to discuss the matter with her. She was further excited about my being an astronomer, for that meant there was twice as much to interest me in her experiences.

It was quite plain to me that her interpretation of her observations was somewhat eccentric. But in her letters she appeared to be a very sweet, elderly woman with a special need in her life to have someone like me talk to her about her experiences. Over several months, I sent her reassuring letters in the hope that I could eventually get her to make more and more rational observations as our correspondence continued. I think it was at this point that I realized a UFO investigator is more like a counsellor or a social worker than a criminologist, as it might seem to the uninitiated.

When I was just starting to get involved in ufology as a teenager, tracking down the identity of UFOs seemed very uncomplicated. A report would come in, get investigated, and I'd find out what had been seen, if I could identify the mystery object. But a UFO investigator does not investigate UFOs; a ufologist studies UFO reports, which is a different matter entirely. A UFO report is made by a witness whose observational capabilities are affected by many things: emotions, attitudes, biases, preconceived notions, religion, etc. These are, of course, apart from the physical problems associated with UFO sightings, like perceptual distortions, mirages, optical illusions, and whatnot. A UFO investigator, therefore, is much like a humanistic behavioural psychologist and deals with the public as would an urban anthropologist.

I never did meet Mrs. W, though I did attempt to do so. It happened that I and another of my ufology associates were invited to speak at a meeting some distance away from Winnipeg, and our route passed close to Mrs. W's town. So, on our way there, we dropped by her house. There was nobody home, so I left a letter in her mailbox and we continued on our way. When we arrived back home after our trip, there was a letter from her already waiting for me. But she wasn't at home anymore. Her husband, of whom she had never spoken highly in her letters to me and who did not share her observations of spacecraft, had committed her to a psychiatric institution. Her letter to me was quite plaintive: "Please tell the doctors that I really am seeing these UFOs, and that I am not crazy." Fortunately, the hospital sent her home after a few days and she was put in a home-care program of counselling. She soon ceased seeing UFOs by the hundreds.

On January 26, 1988, Stanton Friedman gave a talk at the University of Manitoba on the subject of UFOs. Stanton is a nuclear physicist and has worked throughout North America on a number of projects, including nuclear rocket engines and irradiation technology. Formerly of California, he currently lives with his family in New Brunswick and travels around the continent lecturing to schools and colleges. He is one of the most (if not the most) knowledgeable experts on the cover-up of UFO information by several world governments, especially the United States. He has spent hundreds of hours in archives and libraries, uncovering documents that seem to suggest that high-level government or military officials have been withholding information or otherwise misleading the public about the nature of UFOs.

Stanton's evening lecture was well attended (he had earlier been interviewed on both radio and TV), and the crowd of about three hundred people was enraptured by his presentation. At the close of his talk, he introduced me and indicated that I could be approached by anyone wishing to talk later about UFOs. The crowd dispersed, with the exception of a few stragglers who wanted to ask Stanton about some specific UFO cases. I put on my coat and began gathering up my notes, getting ready to go home and unwind after a hectic day. Then I noticed a man hesitantly edging his way towards me. When he had finally wound his way through the empty rows of chairs, he called softly to me. "Could you call me to arrange a time when we can meet privately?" he asked.

His nervousness showed me that he probably had a UFO experience of some sort and that he was very reluctant to tell anyone about it. I reassured him that his conversation with me would be in confidence and that I was sincere in my willingness to listen to his story. He briefly described his experience but said that he would go into detail when we met in person later. When we did meet, I was intrigued to learn that he'd had a classic abduction experience or visitation by some sort of entity in his home. There is of course no physical evidence to support the experience he claims to have had, but he is sure that it did happen, and we must at least accept the position that something happened to him to create a memory of the event. As with many UFO abductees, he seemed to have a history of such experiences throughout his life. He has rarely talked with his friends or family about the incidents and has been worried about their reactions should he reveal his experiences to them.

The most vivid of his memories originated from a night during the middle of November 1987. He was in his bedroom, preparing to go to sleep. He had been thinking about the day's events and had been meditating. He got into bed with the lights out and lay on his back starting to drift off to sleep. After a while, he became aware of a presence in his room that seemed to be in the vicinity of his closet. Almost simultaneously, he felt a peculiar tingling sensation in his body. He was surprised to realize that he was paralyzed and unable to move in any way except to rotate his eyes. He felt that the presence was somehow responsible and that it was approaching his bed.[11]

Although he couldn't recall seeing the entity in its entirety, he did have the distinct recollection of seeing a face not more than a foot in front of his eyes. He drew this face without much difficulty, depicting a cherubic character with skin folds, slit-like eyes and a thin mouth, and wearing some sort of tight-fitting helmet. He also felt that something touched his mind and that images of things he had seen in his life were brought to the surface of his mind and taken from him. He remembers feeling or sensing that whatever was doing this to him was also reassuring him that it meant no harm and that it only wanted certain things from his memory. After a while, the flashes of his past life ceased, the entity seemed to withdraw, and sensation returned to his body. He admitted he was extremely disturbed by this incident.

This was only the most recent of a series of strange events that had occurred throughout his life. He had experienced similar paralytic episodes before, each associated with some out-of-body flight, and on one occasion had seen a UFO radiating pulses of light as if it was signalling to him. And in 1987, he and other members of his family had witnessed some nocturnal light UFOs moving over fields near their house.

Common to many published accounts of alleged UFO abductions is the hypnosis of the abductees, by which they are regressed to the time of the incident in order to uncover suppressed or hidden facts. Sometimes, details of medical examinations on board spacecraft are revealed, or trips with beings from other planets. From a psychological standpoint, hypnotic regressions are sometimes useful as therapy to uncover suppressed feelings or remove mental blocks. Some ufologists use hypnotic regressions to penetrate the witnesses' memories of their experiences, which may have been deliberately clouded by their antagonists. Skeptics note that hypnosis cannot determine the truth of any memory, but instead allow a person's own beliefs to come through, whether they are true or not. That is, if a person believes he or she has been on board a UFO, even if they have not, then their story will still be told under hypnosis. Hypnosis cannot be used to accurately distinguish between fact and fantasy.

Knowing these limitations, it was nevertheless decided to have this abductee, whom I shall call "Dave," be evaluated by a professional psychologist who used hypnosis as part of therapy. Dave agreed to sessions with the psychologist, and the results were interesting.

Under hypnosis, Dave described his experience of the previous November. Some details were added to the account. He now recalled seeing the entire body of the entity that visited him in his bedroom and expressed a great deal of fear as it progressed towards him. In its hand was a rod with a light on the end. When the lighted end touched Dave's forehead, he relived an acutely painful or otherwise traumatic sensation, even while hypnotized, to the point where the clinician had some difficulty in regaining control of his subject.

In his later evaluation of the witness, the clinical psychologist expressed his opinion that Dave had not been abducted aboard a spacecraft, nor had he actually been visited by a strange entity. Instead, he concluded that judging from the way Dave had acted under hypnosis and his reactions to suggestions and questions, he felt that Dave had more likely experienced a very realistic hypnogogic dream that for some reason caused him a great deal of trauma. This type of dream occurs just as we are falling asleep and we are in a very relaxed state, rendering us susceptible to spurious information from our senses. A tingling sensation, for example, is very common during self-hypnosis, as is a feeling of paralysis, and these could be produced by meditation or quiet thought.

Did Dave have a visit from an extraterrestrial entity or did he have a vivid dream? Even today, he believes that he was contacted and that he is still under observation by something or someone. Without physical proof, contact by UFO entities is extremely difficult to prove. Skeptics dismiss such claims, but believers point out that selective observation and sampling is a logical method of contact with new civilizations by anthropologists.[12]

During the summer of 1977, Tim was camping along the shore of Pelicanpouch Lake, near Minaki, Ontario, not far from the Manitoba border. On August 7, 1977, he was relaxing as his campfire burned down and was gazing at the stars. It was becoming cloudy, and after a while, around 10:30 p.m., he went to sleep. He remembered going to sleep on his left side, curled up in his sleeping bag in his tent. He was awakened what he thought was a few hours later by an unusual noise outside his tent. It was a low throbbing or humming sound, and he turned over onto his back to listen to it and determine where it was coming from. When he was on his back, he became aware of another sound: a high-pitched whine that was somewhat painful to his ears. Simultaneously, he felt a burning sensation over his body, "like tiny, hot suction cups." He felt somewhat paralyzed but looked to his right and left with the movement of his eyes and saw a diffuse light coming under the flaps of his tent. He thought this was odd, since he realized that it was also raining, and if this was so, it should have been pitch black outside because his campsite was in an isolated location. But this light enabled him to see the orange colour of his tent quite clearly.

After two or three minutes, the high-pitched noise and heat suddenly stopped, but the original humming continued. Shortly, the volume and pitch of the sound changed, suggesting that its source was moving first away from him and then in an arc in front of his tent. He briefly heard the high-pitched whine again, then it stopped and the original humming seemed to move away and faded from audibility. Tim lay awake for several minutes after this but then went back to sleep.

He thought that some object, perhaps a UFO, had been searching for something in the area by playing a searchlight over the ground. He claimed that he had an unusual string of good luck after his experience and that he felt very aware of sounds in the environment ever since. But a week or so later, back in his home, Tim had another odd experience. It again took place in the evening at bedtime. As he drifted off to sleep, he could hear children playing outside his house. He began dreaming and felt that he could hear the high-pitched sound he had heard in the bush. He then dreamed he could hear metallic-sounding footsteps approaching his bedroom. He saw a small humanoid figure appear on the other side of the room. It was about 5.5 feet tall, with blonde, shoulder-length hair. Though he could not remember its lower portion, it appeared to be wearing a brownish tunic. He could not recall anything about its face.

As the entity came nearer, Tim dreamed that he yelled to the thing to turn on the lights, as he was afraid. In response, the entity reached and flicked on the light switch, but it did not work. The creature came up to Tim's bedside, leaned over him, and put something into his aural canal. At this point, Tim woke up, quite panicky and with a fear that "they" were coming to get him. He had fleeting thoughts of being inside a spaceship but could not remember any details. He also said that during the dream, he was paralyzed (a theme in abductee stories) but could still hear the voices of the children playing outside his house. When he woke from the dream, he could still hear the children as they finished their play and were heading for bed.[13]

Another well-documented and investigated Canadian abduction case occurred in and around Kelowna, British Columbia. The two women involved have now gone public with their account, and one has in fact initiated an abductee support group in the Okanagan Valley. Both women have been labouring with their memories of their experiences, and their coping efforts are ongoing. Their initial UFO encounter appears to be corroborated by a another couple who watched a UFO hovering near where theirs occurred.[14]

Shortly after midnight on July 31, 2003, the two women had been surfing the Internet for a while and decided to take a break. One suggested they drive to a dark spot and do some stargazing, so they got into a car and drove towards Glenmore. Though there had been a considerable amount of traffic on the highway, when they stopped to do their sky watching, the traffic was gone — no lights from any vehicles at all.

As in previous sky-watching trips, one woman shone a flashlight into the sky while the other used binoculars to scan the heavens. Suddenly, three white stars in the sky moved to create a triangular formation and began moving as one unit. They watched the trio glide silently in front of the car, changing to neon green as it flew, and the women thought it was an aircraft of some kind. Then, unexpectedly, the object stopped and hovered just ahead of their car.

They turned the headlights off and shone their flashlight on the road in front of the car. The beam was reflected back from five sets of eyes staring at them from about forty feet away. They initially thought they were cougars but then realized the eyes were on creatures about four feet tall, dark grey in colour, and moving slowly and menacingly towards them. Terrified, they tried to get back into the car but felt as if they were moving through quicksand and as if everything was slowing down.

Finally back in the car, they found its electrical system was going berserk, with the dome light and headlights turning on and off on their own. They managed to start the car and sped off towards home. As they drove, they both felt their bodies tingling, as if they were full of static electricity. They then realized that while it had seemed they were watching the creatures outside the car for only a few minutes, almost half an hour had elapsed.

When they were nearing their home, they turned onto a dark street along a grassy field. They saw another glowing neon green ball flying low over the field, travelling in jerky movements, and then it suddenly flew quickly towards them. It hovered high above their car, but they sped off quickly again and drove into a dark orchard to hide among the trees. From their seemingly safe retreat, they watched as the original single green ball of light was joined by two others moving together in a triangular formation and then they split apart and flew off in different directions. When the lights were gone, they started the car and drove home.

Back in the house, shaken by their experience, it took them a long time to fall asleep. In the morning, one woman discovered a large painful bruise on her left breast and another on the bottom of her foot. The other had a large circular burn on her lower back near her tailbone and had a brief nosebleed. Consulting their physicians, one doctor gave his opinion that the burn near the tailbone looked like a radiation burn.

On the same night the women's experience took place, another couple who couldn't sleep also decided to go out in the evening. They also observed a bright, glowing neon green light moving irregularly in the night sky, very near where the women had been stopped in the orchard, apparently confirming the women's story. And on this same date, nearly 150 separate witnesses observed a series of unusual UFOs flying over the Okanagan, part of a large number of cases that were recorded between July 27 and August 18, 2003.

Both women continued to have odd experiences that they believe to be related to their original encounter and were convinced that contact with aliens of some kind had occurred.

CHAPTER FORTY-FOUR
THE CANADIAN UFO SURVEY

GEOFF DITTMAN

Many books and television documentaries about UFOs focus entirely on alleged alien abductions. Yet abduction cases actually comprise a very tiny fraction of the bulk of UFO data. The bread and butter of UFO research lies not in fanciful discourses about aliens' genetic manipulation of humans but in what UFO witnesses are actually seeing and reporting. With that in mind, since 1989 the authors have been soliciting UFO case data from all known and active researchers in Canada. Our goal has been to provide data for use by researchers as they try to understand this controversial phenomenon.[1]

Why bother to collect UFO reports? In general, the public equates UFOs with alien visitation. However, there is no incontrovertible proof that there is a real connection. In order to determine if there might be signs of extraterrestrial contact, research on the actual characteristics of UFO reports is needed. If one wants to know what people are really seeing in the skies, the answer lies within the reports. To get a feel of what is being seen, we ask participants to provide us with information on certain key characteristics that correspond with data fields in the Canadian UFO Survey database. These fields are:

- the YEAR for the report
- the MONTH of the incident
- the DATE of the sighting
- the local TIME, on the twenty-four-hour clock

- the geographical LOCATION of the incident
- the PROVINCE where the sighting occurred
- the TYPE of report, using the Modified Hynek Classification System
- the DURATION of the sighting, in seconds (a value of six hundred thus represents ten minutes)
- the primary COLOUR of the object(s) seen
- the number of WITNESSES
- the SHAPE of the object(s) seen
- the STRANGENESS of the report
- the RELIABILITY of the report
- the SOURCE of the report
- the EVALUATION of the case
- COMMENTS noted about the case

We feel these are the most basic characteristics of sightings that will allow us to make a reasonable judgement in determining if the report has an easy explanation or if it is truly unexplainable given our current knowledge. Many UFO research groups ask for much more information from their witnesses. We have found, however, that often witnesses are reluctant to take the extra time required to fill out such detailed reports. Furthermore, the additional information is often of limited use, there being a sort of law of diminishing returns on the amount of information in UFO reports. Inputting into the database information such as how clear the sky was at the time of the sighting would prove to be a very time-consuming process.

Unfortunately, obtaining even this limited amount of information from researchers has proven to be a bit of a challenge. Many individuals, associations, clubs, and groups claim to investigate UFO reports. Many solicit reports from the general public. However, it is now known that only a small fraction of active ufologists and self-proclaimed researchers actually investigate cases *and* maintain useable records. Some researchers do not retain quantitative criteria in their investigations (contactee groups, for example). Comparatively few actually participate in any kind of information sharing or data gathering for scientific programs. Some are primarily special interest groups based in museums, planetariums, church basements, or individuals' homes and do essentially *nothing* with the sighting reports they receive.

An added problem is the rapid increase in the number of individuals collecting UFO cases through the Internet. Every few days, it seems, another website is announced, heralding yet another location for witnesses to report and record their sightings from around the world. Tracking down all UFO cases from a given geographical region is therefore a very time-consuming process.

UFOs and IFOs

For the survey, the working definition of a UFO is *an object seen in the sky that its observer cannot identify.*

Studies of UFO data routinely include reports of meteors, fireballs, and other conventional objects. In many instances, observers fail to recognize stars, aircraft, and bolides, and therefore report them as UFOs. Witnesses often report watching stationary flashing lights low on the horizon for hours and never conclude that they are observing a star or planet.

Some UFO investigators spend many hours sorting IFOs (Identified Flying Objects) from UFOs. Historically, analyses of UFO data such as the U.S. Air Force projects Grudge, Sign, and Blue Book all included raw data that later were resolved into categories of UFOs and IFOs. Sometimes, observed objects are quickly assigned a particular IFO explanation even though later investigation suggests that such an explanation was unwarranted. The reverse is also true.

The issue of including IFOs in studies of UFO data is an important one. One could argue that once a sighting is explained, it has no reason to be considered as a UFO report. However, this overlooks the fact that the IFO was originally reported as a UFO and is indeed valid data. It may not be evidence of extraterrestrial visitation, but as UFO data it is quite useful. It must be remembered that all major previous studies of UFOs examined UFO reports with the intent to explain a certain percentage of cases. These cases were the IFOs and are definitely part of the UFO report legacy.

IFOs are problematic in that they are not interesting to most ufologists. In fact, some UFO investigators readily admit they do not record details about UFO reports that seem easily explained as ordinary objects. This may be a serious error. The UFO witness may be conscientiously reporting an object that is mysterious to him or her (the exact definition of a UFO). Therefore, even anonymous late-night telephone calls that are obviously reports of airplanes or planets should be rightly logged as UFO reports. It seems reasonable that all

UFO reports be included in statistical databases and in later studies on the phenomenon, regardless of the cases' later reclassification as IFOs.

The fact that most UFO reports can be explained and reclassified as IFOs attests to the reality of the objects seen. UFO reports actually reflect *real* events. When a UFO is reported, a *real object* has been seen that was not just a fantasy of witnesses' imagination.

Because there is no way to enforce standards in UFO report investigations, the quality of case investigations varies considerably between groups and across provinces. Quantitative studies are difficult because subjective evaluations and differences in investigative techniques do not allow precise comparisons. UFOROM's requests for data from Canadian UFO researchers and investigators include only basic information that can be used in rigorous analyses. This includes things such as date and time of the sighting, duration, number of witnesses, and location. These are facts that are not subjective and can be used in scientific studies before interpretation.

For the purposes of this and other scientific studies of UFO data, UFO sightings that have been made to recognized contributing and participating groups, associations, organizations, or individuals are considered *officially* reported and valid as data in this study. The collection of Canadian UFO data is challenging. However, the data obtained for analysis yields results that can be compared with other studies. This is useful in understanding the nature of UFO reports not only in Canada but also elsewhere in the world.

UFO Reports in Canada

Since we began the survey in 1989, the number of reports has varied from year to year. It has gone from a low of 141 reports in 1989 up to a high of 882 cases in 2004. The annual totals have generally been slowly but steadily increasing over time. From 1998 onwards, the increases in cases from year to year have been escalating, and during the past ten years, between 1994 and 2004, there has been a more than 380 percent increase in the number of UFOs reported annually. The year 2003 alone saw a 39 percent increase over 2002. This increase contradicts comments by some in the media who would assert that UFOs are a passing fad or that the number of UFO sightings is decreasing. In fact, since media coverage of UFOs has decreased in recent years, it is striking that even without media stimuli, UFO sightings are being reported in greater numbers.

The following table shows the numbers of reported UFOs per year since 1989.

Year	Number of cases	Cumulative total
1989	141	141
1990	194	335
1991	165	500
1992	223	723
1993	489	1,212
1994	189	1,401
1995	183	1,584
1996	258	1,842
1997	284	2,126
1998	194	2,320
1999	259	2,579
2000	263	2,842
2001	374	3,216
2002	483	3,699
2003	673	4,372
2004	882	5,254

What can explain this significant increase in UFO reports over the years? Traditionally researchers have believed that only about 10 percent of sightings are reported to researchers or the government.[2] But the percentage of sightings reported might be increasing. With the rising popularity of the Internet since the mid-nineties, it has become easier for UFO witnesses to track down investigators to whom sightings can be reported. Furthermore, it has become easier for said researchers to distribute those reports to colleagues across the country. Whereas in the past one of the authors has had to at times plead with researchers to participate in the study, now it has become as simple as surfing the Web. All one has to do is locate the appropriate websites and download the report information. The rise of email discussion lists, including one devoted to Canadian UFO reports run by one of the authors, has also contributed to the ease in collecting reports. The number of sightings collected for the Canadian UFO Survey is dependent on the ease with which we are able to gather the reports, and in some ways it has become much simpler now to find the reports than it has been in the past.

Another factor contributing to the increase in sightings is the participation of the federal government. Several departments, including the

Department of National Defence and Transport Canada, have agreed to forward any UFO reports they receive to Ufology Research of Manitoba for inclusion in the annual survey.

This increase has been partially offset by several factors. For years, many UFO reports came from the National Research Council of Canada (NRC), which routinely collected UFO reports from private citizens, RCMP, civic police, and other sources. This collection of data was in support of the NRC's interest in the retrieval of meteorites. This practice, however, came to an end in 1995 as a result of budgetary restrictions and the lowered prioritization of meteoric research. The shutting down of this collection has undoubtedly resulted in the loss of many UFO reports.

Further hindering the collection of UFO reports has been the seemingly constant infighting amongst UFO researchers in Canada. There has been much bad blood not only between groups but even within groups as well, resulting in the fracturing of organizations. This has made it difficult to keep track of researchers and any reports they might have. Such conflict also seemingly makes it difficult at times to obtain researchers' agreement to participate in the survey. Furthermore, researchers are often transient. People often come to ufology determined to get to the bottom of it all, only to get bogged down by the large amount of inconclusive evidence. As British ufologist Jenny Randles has noted, in the beginning, many researchers get a sense of excitement from studying UFO reports. The solution to the problem is just around the corner. After a while, though, all cases begin to seem the same. A sense of monotony takes over, and researchers begin to feel they are wasting their time. The answers will never come.[3] Just when researchers begin to become experienced enough to add value to the subject, they grow frustrated with the lack of progress and drop out of the scene, resulting in a vacuum of research. It is not uncommon for there to be no active researchers in an entire province for several years at a time.

Then of course there is the fact that for all UFO researchers in Canada, collecting UFO reports is only a voluntary pastime, subject to changes in lifestyle and financial situations. One cannot make a living researching UFO sightings, and therefore researchers are limited in their investigations by both time and money. Family and career regularly get in the way, resulting in UFO sightings either being missed or not properly researched.

Analysis of UFO Reports

Despite these difficulties, UFO reports are not only continuing but also increasing year after year. This has resulted in a wealth of case data for us to use in our analysis. For the most part, our analysis of the data has been limited to elementary counts, for example, the number of cases with three witnesses, how many reports were made in February, etc. Periodically, more detailed statistical analysis has been done, for example, chi-square analysis. But generally it has been found that little of value has come from such work. This is partially due to limited sample size, which will become less and less of an issue as the database grows with time. For now, however, our analysis has generally been more basic.

Distribution of UFO Reports Across Canada

Analysis of UFO reports by province yielded results somewhat similar to those of international studies. Several European researchers have suggested that there is an inverse relationship of UFO reports to population. In other words, UFOs tend to be reported in greater numbers per capita in areas with low population density than in high-population centres. The Swedish organization Archives for UFO Research did a sophisticated study breaking down their 327 case reports by Sweden's twenty-three political divisions. They first predicted how many sightings each county would have (based on population), assuming the number of sightings would be directly correlated to the number of people living in the region. That is, they assumed that the greater the number of people, the greater the number of sightings. They then compared this estimated number to the actual number of sightings. What they found was that there was more of an inverse relationship. Some 25 percent of the sightings came from the less populated northern divisions, which account for only about 15 percent of the population. Similarly the more populated south had many fewer reports than was expected.[4]

In another study, researchers Dr. Jacques Vallee and Claude Poher found similar results, showing a "pattern of avoidance of population centres."[5] For the purposes of this study the data was examined only at the provincial level, with no attempt made to differentiate in population density any further than that. As such, the results aren't as reliable as those of the Swedish organization. Some Canadian provinces, for example Quebec and British Columbia, have both regions of very high population density and large geographical areas with very few people.

Despite the less detailed examination in our survey, similar results to those of the Swedish study were nonetheless found. Ontario and Quebec, with a population in 2003 of some 19.7 million people, or 62 percent of the national total, had only 32 percent of the total UFO sightings. Similarly, the Yukon, Nunavut, and Northwest Territories, with only 0.32 percent of the national population, accounted for more than 5 percent of the sightings. Significant differences were also found in British Columbia (13 percent of the population versus 34 percent of sightings) and Manitoba (4 percent of the population versus 9 percent of sightings).

It should be noted that the results fluctuate somewhat from year to year. For example, British Columbia has been responsible for as little as 8 percent and as much as 45 percent of the national sightings. But the northern territories have been overrepresented, and Ontario and Quebec have been underrepresented, in most years of the survey.

There are many possible explanations for this finding. One is that the underlying phenomenon tries to avoid population centres. This of course would be expected if it was trying to hide its presence. There are also several more prosaic explanations. How active the UFO groups are in each province is certainly a factor in the number of UFO cases reported each year. One of the largest and most involved groups in the country is located in British Columbia (UFO*BC), which usually has the largest number of UFO sightings in the country. UFO*BC has conducted a relatively aggressive and successful marketing campaign in the province and even set up a telephone hotline for sightings reports. This makes it much more likely that the general public is aware that UFO*BC exists, and it makes it easy for any eyewitnesses to come forward with their reports. In other provinces, which have few if any investigators, the ability of eyewitnesses to report a sighting to a non-government organization is much more difficult.

A confirmation that this is the case is the distribution of UFO reports made to the National UFO Reporting Center (NUFORC) in the United States. NUFORC also has a UFO reporting hotline and is widely recognized in the U.S.A. as a recording centre for UFO reports, although with few staff, its ability to investigate cases is obviously minimal. Though an American organization, NUFORC receives UFO reports from literally all around the world and in fact had 761 Canadian cases reported to it between 1999 and 2004. When we look at the provincial distribution of Canadian cases reported to NUFORC, we see a distribution much more closely related to population. There is now an overrepresentation in Ontario, still an overrepresentation in B.C. and an underrepresentation in Quebec, but the results are close to what is expected for the other ten provinces and territories. Clearly, UFO*BC's telephone hotline and marketing efforts are paying off.

Monthly Trends in UFO Reports

Monthly breakdowns of reports each year tend to show slightly different patterns. For example, in 1999 UFO cases had no clear peaks in monthly report numbers, but the year 2000 saw a very significant set of peaks in August and October and troughs in May and June. UFO reports are generally thought to peak in summer and trough in winter, because of the more pleasant observing conditions during the summer months, when more witnesses are outside. In 2003, a very unusual monthly variation was found. With the exception of a large peak in July and August and a lesser one in October, there was almost a constant level of UFO activity reported throughout the year. The yearly trough in May and June was slightly evident. This is counter-intuitive to the belief that more UFOs are seen when there are more people outside during warmer periods of the year. But in 2004 the summer peak had returned, with the number of sightings peaking in August.

Monthly Report Numbers

Jan.	Feb.	Mar.	Apr.	May	Jun.	Jul.	Aug.	Sep.	Oct.	Nov.	Dec.
402	320	392	381	325	396	599	739	461	548	364	294

Consolidating the data results in a distribution of reports that one would expect, with a clear peak in the summer months and a fairly level trough in the winter months. The fact that the report levels vary considerably from year to year, however, suggests that the number of UFO sighting reports is not directly related to climate. Whatever stimulus causes UFOs to be reported, it is not linked to warmer weather and the increase in the number of potential witnesses outdoors.

UFO Report Types

It became apparent to researchers early on that an accurate means of classifying UFO sightings was required. While several different classifications have been created over the years, one has largely become the de facto standard in ufology. It is known as the Hynek Classification System, after its creator, astronomer J. Allen Hynek. (It is from this classification system that Steven Spielberg's movie *Close Encounters of the Third Kind* got its name. Hynek was in fact a consultant for the movie.) It is a modified Hynek Classification System that was chosen for the Canadian UFO Survey. The classification system is broken down as follows:

- Nocturnal Light (NL) — light source in night sky
- Nocturnal Disc (ND) — light source in night sky that appears to have a definite shape
- Daylight Disc (DD) — unknown object observed during daylight hours
- Close Encounter of the First Kind (C1) — ND or DD occurring within two hundred yards of a witness
- Close Encounter of the Second Kind (C2) — C1 where physical effects are left or noted
- Close Encounter of the Third Kind (C3) — C1 where figures/entities are encountered
- Close Encounter of the Fourth Kind (C4) — an alleged abduction or contact experience

(Note: There are also several other classifications, such as RD for a UFO showing up on radar, that are relatively rare, so for the purposes of this book we have them left out of the analysis.)

An analysis by report type shows a similar breakdown from year to year. The percentage of cases of each type remains roughly constant from year to year, with only minor variations. Nocturnal lights account for some 65 percent of all cases since 1989. Daylight disc reports, on the other hand, are a mere 12 percent. In general, most UFOs are simple lights seen in the night sky, since about 83 percent of all UFO sightings, including both NL and ND cases, occurred at night.

Only about 4 percent of all reported UFO cases were close encounters. Very, very few UFO cases involve anything other than distant objects seen in the sky. This is an important statistic, because the current popular interest in abductions and sensational UFO encounters is based not on the vast majority of UFO cases but on the very tiny fraction of cases that fall into the category of close encounters. The endless speculation of what aliens may or may not be doing in our airspace seems almost completely unconnected to actual UFO reports.

UFO Reports by Type

	NL	ND	DD	C1	C2	C3	C4
#	3,311	998	626	116	52	25	35
%	64	19	12	2	1	1	1

Given the variety of reports, some researchers have looked to statistical analysis to determine whether more than one phenomenon is involved, driving the different kinds of reports. This seems obvious, if one looks at the various solutions for UFO cases found to have natural explanations. Satellites will explain many nocturnal light cases but not any daylight disc or close encounter cases. Nonetheless, several researchers have looked at the distribution of the different kinds of reports based on such things as time of day, duration of the sighting, and the overall strangeness of the sighting. Several ufologists have indicated that they have found significant differences. A preliminary look at the Canadian UFO Survey data, using a simple statistical technique known as chi-square analysis, backs up the claim that unexplained sightings appear to have different underlying characteristics than explained sightings.

Hourly Distribution

This is probably one of the most analyzed UFO statistics. It has been found to be fairly consistent around the world, with a primary peak around 2100 hours and a secondary peak around 0300 hours. The reports die down during the day. Canadian data isn't much different from what's being found elsewhere, although the primary peak is somewhat later, at about 2300 hours. Almost 40 percent of all UFO sightings occur between 2100 hours and midnight. The secondary peak is between 0100 and 0200 hours. The trough is 0900 hours.

What accounts for the large number of sightings during the evening? Since most people work during the day, it only is natural that more people would have free time to be out and about during the evening. And by midnight most people have returned home to sleep, so we would expect observations to decline. Since most UFOs are nocturnal lights, most sightings will occur during the evening hours. Still, one cannot rule out the possibility that it is the phenomenon itself, rather than the viewing habits of witnesses, that is responsible for the larger number of sightings at night.

Duration

The category of duration is interesting in that it represents the *subjective* length of time the UFO experience lasted. In other words, this is the length of time the sighting lasted *as estimated by the witness*. Naturally, these times are greatly suspect because it is known that people tend to badly misjudge the flow of time. However, *some* people can be good at estimating time, so this value has some importance. Although an estimate of one hour may be in error by several minutes, it is unlikely that the true duration would be, for example, one *minute*. Furthermore, there have been cases when a UFO was observed and clocked very accurately, so that we can be reasonably certain that UFO events can last considerable periods of time.

The average duration of a sighting can be calculated as the sum of all given durations divided by the number of cases with a stated duration. This value has varied somewhat, from seven minutes in 1994 to twenty-five minutes in 1996. The total average duration for the cases from 1996 through 2004 is 1,158 seconds, or almost twenty minutes.

The duration of a sighting is one of the biggest clues to its explanation. For example, short duration events are usually fireballs or bolides. Noting this, the U.S. Air Force in its guide to UFO identification indicated, "When the duration of a sighting is less than 15 seconds the probabilities are great that it is not worthy of follow-up.... When a sighting has covered just a few seconds, the incident, when followed up in the past, has almost always proved to be a meteor or a gross mis-identification of a common object owing to lack of time in which to observe."[6]

On the other hand, long duration events of an hour or more are also very likely astronomical objects, usually planets or stars.

Those cases that fall in between very short and very long in duration cannot be defined by duration alone. One study by an Ontario UFO group that timed aircraft observations found that the duration of such sightings varied between fifteen seconds to more than eight minutes. Therefore, sightings with durations in this range could very well be aircraft, providing that other observational data do not contradict such an explanation.

Colour

In cases where witnesses reported a colour of an object, the most common colour was white. The next most common was "multicoloured." Next were orange and red. These results are consistent with other studies, in particular the U.S. Air Force's Project Blue Book. Since most UFOs are nocturnal, starlike objects, the abundance of white objects is not surprising. Colours such as red, orange, blue, and green often are associated with bolides (fireballs).

The "multicoloured" designation is problematic in that it covers a wide range of possibilities. Some studies of UFO data have partitioned the category of colour to include both primary and secondary colours in cases where the observed UFO had more than one colour. The multicoloured label has been used, for example, when witnesses described their UFOs as having white, red, and green lights. (Many of these are certainly stars or planets, which flash a variety of colours when seen low on the horizon. Aircraft are also frequently described as having more than one colour of light.) For our study, the colour classification refers only to the primary colour in the witness's description.

Witnesses

The average number of witnesses per case between 1996 and 2004 is approximately 2.0. This value has fluctuated, reaching as high as 3.1 in 1996 to as low as 1.4 in 1990. When limiting the data to unexplained close encounter cases, the average number of witnesses drops somewhat to 1.7.

This indicates that the typical UFO experience has *more than one witness* and supports the contention that UFO sightings represent observations of real, physical phenomena, since there is usually a corroborator present to support the sighting.

There tends to be more unexplained cases involving multiple witnesses. The average number of witnesses for unexplained cases is 2.23 for the period from 1996 to 2004. Comparing the unexplained cases to all others, 57 percent of the unexplained versus only 41 percent of all others involved more than one witness. Approximately 22 percent of unexplained cases involved three or more witnesses, versus 16 percent for all others. This really isn't that surprising, as one wouldn't expect to find too many cases that involved multiple witnesses that could be easily explained away. Presumably, if the object seen was a mere plane, for example, one of the witnesses would be able to identify it as such.

It seems reasonable to think that witnesses would be more reluctant to report stranger cases, fearing that people would not believe them. Having additional witnesses present might make people more willing to report stranger cases. With this in mind, one would expect a larger average number of witnesses for stranger cases, such as daylight discs and close encounters. Looking at the data, however, this doesn't seem to be the case. Comparing the type of sighting with the average number of witnesses, we find that the average is roughly the same amongst all the types of sightings. The category of daylight discs has the lowest average, with 1.85, whereas nocturnal discs has the highest, with 2.06.

Shape

Witness descriptions of the shapes of UFOs vary greatly. The majority of UFOs, however, are simple points of light. This isn't surprising given that most UFO sightings are of the nocturnal light variety. Some 40 percent of UFO sightings were of this type. Another 11 percent were of fireballs. The classic "flying saucer" or disc-shaped object accounted for only slightly more than 4 percent of all UFO reports, contrary to popular opinion.

The shape of a perceived object depends on many factors, such as the witness's visual acuity, the angle of viewing, the distance of viewing, and the witness's biases and descriptive abilities. Nevertheless, in combination with other case data such as duration, shape can be a good clue towards a UFO's possible explanation.

Strangeness

The concept of a strangeness rating for UFO reports was adopted by researchers who noted that the inclusion of a subjective evaluation of the degree to which a particular case is unusual might yield some insight into the data. For example, the observation of a single stationary light in the sky, seen for several hours, is not particularly unusual and might likely have a prosaic explanation such as a star or planet. On the other hand, a detailed observation of a saucer-shaped object that glides slowly away from a witness after an encounter with grey-skinned aliens would be considered highly strange.

The numbers of UFO reports according to strangeness rating show an inverse relationship such that the higher the strangeness rating, the fewer reports. The one exception to this relationship occurs in the case of *very* low strangeness cases, which are relatively few in number compared to those of moderate strangeness. It is suggested this is the case because in order for an observation to be considered a UFO, it usually must rise above an ad hoc level of strangeness; otherwise, it would not be considered strange at all.

The average strangeness rating for UFO reports from 1996 through 2004 was 3.9, where 1.0 is considered not strange at all and 9.0 is considered exceptionally unusual. Over the years, the average strangeness rating has remained relatively stable at just shy of 4.0. Therefore, most UFOs reported are objects that do not greatly stretch the imagination.

Hollywood-style flying saucers are, in reality, relatively uncommon in UFO reports.

It should be said that highly strange UFO sightings are being *reported* infrequently. Are such high-strangeness cases actually occurring much more frequently but falling within the 90 percent of cases that go unreported in greater numbers than more mundane observations? The potential social stigma attached to seeing incredible events might be too great for many witnesses. Such people would prefer to keep close encounter cases to themselves.

Reliability

The average reliability rating of Canadian UFO reports was 5.2, indicating that there were approximately the same number of higher quality cases as those of low quality. Low reliability was assigned to reports with minimal information on the witness, little or no investigation, and incomplete data or description of the object(s) observed. Higher reliability cases might include those in which there are interviews with witnesses, a detailed case investigation, multiple witnesses, supporting documentation, and other evidence.

Reliability and strangeness ratings tend to vary in classic bell-shaped curves. In other words, there are very few cases that are both highly unusual and well reported. These are the "high-quality unknowns." Most cases are of medium strangeness and medium reliability. However, there are also very few low-strangeness cases with low reliability. Low-strangeness cases, therefore, tend to be well reported and probably have explanations.

Evaluation (Explanations)

After examining the information available on each case, researchers come to a subjective conclusion regarding a possible explanation for each case. There are four operative categories: Explained, Insufficient Information, Possible or Probable Explanation, and Unknown (or Unexplained). It is important to note that a classification of Unknown does *not* imply that an alien spacecraft or mysterious natural phenomenon was observed; no such interpretation can be made with certainty, based solely on the given data (though the probability of this scenario is technically never zero).

In most cases, an evaluation is made subjectively by both the contributing investigators and the compilers of this study. The category of

Unknown is adopted if the contributed data or case report contains enough information such that a conventional explanation cannot be satisfactorily proposed. This does *not* mean that the case will never be explained but only that a viable explanation is not immediately obvious. Cases are also re-evaluated periodically as additional information is brought forward or obtained through further investigation.

Since 1989, the average proportion of Unknowns has been about 13 percent per year. As of 2004, the total percentage of unexplained cases is 15 percent. This is a relatively high figure, implying that almost one in six UFOs cannot be explained. However, there are several factors that affect this value.

The level and quality of UFO report investigation varies because there are no explicit and rigorous standards for UFO investigation. Investigators who are believers might be inclined to consider most UFO sightings as mysterious, whereas those with a more skeptical predisposition might tend to reduce subconsciously (or consciously) the number of Unknowns in their files.

During the first few years of these studies, an evaluation of Explained was almost non-existent. At first, contributors tended to ignore UFO sightings that had a simple explanation and deleted them as actual UFO data. Hence, the only UFO reports submitted by contributors tended to be high-strangeness cases. Contributors were later encouraged to submit data on all UFO reports they received so that a more uniform assessment and evaluation process could be realized. Because many IFO cases such as fireballs and meteors are initially reported as UFOs, the Explained category was considered necessary for a full review of UFO data. As noted previously, early American studies of UFO data included such cases, so present-day comparative studies should include such data as well. Furthermore, since there are no absolutes, the assignation of evaluations is actually a subjective interpretation of the facts by individual researchers.

The process of evaluating UFO sightings is often complex, involving a series of steps that take into account errors of observation and unpredictable but natural phenomena. Checks with star charts, police, air traffic control operators, and meteorologists are often performed. Where possible, witnesses are interviewed in person, and sketches or photographs of the area may be examined. The intent is to eliminate as many conventional explanations as possible before allowing an evaluation or conclusion.

Status of UFO Reports

	Explained	Insufficient Evidence	Probable	Unexplained
1989	0.00%	52.50%	33.30%	14.20%
1990	0.00%	46.40%	40.20%	13.40%
1991	1.20%	48.50%	41.80%	8.50%
1992	8.00%	37.00%	33.00%	22.00%
1993	31.50%	34.80%	23.50%	10.20%
1994/95	19.10%	33.30%	35.20%	12.40%
1996	9.30%	40.70%	33.70%	16.30%
1997	6.00%	37.30%	43.00%	13.70%
1998	5.10%	38.80%	44.80%	11.30%
1999	3.80%	31.50%	52.00%	12.70%
2000	8.75%	35.74%	42.58%	12.93%
2001	5.88%	34.76%	44.12%	15.24%
2002	2.48%	39.75%	39.75%	18.01%
2003	16.34%	24.67%	42.50%	16.49%
2004	8.62%	22.68%	53.17%	15.53%

There were 562 Unknowns out of 3,671 total cases since 1996. If we look only at the Unknowns with a reliability rating of 7.0 or greater, we are left with 176 high-quality Unknowns during this period (about 4.8 percent of the total). This is in agreement with previous studies. As a comparison, USAF Blue Book studies found 3 to 4 percent of their cases were excellent Unknowns.

It should be emphasized again that even high-quality Unknowns do not imply alien visitation. Each case may still have an explanation following further investigation. And those that remain unexplained still are not incontrovertible proof of extraterrestrial intervention or some mysterious natural phenomenon.

Conclusion

After fifteen years of the Canadian UFO Survey, we unfortunately cannot come to any definite conclusions. This perhaps isn't terribly surprising, as many researchers have abandoned ufology as a result of their striking inability to satisfactorily study the subject matter.[7] Despite what many ufologists have claimed, science and UFOs don't seem to want to coexist.

Perhaps this is the result of the ultimate focus of the research; if there are aliens coming here, they very well might not want that fact known and might actively try to discourage any knowledge of their presence.

Another possibility is that the inability of researchers to reach a conclusion on the matter is simply due to the fact that no real money has been thrown at the problem. After all, there would be few scientific advances in the fields of microbiology, astrophysics, or astronomy if millions of dollars weren't spent in research studies and experimentation. The meagre change that part-time ufologists recover from under their sofa cushions just doesn't cut it anymore. Or perhaps the lack of any significant forward momentum in UFO research is something much more logical; one cannot satisfactorily prove a negative. No amount of evidence will ever be enough to prove to hard-core believers in alien visitation that extraterrestrials are, in fact, not coming here.

This doesn't mean we can't learn anything from all of this data. We have, in fact, been able to come to some conclusions. We know that UFO reports are increasing at an incredible rate. These reports are coming from all over the country, though it is unclear whether or not the phenomena behind the reports are actually favouring any particular part of the country. While most UFOs seen are simple lights in the night sky, a nonetheless significant number are objects with a definite shape. There is a greater probability of seeing a UFO during the summer months, particularly between the hours of 8:00 p.m. and 1:00 a.m. Most UFO sightings involve more than one witness. Finally, it should be stated that people who see UFOs come from all walks of life, including people with good observational skills such as pilots and police officers.

Contrary to popular opinion, there isn't any hard evidence of alien visitation to Canada. Similarly, however, one cannot say there definitely aren't any aliens visiting this country. After thousands of reports, including almost two hundred cases without an easy explanation, it would be prudent to keep an open mind on the subject.

CHAPTER FORTY-FIVE
MISIDENTIFIED FLYING OBJECTS

GEOFF DITTMAN

When witnesses inform ufologists of UFO sightings, it is the job of ufologists to then identify as many of those unidentified flying objects as possible. To do this, one needs to be familiar with the possible natural and man-made sources of UFO reports. With this in mind, we have provided a brief description of some of the more common explanations of UFO reports. The explanations have been divided into four basic categories (astronomical phenomena, atmospheric phenomena, man-made phenomena, and miscellaneous). In many cases, these categories are not mutually exclusive.

When reading this list of possible explanations for UFO reports, one might be tempted to think that it would be preposterous to believe that reasonably intelligent people could mistake such mundane things as planes for UFOs. Keep in mind, however, that human perception is notoriously unreliable. Given the right conditions, things seen even on a daily basis can take on an air of strangeness.

1. Astronomical Phenomena

Various astronomical bodies are frequently viewed as unusual. Included in this category would be such things as meteors, stars, and planets. While people see these things on a regular basis, given unusual and unfamiliar circumstances it is surprisingly easy to see a meteor or star as something extraordinary.

Meteors

Our solar system has a large amount of stone and metal within it. After planets, the largest pieces are called "asteroids" or "minor planets." The smaller bodies of rock are referred to as "meteoroids." Asteroids are debris from the universe's early days, leftovers from the creation of the major planets including Earth.[1] There are more than one hundred thousand known asteroids,[2] most of which are within an asteroid belt found between Jupiter and Mars. The smaller meteoroids, however, frequently cross Earth's path, resulting in brilliant light displays as the particles, often not much bigger than grains of sand, burn up from friction. Typically such small pieces burn up in less than a second, but larger pieces are able to survive for longer periods of time. Such larger pieces in the atmosphere are known as "meteors" or, more commonly, "shooting stars." Should the meteor survive the trip through the atmosphere and hit the Earth, the meteor is then referred to as a "meteorite."

Sometimes the meteors are extraordinarily brilliant; they are then called "fireballs." Fireballs are frequently reported as UFOs. In fact, since 1996, almost four hundred UFO sightings over Canada, or more than 10 percent of the total reports, have been explained away as likely being meteors/fireballs.

Luckily it is usually fairly easy for an experienced researcher to identify UFOs that were nothing but meteors/fireballs. Typically meteors are seen for very short periods of time, usually only a few seconds, although occasionally they carry on for ten seconds or more. Meteors are usually seen to travel at a great rate of speed (for they are in fact moving incredibly fast) and should be heading in a downward trajectory. Sometimes, however, their trajectory can be fairly flat and may even give the illusion of being upward in direction. Normally meteors are seen singularly, though less frequently they are seen in small groups, particularly if one breaks apart in flight. Colour can vary quite a bit, though white, yellow, red, and orange are more common; green and blue are less so.[3] Usually witnesses report no sound, but sometimes a roar or a hiss is heard. At night, a glowing trail, and during the day, smoke, might be left in the wake of a meteor. Sometimes meteors explode in mid-air.

Displays involving large numbers of meteors, known as meteor showers, are frequently predictable, thereby making it easier to explain many sightings.

Larger Meteor Showers[4]

Date	Peak	Name	Approx. Hourly Rate
Jan. 1 to 5	Jan. 3/4	Quadrantids	30 to 60
Apr. 16 to 25	Apr. 2/3	Cyrids	8 to 10
Apr. 19 to May 28	May 4/5	Eta-Aquarids	10
Jul. 12 to Aug. 19	Jul. 27 to 30	Delta-Aquarids	15
Jul. 23 to Aug. 22	Aug. 12/13	Perseids	40 to 75
Oct. 1 to Nov. 25	Nov. 4 to 8	Taurids	8 to 10
Oct. 2 to Nov. 4	Oct. 21/22	Orionids	15 to 25
Nov. 14 to Nov. 21	Nov.16 to 21	Leonids	6 to 10
Dec. 6 to 19	Dec. 13	Geminids	50 to 75

Finally, meteor sightings are typically reported by large numbers of people over a wide area, so ufologists should consider meteors as an explanation for any sighting involving several witnesses.

Comets

Comets are chunks of ice, and they become visible when the sun causes them to slowly evaporate. They likely originate from a section of space known as the Oort cloud, which is about halfway to the closest star. Occasionally comets are sent hurtling into the middle of our solar system, perhaps the result of gravitational influences from neighbouring solar systems.[5]

Comets that are visible without the use of a telescope are few and far between. Their scarcity means that people unfamiliar with comets might perceive them as UFOs and report them as such.

Artificial Satellites

There are many man-made objects orbiting around the Earth. The purposes of these satellites are varied, including photography, telecommunications, and studying the environment. They are typically hundreds of miles above the Earth, and with little to no light source of their own, satellites cannot usually be seen during the daytime. At night, however, satellites can frequently be seen when they reflect sunlight.

Satellites have accounted for a lot of UFO reports. Luckily it isn't too hard to identify which UFO sightings are of satellites. They travel at a high altitude and at a high rate of speed, being able to cross the sky in a few minutes. They generally travel a predictable path, usually moving from west to east.[6] Normally they don't change direction, but the phenomena known as "autostasis" can make it seem otherwise. A satellite could appear to hover or move erratically due to irregular eye movements while trying to follow the moving point of light, particularly when there are few points of reference.[7]

Another factor that can sometimes fool an eyewitness is the apparent sudden appearance or disappearance of a satellite. The light from the satellite is nothing but the reflection of sunlight, but the available sunlight will either disappear or appear as the satellite moves in and out of the Earth's shadow.[8]

Finally, satellites have traditionally orbited the Earth alone, but some satellites, notably the U.S. Navy's Parcae satellites, travel in formation. For some time, the Parcae satellites, which travel in a triangular three-satellite formation, puzzled researchers.

While most researchers will generally write off a UFO sighting as a satellite if the behaviour is consistent with one, there is software available that will allow the tracking of satellites should one wish to confirm a sighting.

Artificial Space Debris

While certainly less common than meteors, artificial space debris does rain down on the Earth too. It may take the form of used rockets, satellites at the end of their lives, even space stations. Such debris burns in the atmosphere from the friction. If the re-entry occurs over a populated area, it will usually be well publicized, making it relatively easy to weed out such cases from UFO reports.

Stars and Planets

One wouldn't think that seemingly mundane stars and planets could be viewed as something unusual, but they regularly are. A phenomenon known as "autokinesis" is frequently responsible. Autokinesis is where a stationary point of light appears to move when there are few points of reference. A solitary star or planet against a black sky can appear to be jumping around in the sky. Other factors that can cause the illusion of rapid movement include atmospheric turbulence and clouds. Atmospheric turbulence is caused by heat rising from the ground and can make stars appear to flash or even jump erratically.[9] And clouds moving at a good pace can give the illusion of movement to relatively stationary objects like stars.

Like meteors, the predictability of stars and planets usually makes it easy to weed out such cases from more unusual UFO sightings. Stars and planets are naturally visible for long periods of time. Should a UFO report be of long duration, stars and planets are frequently the answer.

Stars always move from east to west, with the movement being very gradual over the course of the night. There are no bright clusters of stars.[10] Some of the planets, on the other hand, namely Venus, Mars, Jupiter, and Saturn, can get quite bright, depending on how close they are to Earth. Venus in particular is often very bright and has been known to cause quite a few UFO reports. Mars is frequently seen as being red, Venus white, and Saturn and Jupiter yellow in colour.[11]

There is an abundance of software packages out there that enable ufologists to accurately tell where any given star or planet will be in the sky at a particular time and day. These software packages are therefore a valued tool to every researcher.

2. Atmospheric Phenomena

Clouds

Surprisingly, sometimes even clouds are reported as UFOs. One type of cloud, known as "lenticular," is sometimes disc- or cigar-shaped and to a casual observer may appear to be a Hollywood-style flying saucer.[12] This could be particularly true if the observer was in a car, thereby giving the illusion of rapid movement as well.

In the Canadian Arctic, there is the possibility that noctilucent clouds can give rise to UFO reports. Such clouds form at high altitudes around dust and ice particles. They can reflect sunlight, causing the clouds to be easily seen at night around the Earth's poles.[13]

Mirages and Temperature Inversions

Mirages are usually caused by changes in temperature and therefore density of the air, resulting in the bending of light. This can cause objects to appear distorted or warped or even cause the illusion of multiple copies of a single object.[14] Mirages can last for hours but may only be visible to a witness in motion for but a few seconds.[15]

A particular type of mirage is known as a "temperature inversion," which is essentially a mirage higher up in the air. A plane or star behind such an inversion can appear to move erratically. Alternatively, light from the ground can be reflected off the inversion.[16]

Aurora Borealis

More commonly referred to as the northern lights, the aurora borealis is the result of the ionization of particles in the Earth's atmosphere upon being bombarded by electrically charged particles from the sun. Incredible waves of light can be created in the sky over the northern hemisphere at night.[17] There may be electrical interference associated with the northern lights. A researcher should consider the aurora borealis as a suspect for a case involving intermittent waves of light over a period of time up in the night sky, if not associated with a clear physical object.

Parhelia and Paraselenai

More commonly referred to as "sun dogs" and "moon dogs," these are mirages caused by light being refracted off of ice crystals in the air. This gives the illusion of fake suns or moons around the real one.

Ball Lightning

This is a very rare form of lightning. In fact, it was only fairly recently that the scientific community accepted the existence of ball lightning. The irony of one unexplained phenomenon (UFOs) being explained by another unknown phenomenon (ball lightning) by scientists has not been lost on ufologists.

A British paranormal researcher named Jenny Randles has followed the ball lightning controversy for many years and has noted many characteristics.[18] Of course it tends to be ball-shaped. It is generally quite small; only rarely has it been seen to be larger than a basketball. In fact, it is usually not much bigger than a golf ball. The colours of ball lightning range all over the spectrum. It is regularly seen to enter and exit rooms, even aircraft.[19] In fact, its behaviour has been described by many witnesses as being almost intelligently controlled. It is usually silent, although occasionally it gives off a buzzing sound. It typically lasts only a few seconds, and when it does come to an end it may either just disappear or fizzle out. Sometimes it is even seen to explode.

Scientists haven't been able to agree on the cause of ball lightning, or for that matter even the conditions in which it will form. Some researchers have argued that it almost always occurs during thunderstorms. But as an example of just how fractured the scientific community is, one Japanese scientist has claimed that ball lightning only rarely occurs during thunderstorms.[20] In fact, many eyewitnesses do report seeing these balls during calm and dry weather.

While ball lightning is itself a very controversial and unknown phenomenon, it has definitely been the cause of a few UFO reports, and therefore researchers need to keep it in mind when studying UFO cases.

3. Man-Made Artifacts

Airplanes

Even in the vicinity of airports, witnesses frequently report garden-variety airplanes as UFOs. There are several signs to look for when studying UFO reports. Apparent speed will vary depending on the type of aircraft and on distance and altitude. It should take aircraft at higher altitudes several minutes to cross the sky.[21] Planes at lower altitudes should be visible for at least ten seconds, unless objects on the ground block the view.

The colours of airplanes can vary greatly as well, with military aircraft frequently painted grey and civilian aircraft white. Larger passenger planes are now often painted in a multitude of colours. Planes frequently reflect sunlight and as such can often be seen from great distances during the daylight hours.[22] At night, by law all aircraft are required to use navigation lights. For planes, this generally means lights on the wings (red on the left wing, green on the right wing) and several constant white lights. Other lights are also sometimes carried as well. When approaching for a landing, a plane will turn on its powerful white landing lights, which will frequently drown out the form of the aircraft if seen from the front.

The shapes of planes vary somewhat, depending not only on the type of plane but also on the angle and distance it is being viewed at. When viewed from the side, particularly at a distance, the telltale wings may not be seen, making the plane appear to be cigar-shaped. More advanced military aircraft, like the B-2 and F-117 stealth aircraft, can appear to be disc-shaped when viewed from the side.

With regards to sound, the signature roar of a jet engine or hum of a prop will usually allow people to identify a plane. But under certain conditions no sound may be heard coming from planes even when fairly close to an observer.

The behaviour of airplanes is usually predictable. They usually keep steady flight paths and only make gradual turns. While military aircraft (and smaller civilian aircraft) can make more radical turns, such actions usually don't occur over well-populated areas.

Finally, researchers should consider the possibilities of unmanned aerial vehicles (UAVs), sometimes referred to as remotely piloted vehicles (RPVs). Such aircraft are being used more and more by militaries for purposes of reconnaissance. Some of these craft are quite bizarre looking; one Canadian helicopter drone, the CL-227, is nicknamed the "Flying Peanut" because of its distinctive shape.

Balloons and Blimps

Many different kinds of balloons can be the source of UFO reports. Everything from huge hot-air balloons down to tiny children's balloons have resulted in phone calls to the air force and UFO investigators. While they are somewhat less easy for researchers to identify than some of the other explanations, there are some telltale signs to look for. Balloons generally travel at a low rate of speed, usually fairly straight up or down, and when observed to be climbing at an angle, they should be travelling with the wind. One must take into account, however, that wind can be moving in a different direction hundreds of yards above the ground than it is at ground level, thereby fooling observers.[23]

Balloons may or may not carry a light source, such as navigation lights. But they are frequently made of material that is conducive to reflecting light.

Balloons should always be silent. It is, however, possible that other ambient noises in the background might fool some witnesses into thinking the balloon is the source of the noise.

Balloons are generally round, though at lower altitudes some high-altitude balloons can take on all sorts of shapes, given that they are designed to not fully inflate until they reach higher altitudes.[24] Blimps on the other hand are typically cigar-shaped.

Balloons and blimps can come in all sorts of different colours, with some being transparent.[25]

Promotional Lightshows

Bars and carnivals occasionally generate UFO reports through their use of searchlights and lasers. Such promotional displays can be quite a sight, particularly to someone who has never seen one before.

Searchlights will typically be white, but laser lightshows can come in all sorts of colours. The speed of the display can vary considerably, from slow-moving to incredibly fast. The possible trajectories and behaviour is almost limitless. And with cloud cover, there can be the illusion of sudden appearance and disappearance of objects.[26]

Indicators of promotional lightshows as a possible explanation for UFO reports include a long duration of time, a large number of witnesses, seemingly erratic behaviour of the alleged objects (or inversely a repeated pattern), and of course publicity surrounding a new bar or festival. Usually a phone call to the establishment in question can clear up any questions.

Hoaxes

While UFO sightings are often dismissed as hoaxes by our sometimes cynical news media, hoaxes are in reality quite rare. Good hoaxes are even rarer still. But they do happen. Sometimes the behaviour of the "witness" can give it away. Does the alleged witness seem to bask in the attention and be quite happy to talk to the media? Does the witness have expectations of making money off of alleged evidence?

Now with the Internet, researchers have to be more careful watching out for hoaxes. Information on previous UFO sightings is now much more readily available. Hoaxers wanting to mimic real sightings used to have to put some effort into researching reports, but now all they have to do is call up a website. To make matters worse, the World Wide Web is now even being used to help coordinate hoaxing. An individual with a Dallas, Texas–based website organized a hoax recently. The website listed some of the details of the fake sighting to be reported, as well as a drawing of the object people were to report seeing. The perpetrator also recommended phoning the 1-800 number of the Seattle-based National UFO Reporting Center, thereby costing that organization money. In Canada, reports came in from Rosemere, Cambridge, Woodstock, and elsewhere. But by advertising the hoax on the Internet, the organizer not only informed co-conspirators but ufologists as well, and the hoax cases were easily identified.[27]

4. Miscellaneous

Wildlife

Birds can sometimes reflect light in such a way as to hinder people's ability to properly identify them. Signs to look for in recognizing UFOs as birds include formation flying or objects circling one another.[28]

While we have never come across any such cases, an American scientist named Donald Menzel suggested that in some cases, insect swarms, particularly luminescent ones like fireflies, could be reported as UFOs.[29]

Earthlights

Earthlights, or earthquake lights, as part of Tectonic Strain Theory, have been used to explain some UFO sightings. These are lights resulting from electromagnetic discharges from the compression of rock during the normal movement of tectonic plates.[30]

Swamp Gas

No discussion of explanations for UFO sightings would be complete without mentioning swamp gas. One of the first scientists to take UFOs seriously was an astronomer working for the U.S. Air Force by the name of Dr. J. Allen Hynek. Talking to the press in 1966 regarding a series of reports from around Dexter, Michigan, he suggested the sightings were of nothing but swamp gas. While Hynek would come to take UFOs far more seriously later in his life, his dismissive explanation for the Dexter sightings would become the butt of jokes for decades to come.

Swamp gas is methane gas produced from decaying organic matter. One wouldn't expect this to be the source of many UFO reports.

Other Potential Explanations

There are countless lesser explanations for smaller numbers of UFO reports. These include kites, vehicle headlights (off in the distance), psychological hallucinations (caused by mental illness or drug abuse), eye floaters, parachutes, and fireworks.[31]

AFTERWORD

This book has just scratched the surface of the recorded UFO sightings and reports that have been made in Canada. As we have shown, UFOs have been seen in every province and territory, from coast to coast and from southern Ontario to the High Arctic. It is true that many reports of moving lights in the sky can be explained as astronomical or aeronautical objects, but there are also much more puzzling sightings that do not have simple explanations.

There is no incontrovertible proof that aliens from other planets are visiting Earth. There is, however, a wealth of data on observations of unidentified flying objects that demands attention and serious study by researchers in both physical and social sciences as well as fields within medicine.

The study of UFO reports and investigations leads us to wonder about the nature of our world, our humanity, and our place in the universe. If that is the least response dwellers on the rocky ball named Earth have in reaction to the UFO phenomenon, then the UFO mission has been worthwhile.

If you think you have seen a UFO and would like to help the continuing study of UFO reports, let us know by sending us an email to **canadianuforeport@hotmail.com** or a letter to **Box 204, Winnipeg, MB, R3V 1L6.**

APPENDIX A

The Strangest Canadian UFO Reports

Canadian UFO researchers and investigators were polled for their personal picks of the most remarkable Canadian cases of the past century (or so). They are, in chronological order:

Ottawa, Ontario, February 15, 1915
A "phantom invasion" of unusual aerial objects caused enough panic throughout the national capital region that the lights on Parliament Hill were extinguished in order to prevent being targeted by the "enemy."

Gander, Newfoundland, February 10, 1951
A U.S. Navy transport was reported to have nearly collided with a giant circular orange object that almost literally flew circles around the American plane as it flew between Iceland and Newfoundland.

Shirley's Bay, Ontario, August 8, 1954
Wilbert Smith, a Department of Transit engineer, set up a "flying saucer detection station" at a government facility. On this date, his instruments recorded a large magnetic disturbance overhead, which Smith believed to be from an alien craft.

Fort Macleod, Alberta, August 23, 1956
RCAF Squadron Leader Robert Childerhose and his flight lieutenant were attempting to set a cross-Canada speed record in their Sabre jet when they observed and photographed a bright oval object near their plane at an altitude of thirty-six thousand feet.

Falcon Lake, Manitoba, May 20, 1967
Weekend prospector Stefan Michalak was burned by an object that had landed near him. Despite investigations by American and Canadian officials, the case was listed as "unexplained."

Shag Harbour, Nova Scotia, October 4, 1967
Many witnesses observed a bright object fall from the sky into the ocean. Later, a patch of luminous foam was found on the surface of the water.

Langenburg, Saskatchewan, September 1, 1974
Farmer Edwin Fuhr was swathing when he came upon several bowl-shaped objects spinning rapidly in a hayfield. The object took off and left behind circular impressions that predated the "crop circles" found years later in England.

Carman, Manitoba, May 13, 1975
Hundreds of people observed a bobbing, bright reddish orange light in the sky beginning about this date and continuing for several months. The object was seen so frequently, it was affectionately named "Charlie Redstar."

Montreal, Quebec, January 6, 1977
Ms. Florida Malboeuf watched as a saucer-shaped object landed on the roof of a building across from her home. Two spindly creatures in tight-fitting suits appeared on the edge of the roof and then disappeared before the object took off.

Duncan, British Columbia, November 1980
Granger Taylor was a teenager who was obsessed with aliens and UFOs to the point of building his own huge full-size model in his backyard. One day, he announced to his friends he was going to be taken away by aliens and he was never seen again.

Although there are many, many more examples of Canadian UFO cases, these are among the most significantly unusual on record. Whether or not they are "real" is irrelevant. They each have helped fire the Canadian imagination and fascination with the possibility of life elsewhere in the universe.

APPENDIX B

Canadian Cases Listed Among the Blue Book Unknowns

A number of UFO researchers studying historical cases have been able to obtain copies of many documents concerning sightings of unidentified flying objects reported to the United States Air Force. Between July 2, 1947, and January 30, 1970, more than thirteen thousand cases were officially recorded and filed with military projects including those code named Project Sign, Project Grudge, and Project Blue Book. Officially, more than seven hundred were listed by the USAF as "Unidentified." However, when ufologists began going through the reports, some of the cases given explanations were found to be stretching the limits of plausibility, and the number of UFOs based on the official files was increased to about fifteen hundred. Most of these cases involved military observers and many involved radar or other instrument-assisted tracking. Of this set of unknowns, a good number took place in Canada, and they are listed here as an indication of official military sightings of UFOs in our skies.[1]

Project Blue Book Canadian Unknowns

July 10, 1947
Harmon Field, Newfoundland, Canada.
Between 3:00 and 5:00 p.m. local time.
Witnesses: three ground crewmen, including Mr. Leidy, for Pan American Airways. Watched briefly while one translucent disc- or wheel-shaped object flew very fast, leaving a dark blue trail, and then ascended and cut a path through the clouds.

October 27, 1948
Goose Bay AFB, Labrador, Canada
(No details released.)

October 31, 1948
Goose Bay AFB, Labrador, Canada
(No details released.)

November 17, 1948

Peace River, Alberta, Canada (at 56E 10' N, 117E 30' W). 6:18 am PST

Pilot and radio [radar?] operator of military aircraft saw a bright orange flaming egg-shaped object flying on a SW heading.

March 18, 1949

Fort Chimo, Quebec, Canada. 7:50 p.m. EST

USAF and RCAF personnel at Detachment Crystal-I, 1227th Air Base Squadron, including USAF 1st Lt. and Warrant Officer J.G., RCAF Flying Officer/Liaison Officer Brodribb, and a USAF civilian employee, saw a red light like an aircraft light to the S traveling W to E at high speed estimated 10,000 feet and 200-250 mph silently with stops and starts and flickering, and a turn to the S at the end.

September 9, 1949

Goose Bay, Labrador, Canada. 9:56 p.m. AST

Military aircraft pilot saw an egg-shaped object disappear into a cloud at high speed.

Aug. 30, 1950

Sandy Point, Newfoundland, Canada. 1:30 p.m.

Witnesses: three local employees, including Kaeel and Alexander, of the Air Force Base. A dark, barrel-shaped object with a pole down from it into the water, flew at 3-5 mph and 15-20' altitude for 5 minutes.

Sept. 14, 1951

Goose Bay, Labrador, Canada. 9:30 p.m.

Witnesses: T/Sgt W.B. Maupin, Cpl. J.W. Green. Three objects tracked on radar. Two were on a collision course, then one evaded to the right upon the request, by radio, of one of the radar operators. No aircraft were known to be in the area. A third unidentified track then joined the first two. More than 15 minutes.

September 17, 1951

Hudson Strait (at 61E 30' N, 68E 50' W) to Baffin Island, Canada. 10:20-11:55 p.m. EST

USAF B-36 radar operator Major Paul E. Gerhart and navigator

Major Charles J. Cheever on a flight from Goose Bay, Labrador, to Resolute, North West Territories, heading NW at 208 knots (239 mph) over Hudson Strait, picked up radar interference which came from an unidentified aircraft at relative bearing 130E (E) at 28 nautical miles (32 miles) heading away from them. Anti-jamming device on the APQ-24 radar was turned on at 11:20 p.m., but did not affect the jamming on the radar scope. At 11:35 p.m., jamming covered 120E of the right side of the radar scope and then an unidentified aircraft was seen visually on the right side of the B-36, which was then at 18,000 feet at 65E 40' N, 71E 40' W (over SW Baffin Island). Object had "unconventional running lights" all white instead of red-green, with twin white flashing tail-lights, traveling about 30 knots faster than the B-36, crossed the front from right to left heading 334E true towards the NNW, and was in view about 20 minutes (to a distance of about 12 miles). While the object was still visible, at 11:50 p.m., the B-36 autopilot and the APQ-24 radar set went out, the latter returning after a few minutes about when the object disappeared. ECM operators S/Sgt Donald E. Jenkins and S/Sgt Doty T. Larimore on 2 B-36 flights from Goose Bay to Resolute while still over Labrador the next day detected carrier wave signals at several frequencies and some radar-like pulses at other frequencies, all below 1,000 MHz.

April 12, 1952

North Bay, Ontario, Canada. 9:30 p.m.

Witnesses: Royal Canadian Air Force Warrant Officer E.H. Rossell, Flight Sgt. R. McRae. One round amber object flew fast, stopped, reversed direction, climbed away at 30E angle during a 2 minute observation.

April 18, 1952

Corner Brook, Newfoundland, Canada. l0:l0 p.m.

Witness: reporter Chic Shave. One round, yellow-gold object flew south and returned during 1.5 minute sighting.

April 18, 1952

Corner Brook, Newfoundland, Canada. 4 a.m.

Witness: janitor C. Hamilton. One yellow-gold object made a sharp turn and left a short, dark trail during l minute sighting.

June 19, 1952

Goose Bay, Labrador, Canada. 2:37 a.m.
Witness: 2nd Lt. A'Gostino and unidentified radar operator. One red light turned white while wobbling. Radar tracked a stationary target during the 1 minute sighting. The target suddenly enlarged then returned to previous size, possibly a disc rotating to present wider reflective surface.

Sept. 23, 1952

Gander Lake, Newfoundland, Canada. No time shown.
Witnesses: Pepperell AFB operations officer and seven other campers. One bright white light, which reflected on the lake, flew straight and level at 100 mph for 10 minutes.

September 28, 1952

Goose Bay, Labrador, Canada
(No details released.)

November 26, 1952

Goose Bay, Labrador, Canada. 2:30 a.m.
F-94 chased maneuverable disc that changed colour from white or orange to red as it climbed and turned.

December 15/16, 1952

Goose Bay, Labrador, Canada
F-94 chased maneuverable disc that changed colour from white to red, and tracked it on airborne radar. T-33 crew also sighted it.

April 8, 1953

Between Goose Bay, Labrador, and Sondrestrom AFB, Greenland (at 66E 0'N, 53E 30' W). 7 p.m. AST
USAF MATS transport pilot and copilot saw a white light at 15,000 feet on a steady course in a shallow descending turn.

May 1, 1953

Goose Bay AFB, Labrador, Canada. 11:35 p.m.
Witnesses: pilot and radar operator of USAF F-94 jet interceptor, and control tower operator. One white light evaded interception attempt by F-94 during 30 minute sighting.

May 2, 1953

Goose Bay AFB, Labrador, Canada
(No details released.)

June 22, 1953

Goose Bay AFB, Labrador, Canada. 2:10 a.m.
Witnesses: pilot and radar operator of USAF F-94 jet interceptor. One red light, flying at an estimated 1,000 knots (1,100 mph) eluded the chasing F-94 after 5 minutes.

July 5, 1955

About 50 miles west from Lark Harbour on the west coast of Newfoundland, Canada. 3:00-3:56 a.m. AST
USAF Lt. H.H. Speer, pilot of KC-97 Archie 29, and the pilot of KC-97 Archie 91, both at 20,000 feet on a refueling mission out of Harmon AFB, saw two bright objects at 49E 10' N, 59E 50' W. The objects were both stationary and also appeared to be at 20,000 feet. The pilots reported the sighting Harmon AFB at 3:05 a.m., made contact with radar site, USAF ADC site N-23 (Air Defense Direction Center, 640th AC&W Squadron, Harmon AFB, Stephenville, Newfoundland, CPS-6B search and height-finder radar, TPS-502 backup height-finder, at 48E 35.3' N, 58E 40' W). Radar painted an object at 3:07 a.m. with intermittent contact until 3:56 a.m. (and also four or five additional objects). Archie 29 KC-97 was in the best position to close on the object and was ordered to do so by Harmon, at a position 290E from radar site at about 80 miles, 10 o'clock position to the KC-97, but not consistent with the coordinates. As they were approached, the objects started moving NE at 50E true heading accelerating to 275 knots (300 mph) faster than Archie 29 KC-97. Speer maintained visual contact with the object, calling directional changes of the object to the radar site via radio, the changes correlated exactly with those painted on the scope by the controller. The object began climbing at 3:38 a.m. and fighters were scrambled, but no radar or visual contact was made by them. Speer lost sight of the object when it climbed to 40,000 to 50,000 feet. Radar then tracked the object accelerating to 1,600 knots (1,800 mph) moving off to the NE. At the same time, radar also painted five smaller objects 5,000-10,000 feet below the KC-97s at 30E true, 60 miles from the radar, again

inconsistent with the coordinates. These objects were moving very fast, changing direction and azimuth, jumping on and off radar scopes, forming circular patterns, changing to lines abreast of one another, traveling 10-20 miles then changing direction, with speeds in excess of 1,500 knots (1,700 mph). Radar tracked four objects at the point of the initial sighting on 40E true heading, with speeds of 300 knots (350 mph). At 3:40 a.m., the objects were at 50E 10' N, 57E 50' W. One C-119 aircraft en route from Goose Bay passed within five miles of the object, but it is not known if anything was seen.

Feb. 12, 1956

Goose Bay, Labrador, Canada. 11:25 p.m.
Witnesses: F-89 pilot Bowen, radar observer Crawford. One green and red object rapidly circled the aircraft while being tracked on radar during 1 minute sighting. No further details.

December 19, 1957

Pepperell AFB, Newfoundland, Canada
(No details released.)

February 25, 1958

Glenwood, Newfoundland, Canada
(No details released.)

February 25, 1958

Gander AFB, Newfoundland, Canada
(No details released.)

October 31, 1958

Caledon East, Ontario, Canada. 3:50 p.m.
Civilian saw am elliptical, aluminum-coloured object at 6,000 feet altitude, coming down to 12 feet, flying up and down by sudden jumps, stopping at ground level less than 600 feet away for 5 minutes. A red light appeared at one end of the object, which gradually took a fiery colour, then exploded. Witness ran away.

June 18, 1959

Edmonton, Alberta, Canada. 9:30 p.m.

Witnesses: A. Cavelli and R. Blessin, using 7x binoculars. One brown, cigar-shaped object came from below the horizon (close to the witnesses) ascending to 40-50' above the horizon in 4 minutes.

Aug. 10, 1959
Goose Bay AFB, Labrador, Canada. 1:28 a.m.
Witness: Royal Canadian Air Force pilot Flt. Lt. M.S. Mowat, on ground. One large star-like light crossed 53 degrees of sky in 25 minutes.

December 18, 1959
S. Victoria Island, NWT, Canada
(No details released.)

May 7, 1960
Canada, Montana, North Dakota (?)
(No details released.)

April 2, 1962
Goose Bay, Labrador, Canada
(No details released.)

January 8, 1967
Goose Bay AFB, Labrador, Canada
USAF MAC C-97 pilot and ground radar operators tracked object at 2,100 knots (2,400 mph).

NOTES

The Historical Context

1. Jesuit Relations, Volume 48, 1662-1663, Vol. XLVIII. Lower Canada, Ottawa: 1662 C 1664. Cleveland: The Burrows Brothers Company, Publishers, M DCCC XCVIX. Relation of New France, in the years 1662 and 1663. Paris: Sebastien Cramoisy et Sebastien Mabre?Cramoisy, 1664. Relation of what occurred in the Mission of the Fathers of the Society of Jesus in the country of New France, from the Summer of the year 1662 to the Summer of the year 1663. Chapter 1: "Three Suns and Other Aerial Phenomena, Which Appeared in New France." Retrieved from http://puffin.creighton.edu/jesuit/relations/relations_48.html
2. Ibid.
2. Ibid.
3. Tyrrell, J.B., ed. (1916). *David Thompson's Narrative of His Exploration in Western America 1784–1812*. Toronto: The Champlain Society, pp. 118–199.
4. Fergusson, C.B., ed. (1961). *The Diary of Simeon Perkins*. Vol. 3. Toronto: The Champlain Society.
5. Colombo, J.R. (1992). *Dark Visions*. Toronto: Hounslow Press.

Airships Over Canada

1. Bullard, T.E. (1992). *The Airship File*. Bloomington, Indiana: [privately published].
2. *Manitoba Morning Free Press*. (July 2, 1896), p. 4.
3. Retoff, W. (1980, August). *Ideal's UFO Magazine*, #11, p. 53.
4. Cohen, D. (1981). *The Great Airship Mystery*. New York: Dodd, Mead & Co.
5. Clark, J. (1998). "Airship Sightings in the Nineteenth Century." In *The UFO Book*. (pp. 27-39). Toronto: Visible Ink.

The Great Meteor Procession of 1913

1. Millman, P., and McKinley, D. (1967). Stars fall over Canada. *Journal of the Royal Astronomical Society of Canada*, Vol. 61, no. 5, pp. 277–294.
2. Chant, C. (1913). *Journal of the Royal Astronomical Society of Canada*, Volume 7, pp. 146–300.

3. Ibid.
4. Ibid.
5. Ibid.
6. Ibid. Additional information about the event can be found at: http://djvued.libs.uga.edu/text/chanttxt.txt
7. Fort, C. (1941). *New Lands*. New York: Ace Books. Chapter 35, pp. 201–202.

The 1915 Invasion of Canada

1. Campagna, P. (1997). *The UFO Files*. Toronto: Stoddart, pp. 9–10.
2. Some of the information on historical Canadian UFO cases was discovered through the patient and diligent perusal of archives by Mr. X (his legally changed name), a member of the International Fortean Organization and former editor and publisher of the *Res Bureaux Bulletin*. Retrieved from: http://www.100megsfree4.com/farshores/aircan.htm

The Village That Disappeared?

1. Strieber, W. (1989). *Majestic*. New York: Putnam, p. 50.
2. Blundell, N., and Boar, R. (1983). *The World's Greatest UFO Mysteries*. London: Octopus Books, pp. 86–87.
3. Retrieved from: http://www.rense.com/general11/dis.htm
4. Edwards F. (1959). *Stranger Than Science*. New York: Ace Books, pp. 26–28.
5. Kelleher, E. (November 29, 1930). "Tribe Lost in Barrens of North / Village of Dead Found by Wandering Trapper, Joe Labelle." *Halifax Herald*.
6. Colombo, J.R. (1988). *Mysterious Canada*. Toronto: Doubleday.
7. Whalen, D. (November 1976). *Fate Magazine*.
8. Retrieved from: http://www.rcmp. ca/history/anjikuni_e.htm

Saucer-Spotting Parties

1. "Mystery of the Flying Discs Deepens." (July 7, 1947). *Winnipeg Free Press*.
2. "Dr. Murray Scientific Expedition Probes 'Flying Saucers'." (July 8, 1947). *Winnipeg Tribune*.

Sky Cleavage: The First Canadian UFO Photograph

1. USAF Air Intelligence Report No. 100-203-79, April 28, 1949.

Analysis of Flying Object Incidents in the United States. Appendix C. Retrieved from: http://www.project1947.com/fig/1948air.htm
2. Hall, M., and Connors, W. (1998). *Alfred Loedding and the Great Flying Saucer Wave of 1947.* Albuquerque, New Mexico: Rose Press. Retrieved from http://www.nicap.org/harmon.htm
3. Project Blue Book Files, Roll No.2, Case 60, listed as Incident 27a.
4. Hall and Connors, op. cit.

Duck, Duck...

1. Hall, R., ed. (1964). *The UFO Evidence.* Washington, DC: National Investigations Committee on Aerial Phenomena (NICAP), p. 84. Available online at: http://www.nicap.dabsol.co.uk/goose.htm
2. Sparks, B. (2003). *Comprehensive Catalog of 1, 500 Project Blue Book UFO Unknowns.* Work in Progress (Version 1.6, June 18, 2003). Privately published. Case nos. 119, 121, and 123. Retrieved from: www.nidsci.org/pdf/bluebookunknowns-v1-6.pdf
3. Keyhoe, D. (December 1952). "What radar tells us about flying saucers." *True Magazine.* Available online at: http://www.nicap.dabsol.co.uk/whatradar.htm
4. Aldrich, J. (Undated). Project 1947, no. 185.
5. Sparks, B. op. cit. Blue Book Case No. 969.
6. Ruppelt, E. (1956). *The Report on Unidentified Flying Objects.* Garden City, NY: Doubleday, pp. 146–147.
7. Ibid., pp. 147–149.
8. Sparks, op. cit. Case No. 463, Blue Book Case No. 1308.
9. Ruppelt, op. cit., p. 146.
10. Keyhoe, D. (1953). *Flying Saucers from Outer Space.* New York: Henry Holt, p. 52. Available on the net at: http://www.nicap.dabsol.co.uk/goose3.htm
11. Keyhoe, 1952, op. cit.
12. Kanon, G. (April 30, 1975). "Maritimers are 'seeing things' — but some leave their mark." *The 4th Estate.*
13. Jones, B. "1953 UFO Case." Retrieved from http://www.pinetreeline.org/other/other19/other19j.html
14. Jones, Ibid.
15. Aldrich, J., op. cit.
16. Sparks, op. cit. Case No. 772.

17. Ibid.
18. Ibid. Case No. 739, Blue Book Case No. 2601.
19. "Flying Saucers? Yes Says Captain, Crew and Passengers." (July 1, 1954). London, England, *Daily Express.*
20. Retrieved from: http://ufos.about.com/library/bldata/bl3newf.htm
21. Retrieved from: http://www.nicap. org/boacmcd.htm
22. Sparks, op. cit. Case No. 960; Blue Book Case No. 3969.
23. Retrieved from: http://ufos.about.com/library/bldata/bl3newf.htm

The Steep Rock Lake Water Bandits

1. Clark, J. (1998). *The UFO Encyclopedia*, 2nd Edition. Chicago: Ommigraphics, Inc., p. 506.
2. Fowler, R. (1990). *The Watchers.* New York: Bantam Books, pp. 72–74.
3. Edwards, F. (1966). *Flying Saucers — Serious Business.* New York: Bantam, pp. 91–93.
4. Lorenzen, C., and Lorenzen, J. (1967). *Flying Saucer Occupants.* Toronto: Signet, pp. 19–21.
5. Vallee, J. (1969). *Passport to Magonia.* Chicago: Regnery, p. 188.
6. Colombo, J. (1991). *Mysterious Canada.* Torongo: Doubleday, pp. 231–232.
7. Clark, op. cit.
8. Retrieved from: http://www.etext.org/Politics/Conspiracy/Cosmic.Awareness/1993.Issues/Issue_9305

Canadian Saucers in the Fifties

1. *Toronto Telegram* (October 21, 1950).
2. HBCCUFO UFO Report Files. Retrieved from http://www.hbccufo.org/modules.php?name'News&file'article&sid'270
3. Gross, L. (1956). *UFOs: A History.* 1952/6 Books, Book #5, p. 81.
4. Strentz, H. (1970). "A Survey of Press Coverage of Unidentified Flying Objects, 1947–1966." Doctoral Dissertation, Northwestern University, Chicago.
5. UFOROM Files.
6. Michel, A. (1958). *Flying Saucers and the Straight Line Mystery.* New York: Criterion, pp. 248–9.

The Fort MacLeod Incident

1. Retrieved from: http://brumac.8k.com/RJC/RJC.html
2. Charman, W. (1979). "Ball Lightning." *Physics Reports*, V. 54, No. 4, pp. 261–306.
3. Maccabee, B. (1999). "Optical power output of an unidentified high altitude light source." *Journal of Scientific Exploration*, 13(2), 199.
4. Childerhose, R. (1969). "The Childerhose UFO Photograph." In Smith, W. (1969) *The Boys From Topside*. Clarksburg, West Virginia: Saucerian Books, Appendix V, pp. 93–94. Reprinted from: *Flying Saucer Review*, October 1958.

The Falcon Lake Incident

1. Bondarchuk, Y. (1979). *UFO Sightings, Landings and Abductions*. Toronto: Methuen, pp. 37–45.
2. Michalak, S. (1967). *My Encounter with the UFO*. Winnipeg: Osnova Publications.
3. Campagna, P. (1997). *The UFO Files*. Toronto: Stoddart.

Nova Scotia's UFO Crash

1. Many books have been written on the subject, including several by Stanton T. Friedman and Kevin Randle.
2. Movies on the subject include HBO's *Roswell Incident* and Steven Spielberg's *Taken*.
3. Ledger, D., and Styles, C. (2001). *Dark Object*. New York: Dell, pp. 9–11.
4. Ibid., pp. 13–14.
5. Ibid., pp. 14–17.
6. Ibid., p. 6.
7. Ibid., pp. 18–21.
8. Ibid., pp. 24–27.
9. Ibid., pp. 29–31.
10. Ibid., p. 34.
11. Ibid., pp. 39–42.
12. Randle, K. (1997). *The Randle Report*. New York: M. Evans and Company, p. 2.
13. Ledger and Styles, op. cit., pp. 43–45.
14. Ibid., p. 46.
15. Ibid.
16. Ledger, D. (1998). *Maritime UFO Files*. Halifax: Nimbus, p. 88.

17. Ledger and Styles, op. cit., pp. 47, 49.
18. Ibid., pp. 79–80.
19. Ibid., pp. 117–118.
20. Ibid., pp. 120–124.
21. Gillmor, D., ed. (1969). *Scientific Study of Unidentified Flying Objects*. Toronto: Bantam Books, p. 35.

UFOs and Blackouts

1. Blackout History Project. 1965: "Great Northeast Blackout." Retrieved August 17, 2005, from http://blackout.gmu.edu/events/tl1965.html
2. Friedlander, Gordon D. (October 1976). "What Went Wrong VIII: The Great Blackout of '65." *IEEE Spectrum*, p. 83.
3. U.S. Federal Power Commission (1965-12-6). *Report to the President by the Federal Power Commission on the Power Failure in the Northeastern United States and the Province of Ontario on November 9-10, 1965*. Washington, DC: U.S. Government Printing Office, p. 9.
4. Blackout History Project, op. cit.
5. Edwards, F. (1966). *Flying Saucers – Serious Business*. Toronto: Bantam, p. 146.
6. Ibid.
7. Ibid., p. 147.
8. Keyhoe, D. (1974). *Aliens from Space*. Scarborough, ON: Signet, p. 172.
9. Ibid.
10. Ibid., p. 176.
11. Ibid., p. 178.
12. Ibid.
13. Druffel, A. (2003). *Firestorm*. Columbus, NC: Wildflower, pp. 145–146.
14. Ridge, F., and NICAP Interlink: UFO. "Power Outages & UFOs." Retrieved May 9, 2005, from http://members.evansville.net/slk/blackout.htm
15. Trefil, J. (2003). *The Nature of Science*. Boston: Houghton Mifflin, p. 304.

The Landing on Allumette Island

1. UFOROM Files.

The 1973 Invasion of Quebec

1. MacDuff, C. (1974). *The November 1973 UFO Invasion of Quebec*. Dollard-des-Ormeaux, Quebec: UFO-Quebec, pp. 1–17.
2. UFOROM Files.

Did Flying Saucers Create Crop Circles?

1. From the paper "The Langenburg CE2 Case: When UFO's Left Their Mark" by Chris Rutkowski, included in compilation by Evans, H., and Stacy, D., eds. (1997). *UFO: 1947–1997*. London: John Brown, p. 123.
2. Hynek, J.A., and Vallee, J. (1975). *The Edge of Reality*. Chicago: Henry Regnery, p. 268.
3. Ibid.
4. Ibid.
5. Evans and Stacy, op. cit., p. 124
6. Hynek and Vallee, op. cit., p. 276.
7. From N74-067 in the Non-Meteoric Sightings file, as cited in Evans and Stacy, op. cit., p. 127.
8. Hynek and Vallee, op. cit., p. 275.
9. Evans and Stacy, op. cit., p. 126.
10. *Regina Leader-Post* (September 27, 1974) as quoted in Evans and Stacy, op. cit., p. 124.
11. Hynek and Vallee, op. cit., p. 268.
12. Evans and Stacy, op. cit., p. 122.
13. Hynek and Vallee, op. cit., p. 279.
14. Evans and Stacy, op. cit., p. 126.
15. RCMP Langenburg Detachment (1989-10-27, L.89-0791) and National Research Council (1989-10-30, N89/64).
16. Evans and Stacy, op. cit., pp. 128–129.

The Falconbridge Radar/Visual UFO Case

1. Fawcett, L., and Greenwood, B. (1984). *Clear Intent*. NJ: Prentice-Hall, pp. 46–48.
2. Ibid.
3. Ibid.
4. Ibid.
5. Klass, P. (1983). *UFOs: The Public Deceived*. NY: Prometheus Books, pp. 107–109.
6. Fawcett and Greenwood, op. cit.

7. Campagna, P. (1997). *The UFO Files*. Toronto: Stoddart, p. 184.
8. *Winnipeg Tribune* (November 13, 1975).
9. Sparks, B. (2000). Retrieved from http://www.virtuallystrange.net/ufo/updates/2000/dec/m12-002.shtml

Charlie Redstar and Friends

1. All cases cited and described in this chapter are drawn from reports and documentation in UFOROM Files.
2. Grant Cameron's files, personal correspondence.

Into the Eighties

1. Rutkowski, C. (1993). *Unnatural History*. Winnipeg: Chameleon, p. 46.

Angel Hair

1. Rutkowski, C. (1993). *Unnatural History*. Winnipeg: Chameleon, p. 48.
2. Ibid.
3. Singapore Zoological Gardens Docents (2000). *Spiders-Spider Silk*. Retrieved August 14, 2005, from http://www.szgdocent.org/ff/f-ssilk.htm.
4. Obrycki, J., and VanDyk, J. (2000). "Arachnids and Silk Production." Retrieved August 11, 2005, from http://www.ent.iastate.edu/dept/courses/ent201/arthropoda/classarachnidasilk.html
5. There are seven kinds of spider silk, with most spiders being able to produce more than one kind. See Tenenbaum: http://whyfiles.org/shorties/077spidersilk. Each kind of silk is somewhat different, as each is used for a different purpose. For example, one kind is sticky and is used to wrap prey, while another kind is non-sticky and is used as a dragline to help move from one spot to another. But one thing they all have in common is strength.
6. Singapore Zoological Gardens Docents, op. cit.
7. Design in Site. "Material: Spider Silk." Retrieved August 11, 2005, from http://www.designinsite.dk/htmsider/m0609.htm
8. Michel, A. (1974). *The Truth About Flying Saucers*. New York: Pyramid, p. 154.
9. Ibid., p. 155.

The Men in Black

1. See his article "M.I.B. Activity Reported from Victoria B.C.," *Flying Saucer Review* (January 1992), published by Devney.
2. Randles, J. (1997). *The Truth Behind Men in Black*. New York: St. Martin's, p. 131.
3. Barker, G. (1997). *They Knew Too Much About Flying Saucers*. Lilburn, Georgia: IllumiNet.
4. Barker himself was known as a bit of a prankster. In a fascinating book titled *Shockingly Close to the Truth*, written by Barker friend James Moseley and co-authored by Karl Pflock, Moseley described some of the pranks and hoaxes Barker was involved in. Moseley also quoted Barker from a personal letter in which Barker described the mother-of-all men-in-black tales as being a product of the witness's "mind and imagination," as well as a "persecution complex." See Moseley and Pflock (2002), p. 42.
5. Randles, op. cit., pp. 133–134.
6. As quoted in Clark, J., op. cit., p. 426.
7. Keith, J. (1997). *Casebook on the Men in Black*. Lilburn, Georgia: IllumiNet, p. 199.
8. Davenport, M. (1994). *Visitors from Time*. Murfreesboro, TN: Greenleaf, p. 197.
9. Randles, op. cit., p. 132.
10. Davenport, op. cit., p. 197.
11. Randles, op. cit.1997, p. 134.
12. For an original account of this case, see Haines, R. (1987) "Analysis of a UFO Photograph." *Journal of Scientific Exploration*, 1, 129–147. More recently, it was republished in Sturrock (1999), pp. 173–197.

The Strangeness Continues

1. Haines, R. (1999). *CE-5*. Naperville, IL: Sourcebooks, pp. 337–339.
2. RCMP Wesleyville Detachment files (1989-06-13 and 1989-07-26, File 89-326).
3. National Research Council file (1989-10-27, N89/69).
4. RCMP Hall Beach Detachment files (1989-11-04 to 1989-11-06, File 89-300).
5. Distant Early Warning, a series of radar stations run jointly by the U.S. and Canadian militaries, as part of the NORAD agreement. They were on the watch for possible attacking missiles or

bombers from neighbouring Soviet Union/Russia. In 1993 the DEW system was formally replaced by the North Warning System.

6. RCMP Hall Beach Detachment files (1989-11-06, File 89-300).

Electromagnetic Effects Cases

1. For a good summary of such cases, see Hall (1997) and Hall (2001).
2. For example, there have been allegations that the great 1965 northeastern power failure was UFO related. See the "UFOs and Blackouts" chapter.
3. See Hall (2001), pp. 259–260, which in turn quotes McCampbell, J. (1973). *UFOlogy: New Insights from Science and Common Sense*. Belmont, CA: Jaymac.
4. Cardella, P. (November 22, 1989). "Local UFO Sightings Draw Attention of International UFO Group." *Daily Miner*.
5. Ibid.
6. Houston, M. (November 24, 1989). "Hundreds Hear Phones Ring Off Hook, See Bright, Pulsaiting Light." *Winnipeg Free Press*, p. 2.
7. Ibid.
8. Cardella, op. cit.
9. Houston, op. cit.
10. Moche, D.L. (2000). *Astronomy.* 5th Edition. Toronto: John Wiley & Sons, pp. 102–104.
11. Ibid., p. 107.
12. Gillmor, D., ed. (1969). *Scientific Study of Unidentified Flying Objects.* Toronto: Bantam Books, Pp. 724–725.
13. Ibid., p. 680.
14. Houston, op. cit.
15. Moche, op. cit.
16. Ontario Provincial Police File 17-10-89-03676.
17. Ibid.
18. Ibid.
19. RCMP Punnichy Detachment (1989-12-15). File 89-2071.

A UFO Lands in Quebec

1. The names of all witnesses have been changed in this case to protect their privacy.
2. Correspondence from Christian Page.

3. RCMP St-Jean-Sur-Richelieu Detachment (1989-11-23). File 89-610.
4. Ibid.
5. RCMP St-Jean-Sur-Richelieu Detachment (1989-12-19). File 89-610.
6. Ibid.
7. RCMP St-Jean-Sur-Richelieu Detachment (1989-11-23). File 89-610.
8. RCMP St-Jean-Sur-Richelieu Detachment (1989-12-19). File 89-610.
9. Ibid.

The Carp Case

1. Anonymous documents mailed to Chris Rutkowski.
2. Theofanous, T., and Bruce-Knapp, E. (August 1995). "The Carp Case." *MUFON Ontario Newsletter*. Retrieved from http://www.virtuallystrange.net/ufo/mufonontario/archive/car p. html
3. Ibid.
4. Ibid.
5. Ibid.
6. Ibid.
7. Ibid.
8. Anonymous documents mailed to Chris Rutkowski.
9. Meurer, T.D., and Cosgrove, J. (Originally aired on 1993, February 2). *Unsolved Mysteries*. Available in DVD as *Unsolved Mysteries: UFOs*, from Lions Gate Home Entertainment.
10. Theofanous and Bruce-Knapp, op. cit.
11. Ibid.
12. Ibid.
13. Ibid.
14. Ibid.
15. Ibid.
16. Ibid.
17. RCMP FIU Detachment, Federal Policing Section Sub-division, Detachment A (1993-04-01). File 93A-0735, paragraph 4.10.
18. Ibid., paragraph 4.24.
19. Ibid., paragraph 4.25.
20. Ibid., paragraph 4.29.
21. Ibid., paragraph 4.26.

22. Ibid., paragraph 4:35.
23. Ibid., paragraph 4.36.
24. Ibid., paragraph 4.45.
25. Ibid., paragraph 6.1.
26. Theofanous and Bruce-Knapp, op. cit.
27. Ibid.
28. Ibid.
29. Rutkowski, C. (September 30, 2003). Retrieved from http://www.virtuallystrange.net/ufo/updates/2003/oct/m01-014.shtml

Ebenezer's Ice Cream Cone

1. NRC Non-Meteoritic Sightings File, Case N90/66.
2. NRC Non-Meteoritic Sightings File, Case N90/61.
3. NRC Non-Meteoritic Sightings File, Case N90/62.
4. NRC Non-Meteoritic Sightings File, Case N90/63.
5. NRC Non-Meteoritic Sightings File, Case N90/64.
6. NRC Non-Meteoritic Sightings File, Case N90/65.
7. Ibid.
8. Undated newspaper article.
9. UFOROM files and private correspondence.

Giant UFO Alarms Montreal

1. See the authors' Canadian UFO Survey, which can be viewed at http://survey.canadianuforeport.com. This study has found that there was an average of 2.0 witnesses per UFO sighting from 1996 to 2004.
2. Beliveau, J., and Laroche, M. (November 8, 1990). "A UFO in the Montreal Sky?" *La Presse.*
3. Ibid.
4. Haines, R.F., and Guenette, B. (1992). *Details Surrounding a Large Stationary Aerial Object above Montreal.* Privately Published, p. 2.
5. Ibid.
6. RCMP Montreal (1990-11-13). File 90-MSEG-13458.
7. Haines and Guenette, op. cit., p. 3.
8. RCMP Montreal (1990-11-07). Occurrence 90-1392.
9. Haines and Guenette, op. cit., p. 3.
10. RCMP Montreal (1990-11-13). File 90-MSEG-13458.
11. Haines and Guenette, op. cit., p. 4.
12. Michaels, S. (1996). *Sightings.* Toronto: Simon & Schuster, p. 111.

13. Trudel, J. (November 9, 1990). "Did You See The UFO? Was This a UFO?" *Journal de Montreal.*
14. Ibid.
15. Michaels, op. cit., p. 109.
16. Haines and Guenette, op. cit., p. 5.

Resolute

1. UFOROM case files.
2. Retrieved from http://www.wingar.demon.co.uk/satevo/dk46.htm
3. Retrieved from http://www.satobs.org/satintro.html
4. UFOROM case files.
5. Retrieved from http://www.marssociety.org/arctic/index.asp
6. Retrieved from http://exp-studies.tor.ec.gc.ca/e/eureka/eureka.htm

Never Too Cold for UFOs

1. *Winnipeg Free Press* (January 30, 1996).
2. *News/North* (January 29, 1996).
3. Ibid.
4. Ibid.
5. *News/North* (January 22, 1996).
6. Retrieved from http://www.ssimicro.com/~ufoinfo on February 18, 1996.
7. Retrieved from http://ume.med.ucalgary.ca/aufora/nwt on February 18, 1996.
8. UFOROM Files.
9. Ibid.
10. Ibid.
11. Ibid.
12. Ibid.
13. Ibid.
14. Ibid.

Unique Yukon UFO

1. Jasek, M. (2000). *Giant UFO in the Yukon Territory.* UFO*BC Special Report No. 1. June 2000. UFO*BC, Vancouver: Privately published.

The Gypsumville UFOs and Entities of 1996

1. UFOROM Files.
2. Creighton, D., Fidler, B., and Rutkowski, C. (1997). *Mysterious Manitoba*. Brandon, MB: SEEKERS/UFOROM, pp. 12–16.

The Surrey Corridor

1. Boyce, S. (1995). "Lights in the Sky." *South Fraser BC Woman Magazine*, Holiday Issue.
2. UFOROM Files.
3. Ibid.
4. Ibid.
5. Zytarul, T. (May 25, 1999). "Strange Lights Reported Over White Rock." *The Surrey Now*. Retrieved from http://www.rense.com /ufo3/majufo.htm.
6. Persinger, M., and Lafrenière, G. (1977). *Space-Time Transients and Unusual Events*. Chicago: Nelson-Hall.
7. Persinger, M., and Derr, J. (1990). "Geographical variables and behavior: LXI. UFO reports in Carman Manitoba and the 1975 Minnesota quake: evidence of triggering by increased volume of the Red River." *Perceptual and Motor Skills*, V.71, pp. 531–536.
8. Retrieved from http://www.virtuallystrange.net/ufo/updates/1997/m27-001
9. Ibid.

A Hole in the Ground

1. *Calgary Sun* (June 28, 2001).
2. *The Prairie Post* (April 27, 2001).
3. *The Forty Mile County Commentator* (May 1, 2001).
4. Karkanis, P. (2001). *Occurrence of a circular crater-like formation near Etzikom, Alberta*. Department of Geography, The University of Lethbridge. [privately published].
5. Ibid.
6. Ibid.
7. Retrieved from http://www.aufosg.com/kijek/page181.html
8. Private correspondence in UFOROM Files.
9. Poirier, G. (July 1, 2001). "What was it?" *The Prairie Post*. Retrieved from http://www.prairie-post.com/news/072001-1.html

The Okanagan Arch

1. UFOROM Files.
2. Retrieved from http://www.hbccufo.org/modules.php?name'News&file'article&sid'2174
3. Lang, J. (April 8, 2004). "Seeing Things." *Terrace Standard News.* Retrieved from http://www.rense.com/general51/seng.htm
4. As discussed in *UFO Updates*, retrieved from http://www.virtuallystrange.net/ufo/updates/2003/oct/m15-003.shtml
5. UFOROM Files.

The 2004 Flap in New Brunswick

1. UFOROM Case Files.

The Prime Minister and the UFO

1. UFOROM Case Files.

A Curious Chronological Cluster of Consecutive Canadian Cases

1. Personal correspondence in UFOROM Files.
2. UFOROM Case Files.

Government UFO Investigations

1. The Internet for years has been rife with stories of crashed saucers, alien bodies, and secret underground bases where aliens and the U.S. government work hand-in-hand on some unknown genetic project. For example, see Friedman (May 1996), viewable at http://www.abovetopsectret.com/pages/lecture.html.
2. For a brief summary of his career in government projects, see Friedman (1996).
3. Randles, J. (1997). *Alien Contact.* New York: Barnes & Noble, p. 8.
4. The U.S. Air Force began seriously investigating UFOs with the creation of Project Sign in January 1948. Given a classification of restricted, Sign was the responsibility of the Air Technical Intelligence Center (ATIC).
5. Ruppelt, E.J. (1956). *The Report on Unidentified Flying Objects.* Garden City, NY: Doubleday, p. 6.
6. Bondarchuk, Y. (1981). *UFO Canada.* Scarborough: Signet, p. 166.
7. See Keyhoe, D. (1974). *Aliens from Space.* Scarborough, ON:

Signet, pp. 42–43. Also see Mackie, V.J. (1967-07-20). "UFO Landing Site Was 13-Year Secret." *Ottawa Journal.*
8. Campagna, P. *The UFO Files.* Toronto: Stoddart, pp. 49–51.
9. The Joint Intelligence Committee is made up of representatives of the various branches of the military, along with specialists in certain fields, that met to discuss issues of importance with respect to intelligence matters.
10. Campagna, op. cit., p. 50.
11. Project Sign's first attempt at an answer came in the form of the top secret "Estimate of the Situation." This report stated the conclusion that UFOs were in fact alien visitors. This conclusion, however, did not sit well with the military's chief of staff, General Hoyt Vandenberg. Vandenberg, questioning the lack of proof for interplanetary visitation, returned the report to ATIC. Unmoved by ATIC's attempts at changing the general's mind, the report was eventually declassified and the copies destroyed.

    Such a complete rejection of the favoured hypothesis by the Pentagon had an enormous impact on the morale of the Project's staff. Fearing that continued support of the extraterrestrial hypothesis would be a career-limiting move, the staff made a 180-degree turn in their stance, indicating that all UFO sightings were the result of faulty perception, natural phenomena, or hoaxes. See Ruppelt, op. cit., p. 45.
12. Campagna, op. cit., p. 51.
13. Bruce-Knapp, E., ed. *Wilbert Brockhouse Smith.* Retrieved from http://www.virtuallystrange.net/ufo/mufonontario/archive/wbsmith.htm
14. Department of Transport (1950-11-21). *Memorandum to the Controller of Telecommunications.*
15. Ibid.
16. Friedman, S.T., and Berliner, D. (1994). *Crash at Corona.* New York: Marlowe & Company, p. 50.
17. Ibid., pp 48–49.
18. Ibid., pp 50–52.
19. Department of Transport (1950-11-21). *Memorandum to the Controller of Telecommunications.*
20. Ibid.
21. Bush was an influential U.S. government scientist. From 1945 to 1948 he was the Chairman of the Joint Research and Development Board. See Friedman and Berliner, op. cit., p. 62.

22. Department of Transport (1950-11-21). Memorandum to the Controller of Telecommunications.
23. Department of Transport (1952-10-18). *Project Magnet Report — Draft* . Can be viewed at http://presidentialufo.com/new_magnet_documents.htm
24. Department of Transport, Air Services Telecommunications Division (1951-01-03). Letter to Gordon Cox from W.B.Smith.
25. Campagna, op. cit., pp. 37–38.
26. Smith, W. (n.d.). *Project Magnet*. Can be viewed at http://www.presidentialufo.com/project_magnet_article.htm
27. Department of Transport, Air Services Telecommunications Division (1951-01-03). Letter to Gordon Cox from W.B. Smith.
28. Unlabelled memo from Smith, obtained from University of Ottawa Archives by researcher Nick Balaskas. Can be viewed at http://www.presidentialufo.com/flying_saucer_review.htm
29. Bruce-Knapp, op. cit.
30. Defence Research Board (1952-04-30). Project Second Storey memo (from H.C. Oatway). Can be viewed at http://ufo-joe.tripod.com/xfiles/c149.html
31. Defence Research Board (1952-05-19). Minutes of 2/52 Project Second Storey Meeting.
32. Campagna, op. cit., p. 53.
33. Ibid., p. 55.
34. Ibid.
35. Ibid., pp. 55–56.
36. Defence Research Board (1952-05-19). Minutes of 2/52 Project Second Storey Meeting.
37. Campagna, op. cit., p. 56.
38. Smith, W. (1952-06-25). "Interim Report on Project Magnet." As quoted from Good, T. (1989). *Above Top Secret*. Toronto: McClelland & Stewart, pp. 241–142.
39. Good, op. cit., p. 242.
40. *Flying Saucer Review*, Vol. 10, No.4, 1964, as quoted from Good, op. cit., pp. 240–241.
41. "Electronic Observatory to Watch for Flying Saucers" (November 12, 1953). *Globe and Mail.*
42. Good, op. cit., p. 244.
43. Ibid., p. 242.
44. Ibid., p. 244.

45. Michel, A. (1974). *The Truth about Flying Saucers.* New York: Pyramid, p. 83.
46. Vallee, J. (1996). *Forbidden Science.* New York: Marlowe & Company, p. 440.
47. Good, op. cit., p. 242.
48. Ibid., p. 243.
49. Campagna, op. cit., pp. 43–44.
50. Memorandum from Dr. Peter Millman, November 21, 1953, as quoted by Arthur Bray. Can be viewed at http://ufo-joe.tripod.com/gov/pssbray.html
51. Campagna, op. cit., p. 44.
52. Ibid.
53. Department of Transport (1954-06-25). Files 22-12-29 and 22-12-33.
54. Smith, W. (n.d.). "The Day Project Magnet Detected a Flying Saucer." Retrieved from http://www.presidentialufo.com/ufo_observatory.htm. See also Canadian Press (August 10, 1954). "Canadian Scientists First! Did We Trip a Flying Saucer?" *The Globe and Mail.*
55. Campagna, op. cit., p. 46.
56. Department of Transport (1954-08-10). Can be viewed at http://ufo-joe.tripod.com/gov/shbay.html
57. Department of Transport (1969-09-15). Can be viewed at http://www.presidentialufo.com/declassi.htm
58. See for example Vallee (1996), p. 304.
59. Edwards, F. (1966). *Flying saucers — Serious Business.* Toronto: Bantam, p. 47.
60. Ibid.
61. Ibid., pp 49–50.
62. Gillmor, D.S., ed. (1969). *Scientific Study of Unidentified Flying Objects.* Toronto: Bantam Books, p. 91.
63. The effects of this hoax are still being felt to this day. The Sturrock report, put together by a panel of scientists in the late nineties, included this case in their physical trace case studies. It concluded: "Unfortunately there is no report of an independent analysis in the literature, and the sample is not available for further study." See Sturrock, P. (1999), p. 241. There is no mention of the Condon Committee's findings.
64. Gillmor, op. cit., p. 92.

65. Craig, R. (1995). *UFOs*. Denton, Texas: University of North Texas Press, p. 121.
66. Ibid., p. 122.
67. Gillmor, op. cit., p. 92.
68. Craig, op. cit., p. 127.
69. Ibid., pp. 125–126.
70. Smith, W.B. (n.d.). *The Philosophy of the Saucers*. Can be viewed at http://www.presidentialufo.com/saucer_philosophy.htm
71. Ibid.
72. Smith (March 31, 1958). Speech in Ottawa, Ontario. Can be viewed at http://www.presidentialufo.com/new_page_8.htm
73. Automatic writing, according to supporters, involves an external entity, be it alien or a deceased person, somehow taking over the body of an individual and writing notes as a means of communication. Usually the person whose body is taken over is in some sort of trancelike state and is unaware of what is transpiring.
74. Jacobs, D. (1976). *The UFO Controversy in America*. Scarborough, ON: Signet, pp. 153–154.
75. Hall, R., ed. (1997). *The UFO Evidence*. New York: Barnes & Noble, p. 118. Note that this particular edition records the date as 1963 instead of 1953. The 1964 edition apparently listed the date as 1953, as per Bondarchuk, op. cit., p. 170.
76. Gillmor, op. cit., pp. 532–533.
77. Ibid.
78. Campagna, op. cit., p. 86.
79. Gillmor, op. cit., p. 532.
80. Bondarchuk, op. cit.,p. 171-172.
81. Ibid., p. 173.
82. DND, DOPS UFO File, January 1-November 15, 1967. Non-Meteoric Sightings File, DND 24-222. Herzeberg Institute of Astrophysics. As taken from Bondarchuk, op. cit., p. 174.
83. The NRC is a Canadian Government scientific research organization. Their web page is located at http://www.nrc.ca
84. Bondarchuk, op. cit., p. 175.
85. Ibid.
86. As noted by Campagna, the military continued to receive UFO reports until the late eighties, when CFAO 71-6 was finally rescinded. See Campagna, op. cit., pp. 131–132.
87. Rutkowski, C. (1993). *Unnatural History*. Winnipeg: Chameleon, p. 10.

88. Meteor sightings are still being collected by the Meteorites and Impact Advisory Committee (MIAC) of the Canadian Space Agency.
89. In 2000, Transport Canada and the DND agreed to pass on any UFO reports they receive to the Manitoba-based private UFO research group UFOROM. While the government is no longer actively involved in UFO research, at least two departments are out of courtesy helping private researchers conduct their own investigations.
90. It should be noted, however, that Sagan believed this not because of a belief in alien visitation but because of the nature of governments to secretly investigate anything that might result in improved technology or increased national security, regardless of whether or not the UFOs are spacecraft or products of a foreign government. See Sagan, C. (1995). *The Demon-Haunted World*. New York: Random House, p. 83.
91. Randle, K.D. (2002). *Case MJ-12*. New York: HarperTouch, pp. 104–106.
92. Cameron, G. (n.d.). "Wilbert Smith, A Crashed Saucer, and the Ultimate Alien Encounter." Retrieved from http://www.presidentialufo.com/crashed_saucer.htm
93. Vallee, op. cit., p. 272.
94. Keith, J. (1997). *Casebook on the Men in Black*. Lilburn, Georgia: IllumiNet, p. 82.
95. Ibid., pp. 195–197.

Little Pad on the Prairie

1. UFOROM Files.
2. Ibid.
3. St. Paul Chamber of Commerce website: http://www.stpaulchamber.ca/ufolanding.html
4. Curran, D. (1985). *In Advance of the Landing: Folk Concepts of Outer Space*. NY: Abbeville Press, pp. 38–39.
5. UFOROM Files.
6. Ibid.

Science Versus the Flying Saucers

1. Retrievable from http://www.geocities.com/Athens/Delphi/7998/pollsum.txt.rtf

UFOs and Alien Abductions

1. Fuller, J. (1965). *The Interrupted Journey.* New York: Dial Press.
2. Walton, T. (1978). *The Walton Experience.* New York: Berkley.
3. Blum, R., and Blum, J. (1974). *Beyond Earth: Man's contact with UFOs.* New York: Bantam Books.
4. Clark, J. (1976). "UFO abduction in North Dakota." *UFO Report* vol. 3, no. 3, August 1976, pp. 21+.
5. Strieber, W. (1987). *Communion.* New York: Beech Tree Books.
6. Rutkowski, C. (1999). *Abductions and Aliens: What's Really Going On?* Toronto: Dundurn.
7. Haisell, D. (1978). *The Missing Seven Hours.* Markham, Ontario: Paperjacks.
8. Mark-Age (1974). *Visitors from Other Planets.* Miami: Mark-Age. Inc.
9. Ibid.
10. UFOROM Case Files.
11. Ibid.
12. Ibid.
13. Ibid.
14. Vike, B. (2003). "Missing time in Kelowna, B.C." Retrieved from http://www.hbccufo.org/modules.php?name=News&file=article&sid=1072

The Canadian UFO Survey

1. For more information on the Canadian UFO Survey, check out its website at http://survey.canadianuforeport.com
2. This 10 percent number has been widely reported over the years. The Condon Committee made a rough guess of 10 percent: see Gillmor, D., ed. (1969). *Scientific Study of Unidentified Flying Objects.* Toronto: Bantam Books, p. 11. The guess has been more or less confirmed by public opinion polls. Interestingly, the Condon Committee considered conducting a publicity campaign in an attempt to increase the percentage of witnesses who formally report their sightings. In the end, however, they chose not to, fearing the workload associated with more reports would be too much: see Gillmor, op. cit., p. 11.
3. Randles, J. (1981). *UFO Study.* London: Robert Hale, p. 175.
4. Ibid., pp. 192–193. Randle in turn quotes from Liljegren, A. (January–May 1979). "A Statistical Study of 602 Swedish UFO Reports, 1879–1978." *AFU Newsletter.*

5. Vallee, J. (1992). *Revelations.* New York: Ballantine Books, p. 265.
6. *U.S. Air Force Guide to UFO Identification*, Air Technical Intelligence Center, Wright-Patterson Air Force Base, Ohio, as reported in Steiger, B. (1987). *Project Blue Book.* Toronto: Ballantine Books, p. 260.
7. The U.S. Air Force, in its final report on Project Grudge, stated, "Certain conditions are necessary for drawing valid scientific conclusions. These conditions are largely lacking [in UFO reports]." (From the Mapping, Charting, and Reconaissance Research Laboratory. Final Report Project 364, as quoted from Steiger [1987], p. 224.) Condon Committee members as well were quite displeased in the natural limitations placed on their ability to study the subject matter. Like all researchers, they typically wouldn't become aware of a sighting until long after the UFO had disappeared, thereby limiting their ability to study the subject first hand. They had pondered setting up field teams of scientists across the country who would rapidly respond to any UFO sightings. They quickly abandoned this idea, however, given that the duration of UFO sightings are usually measured in minutes, if not seconds. See Gillmor (1969), p. 16. Another study recommended instead having well-equiped roving teams that would be moved to UFO hotspots. See Vallee (1996), p. 440. As far as anyone knows, this recommendation was never implemented by the U.S. Air Force. Supposedly, however, the Brazillian military had some luck with a similar project back in the seventies. See Vallee (1990), pp. 223–226.

   Of course people can study the physical effects caused by UFOs, as well as photographs. It is such cases that the Condon Committee focused on. Nonetheless, the committee tried long and hard to think of different ways to study the subject scientifically, but all methods were "beset with great difficulties." See Gillmor (1969), p. 48. And finally, upon concluding the study, Robert Condon stated the following: "Our general conclusion is that nothing has come from the study of UFOs in the past 21 years that has added to scientific knowledge. Careful consideration of the record as it is available has led us to conclude that further study of UFOs probably cannot be justified in the expectation that science will be advanced thereby." See Gillmor (1969), p. 1.

Misidentified Flying Objects

1. Gribbin, J. (1996). *Companion to the Cosmos*. London: Weidenfeld & Nicolson, p. 274.
2. Discover Magazine (2003). *Discover Science Almanac*. New York: Hyperion, p. 59.
3. Air Technical Intelligence Center, Wright-Patterson Air Force Base, Ohio, U.S. Air Force, "UFOB Guide," as quoted from Steiger, B. (1987). *Project Blue Book*. Toronto: Ballantine Books, p. 265.
4. Discover Magazine, op. cit., p. 77 and Moche, D. (2000). *Astronomy*. 5th Edition. Toronto: John Wiley & Sons, p. 293.
5. Gribbin, op. cit., p. 86.
6. Coomer, D. (1999). *The UFO Investigator's Guide*. London: Blandford, p. 134.
7. Randles, J. (1981). *UFO Study*. London: Robert Hale, p. 114.
8. Coomer, op. cit., p.136.
9. Randles (1981), op. cit., p. 100.
10. Air Technical Intelligence Center, Wright-Patterson Air Force Base, Ohio, U.S. Air Force, as quoted from Steiger, op. cit., p. 266.
11. Randles (1981), op. cit., p. 101.
12. Coomer, op. cit., p. 153.
13. Ibid., p. 154.
14. Viezee, William, "Optical Mirage," as presented in Gillmor, D. (Ed.) (1969). *Scientific Study of Unidentified Flying Objects*. Toronto: Bantam Books. p. 598.
15. Ibid.
16. Randles (1981), op. cit., p. 107.
17. Altschuler, M.D., "Atmospheric Electricity and Plasma Interpretations of UFOs," as presented in Gillmor, op. cit., pp. 724–725.
18. Randles, J. (1994). *Spontaneous Human Combustion*. New York: Berkley, pp. 155–175.
19. Ibid., p. 162.
20. Ibid., p. 163.
21. Air Technical Intelligence Center, Wright-Patterson Air Force Base, Ohio, U.S. Air Force, as quoted in Steiger, op. cit., p. 265.
22. Ibid., p. 264.
23. Randles (1981), op. cit., p. 115.
24. Coomer, op. cit., p. 147.

25. Air Technical Intelligence Center, Wright-Patterson Air Force Base, Ohio, U.S. Air Force, as quoted in Steiger, op. cit., p. 264.
26. Ibid., p. 267.
27. See for example http://www.virtuallystrange.net/ufo/updates/2005/mar/m07-001.shtml
28. Randles (1981), op. cit., p. 108.
29. Menzel, D., "UFOs-The Modern Myth," in Sagan, C., and Page, T., eds. (1996). *UFO's: A Scientific Debate*. New York: Barnes and Noble Books, p. 142.
30. Paul Devereux and Michael Persinger are two supporters of this hypothesis.
31. Sagan and Page, op. cit., p. 142–143.

Appendix B: Canadian Cases Listed Among the Blue Book Unknowns

1. The UFO cases listed here have come from a variety of sources, including the files of Brad Sparks and Jan Aldrich.

BIBLIOGRAPHY

Barker, Gray. *They Knew Too Much About Flying Saucers*. Lilburn, Georgia: IllumiNet, 1997.

Bondarchuk, Yurko. *UFO Sightings, Landings and Abductions: The Documented Evidence*. Toronto: Methuen, 1979.

———. *UFO Canada*. Scarborough: Signet, 1981.

Campagna, Palmiro. *The UFO Files: The Canadian Connection Exposed*. Toronto: Stoddart, 1997.

Clark, Jerome. *The UFO Book*. Toronto: Visible Ink, 1998.

Colombo, John Robert. (Ed.) *Close Encounters of the Canadian Kind: Personal Accounts of UFOs in Canada*. Toronto: Colombo & Company, 1994.

———. *Mysterious Canada*. Toronto: Doubleday, 1988.

———, ed. *True Canadian UFO Stories*. Toronto: Prosper Books, 2004.

———. *UFOs Over Canada*. Willowdale, ON: Hounslow Press, 1992.

———. *The UFO Quote Book*. Toronto: Colombo & Company, 1999.

Coomer, David. *The UFO Investigator's Guide*. London: Blandford, 1999.

Craig, Roy. *UFOs: An Insider's View of the Official Quest for Evidence*. Denton, Texas: University of North Texas Press, 1995.

Creighton, David, Brian Fidler, and Chris Rutkowski. *Mysterious Manitoba*. Brandon, MB: SEEKERS, 1997.

Curran, Douglas. *In Advance of the Landing: Folk Concepts of Outer Space*. New York: Abbeville Press, 1985.

Davenport, Marc. *Visitors from Time: The Secret of the UFOs*. Murfreesboro, TN: Greenleaf Publications, 1994.

Discover Magazine. *Discover Science Almanac*. New York: Hyperion, 2003.

Druffel, Ann. *Firestorm: Dr. James E. McDonald's Fight for UFO Science*. Columbus, NC: Wild Flower, 2003.

Edwards, Frank. *Flying Saucers-Serious Business*. Toronto: Bantam, 1966.

Evans, Hilary, and Dennis Stacy, eds. *UFO 1947–1997: Fifty Years of Flying Saucers*. London: John Brown, 1997.

Fowler, Raymond E. *The Watchers: The Secret Design behind UFO Abduction*. Toronto: Bantam Books, 1990.

Friedman, Stanton T., and Don Berliner. *Crash at Corona: The U.S. Military Retrieval and Cover-Up of a UFO*. New York: Marlowe & Company, 1994.

Friedman, Stanton T. *Top Secret/Majic*. New York: Marlowe & Company, 1996.

Gillmor, D., ed. *Scientific Study of Unidentified Flying Objects*. Toronto: Bantam Books, 1969.

Good, Timothy. *Above Top Secret: The Worldwide UFO Cover-Up*. Toronto: McClelland & Stewart, 1989.

Gribbin, John. *Companion to the Cosmos*. London: Weidenfeld & Nicolson, 1996.

Haines, Richard F. *CE-5: Close Encounters of the Fifth Kind*. Naperville, IL: Sourcebooks, 1999.

Hall, Richard H., ed. *The UFO Evidence*. New York: Barnes & Noble, 1997.

———. *The UFO Evidence V.II*. Kent, England: Scarecrow, 2001.

Hynek, Joseph Allen, and Jacques Vallee. *The Edge of Reality: A Progress Report on Unidentified Flying Objects*. Chicago: Henry Regnery, 1975.

Jacobs, David M. *The UFO Controversy in America*. Scarborough, ON: Signet, 1976.

Keith, Jim. *Casebook on the Men in Black*. Lilburn, Georgia: IllumiNet, 1997.

Keyhoe, Donald E. *Flying Saucers from Outer Space*. New York: Henry Holt, 1953.

———. *Aliens from Space*. Scarborough, ON: Signet, 1974.

Ledger, Don. *Maritime UFO Files*. Halifax: Nimbus, 1998.

Ledger, Don, and Chris Styles. *Dark Object: The World's Only Government-Documented UFO Crash*. New York: Dell, 2001.

Lorenzen, Coral, and Jim Lorenzen. *Flying Saucer Occupants*. New York: Signet Books, 1967.

MacDuff, Claude. *The November 1973 UFO Invasion of Quebec*. Dollard-des-Ormeaux, Quebec: UFO-Quebec, 1974.

Michaels, Susan. *Sightings*. Toronto: Simon & Schuster, 1996.

Michel, Aime. *Flying Saucers and the Straight-Line Mystery.* New York: Criterion Books, 1958.

———. *The Truth about Flying Saucers.* New York: Pyramid, 1974.

Millman, P.M., and D.W.R. McKinley. "Stars Fall Over Canada." In *Astronomy in Canada: Yesterday, Today and Tomorrow.* Edited by Ruth Northcott. Toronto: Royal Astronomical Society of Canada, 1968.

Moche, Dinah L. *Astronomy.* 5th Edition. Toronto: John Wiley & Sons, 2000.

Moseley James W., and Karl T. Pflock. *Shockingly Close to the Truth!: Confessions of a Grave-Robbing Ufologist.* Amherst, New York: Prometheus, 2002.

Persinger, Michael A., and Gyslaine F. Lafrenière. *Space-Time Transients and Unusual Events.* Chicago: Nelson-Hall, 1977.

Randle, Kevin D. *The Randle Report: UFOs in the '90s.* New York: M. Evans and Company, 1997.

———. *Case MJ-12: The True Story behind the Government's UFO Conspiracies.* New York: HarperTorch, 2002.

Randles, Jenny, and Peter Hough. *Spontaneous Human Combustion.* New York: Berkley, 1994.

Randles, Jenny. *Alien Contact: The First Fifty Years.* New York: Barnes & Noble, 1997.

———. *The Truth behind Men in Black: Government Agents — or Visitors from Beyond.* New York: St. Martin's, 1997.

———. *UFO Retrievals: The Recovery of Alien Spacecraft.* London: Blandford, 1995.

———. *UFO Study: A Handbook for Enthusiasts.* London: Robert Hale, 1981.

Ruppelt, Edward J. *The Report on Unidentified Flying Objects.* Garden City, New York: Doubleday, 1956.

Rutkowski, Chris. *The Falcon Lake Incident.* Winnipeg, MB: Ufology Research of Manitoba, 1980.

———. *Visitations? Manitoba UFO Experiences.* Winnipeg, MB: Winter Press, 1989.

———. *Unnatural History: True Manitoba Mysteries.* Winnipeg: Chameleon, 1993.

———. *Abductions and Aliens: What's Really Going On?* Toronto: Dundurn Press, 1999.

Sagan, Carl. *The Demon-Haunted World: Science as a Candle in the Dark.* New York: Random House, 1995.

Sagan, Carl, and Thornton Page, eds. *UFOs: A Scientific Debate.* New York: Barnes and Noble Books, 1996.

Steiger, Brad, ed. *Project Blue Book.* Toronto: Ballantine Books, 1987.

Strentz, Herbert Joseph. "A Survey of Press Coverage of Unidentified Flying Objects, 1947-1966." PhD thesis, Northwestern University, Department of Journalism, Evanston, Illinois, 1970.

Strieber, Whitley. *Communion: A True Story.* New York: Avon, 1988.

Sturrock, Peter A. *The UFO Enigma: A New Review of Physical Evidence.* New York: Time-Warner, 1999.

Trefil, James. *The Nature of Science: An A–Z Guide to the Laws and Principles Governing Our Universe.* Boston: Houghton Mifflin, 2003.

Vallee, Jacques. *Passport to Magonia: From Folklore to Flying Saucers.* Chicago: Regnery, 1969.

———. *Confrontations: A Scientist's Search for Alien Contact.* New York: Ballantine Books, 1990.

———. *Revelations: Alien Contact and Human Deception.* New York: Ballantine Books, 1992.

———. *Forbidden Science.* New York: Marlowe & Company, 1996.

Wilkins, Harold T. *Flying Saucers on the Attack.* New York: Ace Books, 1954.

INDEX